Doing Good and Doing Well

Doing Good and Doing Well

An Examination of Humanitarian Intervention

STEPHEN A. GARRETT

PRAEGER

Westport, Connecticut
London

Library of Congress Cataloging-in-Publication Data

Garrett, Stephen A., 1939–
Doing good and doing well : an examination of humanitarian intervention / Stephen A. Garrett.
p. cm.
Includes bibliographical references (p.) and index.
ISBN 0–275–96581–3 (alk. paper)
1. Intervention (International law). 2. Humanitarian assistance.
I. Title.
KZ6369.G37 1999
341.5′84—dc21 99–21599

British Library Cataloguing in Publication Data is available.

Library of Congress Catalog Card Number: 99–21599
ISBN: 0–275–96581–3

First published in 1999

Praeger Publishers, 88 Post Road West, Westport, CT 06881
An imprint of Greenwood Publishing Group, Inc.
www.praeger.com

Printed in the United States of America

The paper used in this book complies with the Permanent Paper Standard issued by the National Information Standards Organization (Z39.48–1984).

10 9 8 7 6 5 4 3 2 1

Contents

Preface

> We are members of one great body planted by nature in a mutual love, and fitted for a social life. We must consider that we were born for the good of the whole.
>
> —Seneca

> If a people, in the formation of their government, have been ill-advised, if they have fallen into error, if they have acted iniquitously and unjustly toward each other, God is their only judge; it is not the province of other nations to chastise their folly, or punish their wickedness, by choosing who should rule over them, or in what manner and form they should be governed.
>
> —Charles James Fox, to the House of Commons (April 17, 1794)[1]

This book has to do with foreign policy and, in particular, with the concept of "humanitarian interventions." Much of what follows will discuss such interventions in general terms as they impact on all states within the international system, but there will also be some special attention given to the role of the United States in this arena of activity. The rationale for doing so is plain enough: as the old saying has it, those to whom great power is given are also entrusted with great responsibilities. If a regime of appropriate international humanitarian activity is to be secured and even expanded, clearly the United States must play a crucial role in such a development. The question that presents itself is whether this challenge will be met, given that certain current powerful voices in American opinion and politics argue against a wider international role for the United States.

Humanitarian interventions are a response to particularly severe cases of human suffering, and are defined more precisely in Chapter 1. As a general matter, however, they involve the injection of the military power of one or more outside powers into the domestic affairs of a sovereign state in the face of significant human-rights violations. At their core, humanitarian interventions are, in the words of one writer, actions "primarily guided by the sentiment of humanity, compassion or fellow-feeling."[2] That the issue of humanitarian action generally in world affairs will continue to be a pressing matter for the international community is suggested by the latest figures on what the specialists usually call "complex humanitarian emergencies." The typical characteristics of such emergencies are several: widespread civil conflict (often accompanied by serious atrocities), an erosion of central governmental authority and an accompanying breakdown of public services, mass refugee movements both within and beyond the country's borders, general economic collapse (including hyperinflation, mass unemployment, and disappearance of markets), and, finally, severe malnutrition and even starvation brought on by a combination of the first four elements.[3]

The U.S. Mission to the United Nations released a report in 1997 summarizing the current spread of complex humanitarian emergencies. The report addressed only those situations in which more than 300,000 people were considered to be in dire need of humanitarian assistance. A total of twenty such emergencies were identified. When these cases are added to others that fall below the 300,000 threshold, some 36 million people around the world were at risk (triple the number of the early 1980s). The majority of these emergencies occurred in countries where there was major ethnic strife, and they tended to be concentrated in Sub-Saharan Africa, and in the former Soviet republics in Central Asia and the Caucasus.[4]

Now not all, or even a majority, of the twenty major humanitarian emergencies identified in that report are necessarily a type that makes them candidates for humanitarian interventions, as will be defined here. Indeed, there is a wide range of humanitarian measures that can be contemplated in these cases that do not involve forceful intervention by outsiders, including the provision of food and medicines, traditional relief work by non-governmental organizations, and diplomatic mediation to secure a political settlement that will stabilize conditions in the affected country.[5] Clearly, humanitarian interventions stand as a special class of international action that will continue to be "measures of last resort" and in only the most extreme situations.

As an issue in the relations among nations, humanitarian interventions ultimately have to do with the responsibility that each of us has (or should have) to the well-being of others. As such, they touch on some basic questions concerning the conduct of foreign policy and, even more, on the potential evolution of international politics more generally. One of the most important of these issues concerns the question of what duties a government has beyond those it traditionally owes to its own people. Does it have *any* responsibility for the welfare of others, that is, non-nationals, and if so, to what extent can these—or should these—derogate from the material well-being or even the physical security of the citizenry which that government represents? There is also the distinction often drawn between an "act" and an "omission." Thus, I may accept that I, myself, must not abuse another human being, but is my duty to *prevent* such an act being committed by others equally compelling? Clearly, there are some who doubt that it is, particularly when the act involves situations considerably removed from their own.[6]

Then there is the perennial matter of "order versus justice." A common assertion in analyses of world politics is that there is a fundamental tension between these two values, and that when all is said and done, the claims for justice can only be realized if order is assured. This somewhat paradoxical notion suggests that disorder is in itself the principal threat to human rights broadly defined and, rarely, if ever, provides an environment in which moral norms can be even partially secured in the affairs of individuals. To the extent that a series of humanitarian interventions contribute to instability in the world system, they must, therefore, be regarded as a potentially threatening trend in international relations. Thomas Hobbes is perhaps the best-known progenitor of this position. Hobbesian "political morality consists in ranking peace and stability over all other values, especially those associated with rights and justice."[7] Given Hobbes's gloomy vision of the essence of human nature—naturally anarchical and predisposed toward aggression and violence—it is only through a fixed and predictable political order that a minimally tolerable human existence can be achieved.

The alternative argument is that order basically has to depend on the prevalence of justice, and that in its absence, the "stability" that obtains will only be illusory and short term. From this perspective, there is no contradiction between "doing good" and "doing well": By working for human rights, we are also laying the foundation for a more stable international system. Even if such a happy marriage of goals doesn't always occur, however, there is the further suggestion that, after all, the ultimate peace is the peace of the grave and that, in this mortal realm, we have to make choices at times between opposing values. As Mark Wicclair argues, "it cannot be denied that world peace and stability are desirable ends. But from a moral perspective, considerations of justice must be taken into account as well. Thus, depending upon the extent to which injustice prevails in the world, it is conceivable that a period of conflict and instability would be justified, all things considered."[8]

Underlying the whole debate over humanitarian intervention are some basic empirical questions as well that concern some possibly profound changes in the very character of international relations in the contemporary age. It has been argued that we may indeed be at a turning point in which at least *inter-state* war will become increasingly obsolete. Some of the factors that would lead to this potential outcome would include the increasing globalization of the world economy, the creation of a new international society marked by the proliferation of non-governmental and multilateral organizations, and new and complex forms of interdependence between states and societies in ecological and biospheric areas. The further suggestion, then, is that current and future military conflict will lie mostly *within* states, and in the face of this, the old modalities of deterrence and coercion, especially as practiced by the great powers, will be of increasingly limited utility. Under the circumstances, then, the best chance for peace and stability in the world lies in developing the resources of the world community, perhaps especially under the auspices of the United Nations, for measures such as preventive diplomacy, peacekeeping, and—where necessary—various types of humanitarian intervention.[9]

The basic idea of this book is to subject the concept of humanitarian intervention to a systematic analysis in terms of its implications, its limitations, and its ambiguities. In offering such an analysis, we will be entering the realm of what is generally called "applied ethics." Particularly as it relates to international affairs, applied ethics straddles both the concerns of the moral philosophers and the political theorists and those of actual policymakers and political operatives. It represents an attempt to attach some of the insights of the moral philosophers to the practical concerns of the policymakers. Above all, the concept endeavors to marry certain principles of moral conduct to the real world of affairs, and to offer judgments on the degree to which states or individual decision makers may or may not have demonstrated an appropriate ethical probity, given the constraints facing them. It is evident from this description that if applied ethics is to mean anything, it has to have some ultimate utility in shaping actual conduct. As the philosopher Peter Singer says, "An ethical judgment that is no good in practice must suffer from a theoretical defect as well, for the whole point of ethical judgments is to guide practice."[10]

It may well be said that the topic of humanitarian interventions represents one of the most challenging current issues facing the community of applied ethicists—and not only them, but anyone concerned with the possibilities of moral action in a complicated and violent world. In the biblical passage from Isaiah, we are enjoined "to loose the bands of wickedness, to undo the heavy burdens, and to let the oppressed go free." As a commanding moral principle, it is hard to argue with such an injunction. The questions remain: Which wickedness and burdens should receive our special attention?, and How are we really going to let the oppressed go free? These are not easy questions to answer, but not even to ask them would represent a rejection of our identity as members of a caring collective humanity.

NOTES

1. Cited in Ernst Haas, "Beware the Slippery Slope," in *Emerging Norms of Justified Intervention*, eds. Carl Kaysen and Laura W. Reed (Cambridge, MA: American Academy of Arts and Sciences, 1993), 63.

2. Bhikhu Parekh, "Rethinking Humanitarian Intervention," *International Political Science Review* 18 (1997), 49–70.

3. Andrew Natsios, *U.S. Foreign Policy and the Four Horsemen of the Apocalypse* (Westport, CT: Praeger, 1997), 7.

4. United States Mission to the United Nations, *Global Humanitarian Emergencies, 1997* (Washington, DC: GPO, April, 1997), 1–6.

5. Nicholas Wheeler refers to a category of "non-forcible humanitarian intervention" that emphasizes "the pacific activities of states, international organizations and non-governmental organizations in delivering humanitarian aid and facilitating third party conflict-resolution and reconstruction." Such interventions need not necessarily be "consensual." Thus, the well-known group Doctors Without Borders often operates without the formal

agreement of governments even while its methods are non-violent. Nicholas Wheeler, "Humanitarian Intervention and World Politics," in *The Globalization of World Politics*, eds. John Baylis and Steve Smith (New York: Oxford University Press, 1997), 405.

6. David Fisher, "The Ethics of Intervention," *Survival* 36 (Spring, 1994), 56.

7. Cited in Fernando R. Tesón, *Humanitarian Intervention* (Irvington-on-Hudson, NY: Transnational Publishers, 1985), 80–81.

8. Mark R. Wicclair, "Human Rights and Intervention," in *Human Rights and U.S. Foreign Policy*, eds. Peter G. Brown and Douglas MacLean (Lexington, MA: Lexington Books, 1979), 150.

9. Professor Gordon Craig offers an interesting case for these propositions in "No More Parades," *New York Review of Books* (April 20, 1995), 9.

10. Peter Singer, *Practical Ethics* (Cambridge: Cambridge University Press, 1979), 2.

Acknowledgments

I want to extend my thanks to Professor Cathal Nolan of Boston University and to Professor William Felice of Eckerd College for their careful reading of this manuscript. Their sympathetic criticism and suggestions for improvement have been of great value. For all of us writing on normative issues in international relations, the support of the Carnegie Council on Ethics and International Affairs has also been exemplary. Through its various publications and conferences, the Council has been a driving force in expanding the degree of attention that moral questions in world affairs have received in recent years by both academics and foreign-policy practitioners. Special thanks should go in this regard to the Council's President, Joel Rosenthal, and to its former Director of Educational Programs, Matt Mattern. I am also grateful to the members of my graduate seminar on humanitarian intervention at the Monterey Institute of International Studies for the stimulating insights they provided as I strove to establish my own position on this very important question. Gratitude as well to the Monterey Institute administration for providing me with a research sabbatical that greatly assisted in the final completion of this book. My editor at Praeger, Heather Ruland Staines, has held me to a high standard in revising the manuscript, but at the same time she has been unfailingly cheerful in urging me on. Finally, my beloved wife, Marta, has supported me through thick and thin as I have worked to bring this project to a conclusion. She has indeed been a companion faithful and true, and it is to her that I dedicate this book.

CHAPTER 1

Initial Considerations

In discussing the idea of humanitarian intervention, there are some important preliminary matters that need attention before we proceed further. The terms "humanitarian" and "intervention" are typically embued with such a variety of nuances and differing interpretations that to join them together into a single concept almost inevitably produces ambiguity and perhaps even tension, especially since both words inherently carry a lot of emotional baggage.

The chief complicating factor in addressing humanitarian intervention is that it really stands as a specific subset of a much broader range of activities that can legitimately be described as either humanitarian or interventionist, and some of which are relatively uncontroversial. The tendency in some quarters is to define "humanitarian intervention" simply as a coming together of these two generic types of behavior, but this makes any intelligent discussion of humanitarian intervention as a discrete phenomenon exceedingly difficult. "Humanitarianism" in international relations, for example, can cover a large number of items, such as the work of the International Committee of the Red Cross, famine-relief efforts by private or governmental organizations, international assistance to victims of floods or earthquakes, and even essentially private and individual matters such as family reunification. It is striking, in fact, how constantly the term "humanitarian" is used in public pronouncements by governments to explain their various policies, whether to plea for the release of hostages on humanitarian grounds or to explain the dispatch of personnel or resources to a foreign land as being spurred by humanitarian motives. Indeed, the mantra of "humanitarianism" now seems to have assumed almost equal standing with more traditional terms in foreign policy, such as "the national interest" and "legitimate self-defense," as standard coins of the realm.

The notion of "intervention" also has been subject to a widespread transformation in its usage and even more in its practice. In traditional international relations theory, intervention basically referred to the injection by one state of its military forces into the sovereign territory of another, either for determining the latter's political character or even, in the most extreme examples, for outright subjugation. Defined in this way, the idea of intervention was the bogeyman of international law and was universally condemned as a practice by both customary and conventional norms. In the contemporary world, however, various forms of what can legitimately be called intervention (albeit non-military) by one state or society into the affairs of another state have become virtually commonplace and, as such, have come to be accepted as a normal feature of international relations. One recalls in this context the famous comment of the French diplomat Talleyrand that "non-intervention is a term of political metaphysics signifying almost the same thing as intervention."

The realm of economic activity is a prime example. National firms routinely attempt to penetrate the home markets of foreign competitors and, in many instances, inject their own capital and resources to set up local production centers; meanwhile governments manipulate their tariff and export policies and adopt other measures to influence the economic behavior of other states. The International Monetary Fund often "intervenes" in the economic affairs of states that request loans through its use of "conditionality," which stipulates that applicant states have to adjust their fiscal and monetary policies to the IMF's satisfaction before receiving funds from the organization.

The new interventionism doesn't exist only in the sphere of economics, however. American cultural products, for example, particularly in the area of music and films, have penetrated virtually every society around the world and in some instances have raised alarums about "cultural imperialism." The French government, in response to this supposed unwarranted intrusion, has even established regulations that restrict the amount of material on French television that can be attributed to "foreign" sources. Broadly defined, other examples of the prevalence of intervention in the affairs of the world today stretch out almost endlessly. They include a steady drumbeat of criticism by various governments of the supposedly unsatisfactory diplomatic positions taken by other states, as well as something as theoretically mundane as the work of international journalists in attempting to penetrate the veil of secrecy that many governments strive to maintain over their activities. The point seems evident enough: "Intervention" of various types is today not just a relatively rare—and legally proscribed—activity among states, but it is a virtual norm in the conduct of international relations. John Herz was one of the first observers many years ago to point out that the idea of the impermeable nation-state totally in control of its own affairs and destiny was essentially a thing of the past.[1]

If the concepts of humanitarianism and intervention in world affairs are inherently broad and protean, then it is important to operationalize the concept of "humanitarian intervention" in a way that makes it an analytically distinct phenomenon and thus subject to focused assessment.[2] Humanitarian intervention, as used here, may be defined as the injection of military power—or the threat of such action—by one or more outside states into the affairs of another state that has as its purpose (or at least as one of its principal purposes) the relieving of grave human suffering. The latter may involve, inter alia, the systematic abuse of basic human rights by a cruel and repressive regime, or it may be a consequence of a general breakdown of central governmental authority, leading to a condition of anarchy that in itself threatens those rights. Humanitarian intervention, it will be observed, is inherently *political* in nature. It is the result not of some natural disaster, but rather is instigated by the conscious policies of a particular political authority. Or it results from the *absence* of any such authority that can provide minimal protection for a community of people and in particular ensure that basic standards of civilized treatment are afforded to them. In what follows we will offer a fairly extensive list of what can be regarded as humanitarian interventions both in the distant and more recent past. Suffice it to say at this point that the international community's activities in Somalia and Liberia are good examples of the second type of humanitarian intervention, while the French dispatch of troops to Rwanda in 1994 and the American intervention in Haiti in the same year represent the first model.

Such interventions do not inherently depend on the "consent" of the affected party for their legitimacy. On the one hand, it may be the country's prevailing regime that is the source of the outrages that occasion the intervention, and to seek their consent for the international community's action would effectively be a non sequitur. On the other hand, the human suffering that prompts humanitarian intervention may result from the general breakdown of central authority in a country, and in this instance as well, the requirement of consent is virtually a contradiction in terms. The famous British legal scholar Hersch Lauterpacht summarizes the special character of a humanitarian intervention. Such a step, he says, "signifies dictatorial interference in the sense of action amounting to a denial of the independence of the State. It implies a peremptory demand for positive conduct or abstention—a demand which, if not complied with, involves a threat of or recourse to compulsion . . . in some form."[3]

It should almost be self-evident by now that humanitarian intervention does not equate with what is usually called "peacekeeping" as practiced especially under the auspices of the United Nations. The latter practice makes no real moral distinction between the conflicting parties in a situation, and assumes that at least some tentative agreement on ending hostilities has been previously agreed to by these parties. Peacekeeping, thus, inherently involves an effort to maintain the status quo or at least the status quo as it has now come to be after a previous period of instability. Humanitarian intervention, by contrast, is an attempt to shape and define a new order within the affected country that will end the abuses occasioned by the old order.

In this formulation, the international community's activities in the former Yugoslavia—first with UNPROFOR (United Nations Protection Force) and later with the dispatch of IFOR (Inforcement Force) and then with SFOR (Stabilization Force)—to consolidate the Dayton accords were not a true example of humanitarian intervention. Their primary political purpose was simply to facilitate or maintain a negotiated settlement of political and territorial issues among the Serbs, Croats, and Moslems without passing judgment about who had the superior moral claim in this conflict.[4] It is of some importance in this regard that the Deputy Force Commander of UNPROFOR argued that if humanitarian goals were added to his military mandate, such goals would be "dangerously linked" to the conflict and would jeopardize its impartiality, or else it would create an impression that humanitarian aid could be "punched through" by force.[5]

Another important aspect of UNPROFOR's and IFOR's/SFOR's mission in the former Yugoslavia has been to facilitate the supply of humanitarian aid such as food and medicine to civilians within the war zone. In the case of UNPROFOR, because of the nature of the military situation, most of these supplies inevitably went to the Moslems, particularly those trapped in the so-called safe zones such as Sarajevo and Goradze. But there was nothing inherent in the UN's humanitarian aid mission that limited the provision of this aid solely to the Moslems. Indeed, the Bosnian Serbs, whom most considered the primary aggressor in this struggle, also received at least some food and medicine from the United Nations.

A genuine humanitarian intervention in the former Yugoslavia would not have concentrated simply on offering humanitarian aid, although that could have been one of its subsidiary purposes, or on supporting the parties' agreements at Dayton. Rather, it would have been predicated on a judgment about perpetrators and victims in the war, and would have been avowedly devoted to restraining (and perhaps punishing) the perpetrators protecting the victims. Once again, it would have been an essentially political action. The closest the international community came to such action was the series of air strikes against Serbian positions around Sarajevo in August, 1995, that evidently persuaded the Serbian leadership to enter the Dayton negotiations. While it was perhaps long overdue, this hardly constituted the full sort of humanitarian intervention that is the main focus of this book.

AN INITIAL DEFENSE OF HUMANITARIAN INTERVENTION

In the next chapter, we will analyze in some detail the various and relatively abstract philosophical arguments that are typically advanced to support or to oppose the concept of humanitarian intervention. Before we do that, however, it might be well to offer at least a few initial observations about the logic of and impetus to humanitarian intervention. After all, on its face, such a call to action seems to go against many of our practical and moral intuitions about the conduct of foreign policy and international relations. Aren't states traditionally concerned almost entirely with their own security and personal advancement? Can we really expect states to have any serious concern about the welfare of others, except as may be conducive to their own self-interest? And what about the morality of committing the nation's resources to foreign rescue missions when these resources are badly needed to deal with problems close at hand? Are the homeless in Chicago less worthy of attention than the homeless of Bosnia? Above all, is it right to ask our young men and women to shed their blood on behalf of foreigners when their own country's security is not at stake? Can we truly justify their sacrifice—and explain this sacrifice, for example, to their grieving parents—by suggesting that after all they died trying to achieve "justice" for some obscure and distant land.

These are not trivial queries, and they require a serious response. Those who assert the legitimacy of—and even more the need for—a regime of humanitarian intervention make a beginning at answering them by offering a reflection on the very nature of the human condition. They insist that "humanitarianism," broadly defined, is an integral ingredient of our existence, that there is a basic interconnectedness to humankind, and that a proper regard for the welfare of others is indeed central to our identity as human beings. Aristotle argued that an individual who is "sufficient for himself" must be either a "beast or a god." An Ethiopian scholar and classicist of Jewish heritage, Ephraim Isaac, refers to a traditional Ethiopian proverb to the effect that "he who eats alone, dies alone." He goes on to make an eloquent case for the proposition that none of us can—or want to—ignore the suffering of others, regardless of their status or origin.

> "Humanitarianism" is a feeling of concern for and benevolence toward fellow human beings. It is a universal phenomenon manifested globally and throughout the ages. Humanitarianism as practical generosity or philanthropic activities to promote the well-being of others is also a universal phenomenon. All peoples respect and appreciate humanitarian activities that form part of a common human vocabulary.[6]

Of course, Isaac's argument for the inherent existence of feelings of humanitarianism among all individuals does leave a range of questions to be addressed, notably whether such feelings are or necessarily can be translated into the official activities of those entities we call states. In our individual lives, we may indeed display benevolence toward the suffering of others; does that mean that we insist—or expect that—our governments follow similar standards?

In partial response to this question, those who support humanitarian intervention offer an additional and essentially prudential argument. They make much of the fact that in the currently integrated international system, the travails of one society almost inevitably spill over into difficulties for others as well. It is common knowledge that this system has become increasingly intertwined through economic exchange, movement of peoples across borders, global communications systems, mass transportation, and so forth. We may not have quite arrived at the "global village" of which Marshall McLuhan spoke, but the momentum is clearly in that direction. Under these circumstances—the growing interconnectedness of national communities—societal upheavals that might have passed unremarked on in an earlier era thrust themselves onto the international consciousness, whether for reasons of principle or prudence. From this perspective, international instability is inherently infectious and is not likely to be as quarantined as in past days.

One obvious example is the growing problem of the international flow of refugees. According to figures compiled by the United Nations High Commission on Refugees, total cross-national population movements have increased from 17 million in 1991 to 23 million in 1993 and to more than 27 million at the beginning of 1995. Of this number, some 14.5 million can legitimately be classified as "refugees," that is, people crossing international borders and being granted asylum in another country. The UNHCR also counts some 5.4 million internally displaced persons and another 4 million former refugees who have returned to their homeland.[7] Now, many of these fleeing their homelands may be regarded as essentially economic refugees searching for better material opportunities in other lands. Still, it is unmistakable that many, if not most, of those in flight are escaping unbearable political conditions in their own lands. The exodus from Haiti before the American intervention in that country in the fall of 1994 perhaps is a representative example. To this extent, so the argument goes, humanitarian intervention is really quite a practical response to prevent what might be the effects on one's own society of the troubles in a distant one.

The argument for such interventions also frequently rests on a simple assertion of relative advantage and opportunity, a variety of what can be called distributive ethics.[8] In a world where the United States and other advanced industrial societies dispose of so many resources, and enjoy such disproportionately high standards of consumption compared to many other societies, there is, at the very least, a case to be made for devoting some share of these resources to formal efforts to assist others. This doesn't mean just disaster relief in response to natural calamities, although this is certainly an important function in itself, but a broader effort to bring some of the benefits of a civil society and responsible government to those currently suffering without (again, both ethical and utilitarian reasons can be advanced for doing so). Abraham Lincoln once advanced the compelling proposition that the American nation could not long endure half-slave and half-free. The wisdom of his words—it is suggested—has as great an application today as it did during the great crisis of the Civil War.

Finally, advocates of humanitarian intervention sometimes broach the theme that was compellingly presented by the Polish writer Joseph Conrad in *Heart of Darkness*. This novella dealt with the journey of its unnamed narrator (a suitably correct European) along the Congo River in search of a certain Kurtz, a representative of a British trading company who had descended into unspeakable savagery. Kurtz's tragedy was that, far from opposing the often barbarous customs he found in his remote outpost, he first tolerated and then actually embraced them. The whole point of Conrad's work was to suggest that an acceptance—even a passive acceptance—of cruelty and inhumanity was to invite an increasing corruption of one's own character. John Donne made a somewhat similar argument to the effect that "no man is an island entire of itself . . . any man's death diminishes me, because I am involved in mankind." If we expand the definition of "death" here to include, among other things, the calculated physical abuse of whole categories of individuals, the absence of basic elements of democratic self-governance, and the systematic denial of a wide range of other basic human rights as well, then a compelling case may exist for defining, expanding, and consolidating the whole notion of humanitarian intervention in the interests of the oppressed and the suffering. To shirk this responsibility and this calling—the argument goes—is ultimately to call into question our identity as caring human beings and our own self-respect.

HISTORICAL HUMANITARIAN INTERVENTION

What we have so far is a fairly abstract definition and a set of rather lofty generalizations about the importance of an ideal. It is not unreasonable to ask at this point whether there is really much more to discuss about this "ideal," at least in terms of there being any significant historical evidence that it has sometimes been translated into a reality. One of the criticisms sometimes leveled at proponents of humanitarian intervention is that they are essentially arguing for states to behave in ways that they never have. In other words, they are making an essentially normative argument about what *should be* rather than what has been and currently is. The philosopher David Luban has suffered more than his share of dismissal on these grounds. Typical is the comment by one writer that Luban's "basis for recommending a universal right to intervention is more the [result of] wrath and a feeling of righteousness" than of any very serious consideration of the problem of "rights" and their enforcement.[9]

The assertion that there is almost no empirical record of previous humanitarian interventions, however, can hardly be sustained. The problem seems to be that the critics have typically sought to find instances in which a state or states intervened entirely on the grounds of humanitarian concern, and finding very few, if any, in the historical record, they have basically concluded that the whole notion of humanitarian intervention is a chimera. Yet it doesn't seem unreasonable to suggest that this is setting the standard too high. The idea that governments typically have mixed motives in undertaking any important foreign-policy action is hardly a breakthrough in scholarly analysis. Should it come as a shock that a government may be trying to do well even as it may do good? The real issue here—perhaps the real surprise, at least to some people—is not that governments have their own self-interest in mind when they undertake any foreign-policy venture, but that this self-interest is sometimes supplemented by at least some attention to genuinely altruistic goals.

If we accept, then, that totally "pure" examples of humanitarian intervention are extremely hard to find—if they exist at all—it is possible to identify various historical episodes in which at least some measure of humanitarian concern seems to have been present in forceful interventions by outside forces into a separate sovereignty. In detailing putative examples of such interventions, it is convenient to consider, first, some relatively distant historical cases and then turn to the more contemporary period.

Humanitarian Intervention before 1945

Perhaps the main body of evidence in support of the notion that humanitarian intervention has a significant historical pedigree may be found in the various measures taken by the European powers in the nineteenth century to curb supposed abuses within the Ottoman Empire. In 1827, for example, Great Britain, France, and Russia intervened on the side of the Greeks in their struggle for independence from the Turks. The object of this action was, in the words of one authority, "to prevent the complete subjugation of the Greek people . . . and to protect [their] rights of self-determination."[10] A strong motivating factor in this instance were reports of the unusually cruel, even barbarous, steps taken by the Porte in crushing Greek freedom-fighters. The fact that Greece was considered an integral part of the Western cultural tradition presumably played an important role as well.

Still another example of a European intervention to stem Turkish outrages was the effort undertaken by Russia in the early 1850s to protect the rights of oppressed Orthodox Christians within the Ottoman Empire. In this case, however, the unilateral character of the Russian action led eventually to the Crimean War, in which France and Britain actually allied themselves with the Sultan to maintain the balance of power in southern Europe. In 1860, however, a French force was landed in Lebanon, by agreement of all the major powers, in order to protect the Christian Maronite community there against Moslem attack. This action is generally identified as perhaps the prime exemplar of humanitarian intervention in the nineteenth century. It was sparked by the massacre of some 6,000 Maronites by the Moslem Druze sect while the Ottoman authorities stood aside. The collective endorsement of the landing of French troops included a provision that they would leave after a period of six months. The French also received the reluctant endorsement of the Porte, thus placing this episode in a special category as far as humanitarian intervention is concerned.[11] There was a further Russian intervention in 1877–78 in the Balkans to aid the revolutionary movements in that region and in particular to end what were called the "Bulgarian horrors" (atrocities committed by Turkish troops in that country), an action that led to independence for the Bulgarians and autonomy for Bosnia-Herzegovina. Sanctioned by Austria, Prussia, France, and Italy, the Russian move was described as being motivated by religious sentiment and elementary considerations of humanity.[12]

The above episodes seem to represent almost an ideal paradigm of the mix of both practical and moral concerns evident in almost all real-world examples of humanitarian intervention. On the one hand, the European powers were intent on exploiting Turkish weakness for their own advantage—and with keeping their competitors from making undue gains at Turkish expense in the bargain (e.g., the Crimean War). At the same time, public accounts of some of the genuine atrocities being inflicted by Ottoman authorities on their recalcitrant subjects were sufficiently gruesome that the relevant governments seemed compelled to act in response. Perhaps they were "doing good and doing well" at the same time, but under the criteria established earlier, it seems hard to deny that their actions were at least a *type* of humanitarian intervention that we can legitimately identify. One cautionary note that might be offered here, however, is that in some ways, they constituted the very sort of behavior that contemporary developing countries have found so noxious—and threatening. The Sultan's regime was seen by the more "advanced" European countries as essentially retrograde and outside the pale of civilized society. This made it all the easier for the European regimes to comfort themselves that they were doing the Lord's work in intervening against such a regime, even though some of the intervenors—notably the Russians, with their history of anti-Semitic measures—hardly were models of rectitude in their own human-rights performance.

A special category of humanitarian concern during this period concerned the treatment of Jews within the countries of Eastern Europe as well as Russia itself. The various manifestations of anti-Semitism there, ranging from outright pogroms to certain legal and social disabilities, did not lead to the actual use of outside force, or even to an explicit threat of its being used. Nevertheless, it stands as an example of the concerns of the period. Thus, the British government made strong representations to the regime in Romania in 1867 to take appropriate steps to curtail the widely reported oppression of Romanian Jews. The United States at times added her own voice to these demands, notably in 1872, when the American consul in Bucharest was instructed "due to humanity to remonstrate against any license or impunity which may have attended the outrages in that country." In 1891, Secretary of State James Blaine protested against the Czarist government's harsh treatment of Russian Jews, in part because of "the universal and innate sentiment of humanity," but also because of concerns that such treatment would lead to a flood of Russian-Jewish emigration to the United States. Some twenty years later, Washington went so far as to abrogate an earlier Russo-American friendship treaty of 1832 as a symbol of its disapproval of Russian oppression of its Jewish citizenry.[13]

There are various other pre-1945 cases of humanitarian intervention that are often referred to, including the five-power naval blockade of Antwerp in 1830 in support of the Belgian drive for independence from the Kingdom of the Netherlands. This had the effect of securing the claim of the Belgians to self-determination. A better-known instance of supposed humanitarian intervention came later in the century with American actions in Cuba in 1898. For some years, the Spanish authorities there had been engaged in a ruthless suppression of the Cuban independence movement and in the process had developed among other things the concept of the "concentration camp." President McKinley, in his address to Congress calling for a state of war against Spain to free Cuba, argued that the United States needed to act "in the cause of humanity and to put an end to barbarities, bloodshed, starvation, and horrible miseries." One well-known writer of the time, Professor Theodore S. Woolsey, defended the legitimacy of American behavior: "That intervention on the ground of humanity is justifiable is a matter of precedent . . . as well as a theory. And so far as facts go, our action in behalf of Cuba is as fair an instance of it as any of the earlier examples."[14] As with the earlier interventions by European powers against the Ottomans, there were, to be sure, ulterior motives that historians have identified in both the Belgian and Cuban cases. In Belguim, there was a concern with maintaining the European strategic balance, and in Cuba, an interest in the economic benefits to be had from a free Cuba. President McKinley supplemented his humanitarian rhetoric by adding that "the right to intervene may be justified by the very serious injury to the commerce, trade and business of our people" if nothing were done.[15]

In considering historical examples of interventions based at least partly on the advancement of certain principles or norms, there are two other contrasting cases that deserve attention. The first of these concerned the abolition of the international slave trade in the nineteenth century. Driven by a powerful domestic antislavery movement, Great Britain, then the preeminent maritime power in the world, used its naval power to force an end to the transport of slaves from Africa. Particular pressure was placed on Portugal and Brazil in this regard. After unsuccessful attempts to gain Lisbon's assent to a treaty outlawing all slave traffic, the British navy was given leave in 1839 to unilaterally board and seize Portuguese ships bearing slaves and to free their unfortunate passengers. Brazil had agreed, following its independence in 1822, to end importing slaves from Africa, but the traffic continued and even increased in subsequent years. British ships eventually entered Brazilian ports in 1850 in order to seize and burn those vessels that were suspected of slave trafficking. Given this degree of pressure, the Brazilian legislature at last passed and enforced laws designed totally to end the slave trade. It is important to note that British actions, while unilateral in military terms, did receive the imprimatur of the international community in the form of various treaties that outlawed traffic in slaves. Such activity was indeed defined in these conventions as "piracy" and was thus subject to suppression by any of the seagoing powers. It is also germane to observe that there seemed little pragmatic benefit to Britain deriving out of her actions, especially in the economic sense, since many British plantations in the Caribbean had been heavily dependent on slave labor.[16]

In sharp contrast to the above exercises in intervention for principle—in content, if not in form—there are the activities of the Concert of Europe and, more especially, the so-called Holy Alliance, in the early part of the nineteenth century. By the Treaty of Chaumont in 1814, which was designed to establish the post-Napoleonic European order, it was agreed that there would be periodic congresses of the major European powers (Britain, Prussia, Austria, Russia, and, later, France) to consider joint action to sustain continental peace and security. For Britain, this meant simply maintaining a rough balance of power in Europe, but for Prussia, Austria, and Russia, Chaumont had a rather different implication. The latter three countries formed the Holy Alliance in 1815 in order to suppress dangerous republican tendencies within Europe—by collective force if necessary—which they regarded as dangerous to European stability generally. A protocol that emerged out of the Conference of Troppau in 1820 offered the following:

> States which have undergone a change of government due to revolution, the results of which threaten other states, ipso facto cease to be members of the European Alliance, and remain excluded from it until their situation gives guarantees for legal order and stability. If, owing to such alterations, immediate danger threatens other states, the parties bind themselves, by peaceful means, or if need by arms, to bring back the guilty state into the bosom of the Great Alliance.[17]

Following the Conference at Troppau, there were a series of actual or threatened measures by the Holy Alliance to stem the republican tide in Europe, notably in Piedmont, Portugal, Naples, and Spain. Even after the Alliance collapsed in the mid-1820s, because of disagreements over policy toward the Greek rebellion against the Turks, the guiding spirit of the Troppau declaration continued to exist in various instances. Russia intervened to crush nascent democratic movements in Poland in 1830 and in Hungary in 1848; Austria did the same in Northern Italy in the early 1830s. Even Britain condoned some of these measures, depending on her estimation of their contribution in maintaining the European balance of power. Altogether, it has been calculated that there were some fourteen interventions against republican movements in the weaker European states located in what is now Italy, Spain, and Germany between 1815 and 1850.[18] It might seem bizarre to include the activities of the Holy Alliance alongside those of Britain in ending the slave trade as examples of "humanitarian intervention," but both actually partook of some similar features: Each set of interventions was based on a conviction about upholding certain principles or ideals, each had at least a putative collective character, and, finally, each involved the use or threat of force.

Humanitarian Intervention after 1945

In the more contemporary period, there has been a surprisingly broad series of what might be defined as humanitarian interventions, although, inevitably, there continues to be much controversy about some or all of these cases, to which we will give an airing in due course. Among the best-known was the Indian government's invasion of East Pakistan in 1971 ostensibly in order to end the barbarities being inflicted on the Bengali people by Pakistani authorities and to secure the right of the Bengalis to self-determination. A more modest example of Dehli's use of intervention for humanitarian purposes was its decision to airdrop relief supplies to the Tamil population in northern Sri Lanka in 1987 because the Tamils were suffering from the civil war in that country, a suffering to which, the Indians claimed, the government in Colombo remained indifferent.

Aside from Indian support of the Bengalis, the two other most frequently cited examples of humanitarian intervention in the contemporary era include the Tanzanian intervention in Uganda in 1979 in order to topple the regime of Idi Amin, and the Vietnamese invasion of Cambodia in the same year that had the effect of ending the murderous rule of the Khmer Rouge. There are a number of other cases, however, that deserve at least some mention. The French government, for example, has been involved in several interventions in Africa that had at least some ostensible humanitarian motive. Among these were sending troops to the so-called Central African Empire to topple the bloody regime of Emperor Jean Bedel Bokassa in 1979 and, more recently, the French intervention in Rwanda in June, 1994 that was designed to set up a "safe area" for potential victims of the ethnic bloodletting taking place there.

American foreign policy over the last decade has also featured several nods in the direction of using force to uphold certain principles of human rights and self-governance. We have already mentioned the American threat (and impending application) of force against the Cedras regime in Haiti in the fall of 1994, described as necessary to end the oppression being visited on the Haitian people and to restore the legally elected Aristide government. The Bush administration perhaps set a precedent for President Clinton's actions by undertaking Operation Just Cause against Panamanian dictator Manuel Noriega in December, 1989, the supposed rationale once again being Noriega's subversion of Panamanian democracy as well as his use of a private army of thugs against his political opponents. The United States was also heavily involved, of course, in the United Nations force sent to Somalia in December, 1992 to ensure the delivery of famine relief to Somalis who were facing starvation because of the ongoing war between the various tribal factions in that country.

Other cases of humanitarian intervention in the contemporary period that might be cited include the insertion of forces from ECOWAS (Economic Community of West African States) into Liberia in August, 1990, which was prompted by the virtual breakdown of central authority in Monrovia as a consequence of the Liberian civil war and the accompanying massive suffering of the Liberian population. There has also been the United Nations-sponsored intervention in northern and southern Iraq dating from the spring of 1991 to provide protection for the Kurds and Shiites, respectively, against efforts by the Saddam Hussein regime to crush their desire for at least some measurable autonomy and decent living conditions.

THE SHADOW OF HYPOCRISY

During the United Nations debate over the Indian intervention into East Pakistan in 1971, the Indian ambassador waxed poetic over the bona fides behind his country's action: "We have on this particular occasion absolutely nothing but the purest of motives and the purest of intentions: to rescue the people of East Bengal from what they are suffering."[19] When governments speak of the "purity" of their motives and intentions, even the most sanguine (or innocent) observers are likely to have some worries—and not without reason. For those who are skeptical about the reality—and the utility—of true humanitarian interventions, there are ample cases in which military interventions have been taken for ostensibly humanitarian reasons, but whose real, less elevated motivations have not been hard to discern.[20] The evident hypocrisy found in these cases provides grist for the mill of those who question whether *any* intervention in the internal affairs of a state can ever be taken at face value, at least in terms of its supposed service to a basic moral purpose. It is not an issue that can be easily set aside even by the most fervent supporters of the concept of humanitarian intervention.

Take, for example, the Soviet crushing of the Hungarian rebellion in 1956. The effort of the Hungarian people to throw off the yoke of Soviet domination and to remove the oppressive rule of the Hungarian Communist regime in the bargain, resulted in a Soviet intervention that eventually led to some 30,000 Hungarian casualties and the exodus of another 60,000 Hungarians to refuge in the United States alone. This exercise in bloodletting was hardly represented by Moscow as an example of Soviet imperialism. On the contrary, Soviet representatives at the United Nations styled their actions as an exalted attempt at "helping to put an end to the counter-revolutionary intervention and riots" and as a response to a foreign plot "to stab the Hungarian people in the back."[21] The same type of convoluted rhetoric was used to "explain" the Soviet move into Czechoslovakia some twelve years later. Far from being an attempt by Moscow to crush the reformist government of Alexander Dubcek in the interests of the Soviet *imperium* in Eastern Europe, it turns out that the intervention was undertaken because "enemies were . . . shaking the foundations of law and order and . . . trampling laws underfoot . . . preparing to seize power." Under the circumstances, there was a need for fraternal forces "to clean up the atmosphere . . . and to create the necessary calm and serenity to allow the Czechoslovak people to put order in their home."[22] The reality behind both of those Soviet actions was that they dealt almost entirely with maintaining the cohesion of Moscow's East European security system and with preventing any spillover of "unhealthy" liberal bourgeois thinking into the Soviet Union itself.

Other egregious examples of the corruption of language to paint an exercise in naked aggression as a humanitarian enterprise could be cited almost endlessly. Two pre-1945 cases involved the Japanese invasion of Manchuria in 1931, and Hitler's demand in September, 1938 that the Sudeten area of Czechoslovakia be given over to Germany. Tokyo represented its action to the League of Nations as an acceptance of its duty to "stabilize" the chaotic situation then existing in Manchuria: "It would have been a breach of that duty to have left the population a prey to anarchy—deprived of all the apparatus of civilized life."[23] The Japanese move was, of course, only the initial step in a calculated plan to bring all of China under its control. Similarly, the real purpose of the German action against Prague was effectively to destroy Czechoslovakia—the one genuinely democratic regime in the area at the time—as an independent entity and, in the process, to open the whole Danube valley to Nazi domination. One would never guess this, however, from the tone of Hitler's remarks to British Prime Minister Neville Chamberlain. Writing to Chamberlain on September 23, the German dictator expressed moral outrage at the fact that ethnic Germans and "various nationalities in Czechoslovakia have been maltreated in the unworthiest manner, tortured, economically destroyed and, above all, prevented from realizing for themselves also the right of nations to self-determination."[24] The subsequent German move into the Sudetenland—from this perspective—could only be applauded as a contribution to the net happiness of mankind.

It is only honest and realistic to recognize that a gap between stated purpose and actual motivation has hardly been absent from American foreign policy as well. For example, American spokespersons made much of the humanitarian motives behind Washington's dispatch of forces to the Dominican Republic in 1965 and, of course, to Vietnam throughout the 1960s. In each instance, a major goal of these measures was supposedly to secure the safety and freedom of a country under assault by totalitarian outside forces. The Reagan administration's sending troops to Grenada in 1982 must also be mentioned in this context, although the rhetoric that emanated from Washington on this occasion tended to emphasize the rescue of American nationals from imminent harm more than securing a better life for the Grenadian people.

In the case of the Dominican Republic, the real basis for the Johnson administration's policy seems to have been a fear of a domino effect in the Caribbean. If an avowedly leftist regime were allowed to establish itself in Santo Domingo—especially one that had close ties with Havana—the repercussions in the region were seen as potentially disastrous. On April 30, Ambassador Ellsworth Bunker, addressing a Meeting of Consultation of American Ministers of Foreign Affairs, stressed that the American action had actually been a type of humanitarian intervention in response to the threat of anarchy:

> We are . . . faced with an immediate problem of how to restore law and order in order to protect not only the citizens of foreign countries . . . but also to stop the excessive vandalism which many people are wreaking on their fellow Dominican citizens. . . . We are not talking about intruding in the domestic affairs of other countries, we are talking simply about the elementary duty to save lives in a situation where there is no authority able to accept responsibility for primary law and order.[25]

It wasn't long, however, before President Johnson began to outline the real reasons for American policy. "There are signs that people trained outside the Dominican Republic are seeking to gain control. . . . What began as a popular democratic revolution . . . was taken over and really seized and placed into the hands of a band of Communist conspirators. . . . The American nations cannot, must not, and will not permit the establishment of another Communist government in the Western Hemisphere."[26] Along the same lines, the long, sorry story of the American role in Vietnam suggests that even though there may have been some genuine concern for the future of the South Vietnamese people, Washington's overwhelming emphasis was to counter the threat of Chinese expansion, to minimize the encouragement that a Communist victory in Vietnam could give to others contemplating wars of national liberation, and, finally, the overall military-strategic calculations about defending the Western presence in Southeast Asia and the Western Pacific more generally.

The examples of dissimulation in foreign policy shown above may be regarded as only routine by many experts on the subject, but the issue they raise for proponents of humanitarian intervention is a difficult one. There is a tendency in some quarters to minimize the range of cases in which such insincerity has been present, but to do so seems to play into the hands of those who would deny that genuine humanitarian intervention can ever be a reality. A far better strategy would be to accept that there *are* numerous instances of bogus intervention, but at the same time to insist that such examples can't be used as a rationale for throwing out the baby with the bathwater. In other words, despite these dispiriting exercises in hypocrisy, it is still possible to identify cases of *genuine* intervention for humanitarian purposes. The challenge here, then, is basically empirical and not theoretical: a close examination of the actual details of an interventionary action to determine its real character and actual humanitarian content.

Separating the sheep from the goats in this manner is sometimes quite difficult if we accept that the foreign-policy actions of governments *are* inevitably a mixed bag where their motivations and goals are concerned. Determining the motivations is particularly problematic. Powerful political leaders are adept in applying a humanistic garb to even the most obviously self-interested of their actions, and it is not easy, in most cases, to delve beneath the rhetoric to determine what genuinely humanistic impulses may have been present in their actions. One way in which we can possibly deal with this conundrum is, in effect, to work backward, that is, to focus not so much on ostensible motivations as on results. Assuming that the latter are obviously beneficial for the affected peoples, this may provide at least some intuitive evidence that the original purpose of the intervention did have some altruistic aspect. From a somewhat different perspective, even if a government's motivations per se may have been self-interested, if the *effect* of their actions is good, then a given intervention may rightly be defined as having at least some humanitarian quality to it.

Applying these criteria to the cases mentioned above, the Soviet moves against Czechoslovakia and Hungary resulted in the imposition of hardline domestic regimes that, if anything, increased the suffering of their captive populations. Equally, the American role in Vietnam may rightly be summarized by reference to the famous line by an American officer, in describing an action in the Mekong Delta, that "it became necessary to destroy the village in order to save it." The United States didn't literally "destroy" Vietnam, but it does not seem for want of trying: More bombs were dropped on that hapless country than were dropped in all the theaters of war by all sides in World War II. To take only the four cases of Rwanda, Uganda, East Pakistan, and Haiti, on the other hand, there seems no question that a great many lives were saved by the interventions in those countries. This doesn't mean that there weren't any problematical aspects to them, nor that the pronouncements of the intervenors in each case concerning their reasons for action didn't have to be taken with a certain grain of salt. From a consequentialist standpoint, however, they clearly seem to stand out from some of the more dubious examples of "humanitarian intervention" that we have detailed.

However one uses history to demonstrate either the regularity or the paucity of interventions with a humanitarian motive, it is necessary to turn now to a closer examination of two sets of questions that bear on the very concept of humanitarian intervention. The first of these conserns matters of philosophy and ethical reasoning, while the second involves issues of international law. The basic philosophical and legal arguments that lead either to an assertion or a denial of the right of humanitarian intervention are, of course, hardly unrelated. Indeed, all but the most extreme positivists within the international legal community accept that general notions of ethical principle do have a rightful place in discussions of the "legality" of various actions. For present purposes, however, we will distinguish between the philosophical and legal questions that bear on humanitarian intervention in an effort to render the arguments more clearly.

NOTES

1. John Herz, *International Politics in the Atomic Age* (New York: Columbia University Press, 1962).

2. The origins of the term "humanitarian intervention" are somewhat obscure, but it appears that William Edward Hall was one of the first to use it in his famous treatise on international law published in 1895. See W. E. Hall, *A Treatise on International Law,* 4th ed. (Oxford: Clarendon Press, 1895), 304. Hall defended the notion of such intervention by saying that when "a state grossly and patently violates international law . . . it is competent to any state, or to the body of states, to hinder the wrongdoing from being accomplished, or to punish the wrongdoer." Ibid., 57–58. Perhaps the first full discussion of the concept of humanitarian intervention in the modern period was Antoine Rougier's "La théorie de l'intervention d'humanité," *Revue Générale* 17 (1910), 468–526.

3. Cited in Thomas Buergenthal, "Domestic Jurisdiction, Intervention, and Human Rights: The International Law Perspective," in *Human Rights and U.S. Foreign Policy*, eds. Peter G. Brown and Douglas MacLean (Lexington, MA: Lexington Books, 1979), 116.

4. Richard Betts does suggest that even in the case of "peacekeeping," it is hard to argue that the outside powers are being totally neutral, since their activities inevitably result in at least some change in the local balance of power. Richard K. Betts, "The Delusion of Impartial Intervention," *Foreign Affairs* 73 (November/December, 1994).

5. Raimo Väyrynen, "Introduction: How Much Force in Humanitarian Intervention?" in *The Ethics and Politics of Humanitarian Intervention*, Stanley Hoffman et al. (Notre Dame, IN: University of Notre Dame Press, 1996), 7.

6. Ephraim Isaac, "Humanitarianism Across Religions and Cultures," in *Humanitarianism Across Borders*, eds. Larry Minear and Thomas G. Weiss (Boulder, CO: Lynne Rienner Publishers, 1993), 13.

7. United Nations High Commissioner for Refugees, *The State of the World's Refugees 1995: In Search of Solutions* (New York: Oxford University Press, 1995). The UNHCR identifies another 3.5 million people outside

their native country who have not been classified as refugees, but who are of concern to the organization as well.

8. An interesting discussion of distributive ethics may be found in Edward Weisband, ed., *Poverty Amidst Plenty: World Political Economy and Distributive Justice* (Boulder, CO: Westview Press, 1989). See also Henry Shue's *Basic Rights: Subsistence, Affluence, and U.S. Foreign Policy*, 2nd ed. (Princeton, NJ: Princeton University Press, 1996).

9. Friedrich Kratochwil, "Sovereignty as *Dominium*," in *Beyond Westphalia?* eds. Gene Lyons and Michael Mastanduno (Baltimore, MD: Johns Hopkins University Press, 1995), 38.

10. Ellery Stowell, *Intervention in International Law* (Washington, DC: John Byrne and Co., 1921), 126–27.

11. Ibid., 63–65.

12. Thomas Franck and Nigel Rodley, "After Bangladesh: The Law of Humanitarian Intervention by Force," *American Journal of International Law* 67 (1973), 281–83.

13. Stowell, *Intervention in International Law*, 67–79. On this issue, see also Cathal Nolan, "The United States and Tsarist Anti-Semitism, 1865–1914," *Diplomacy and Statecraft* 3 (November, 1992), 438–67.

14. Theodore S. Woolsey, *American Foreign Policy* (New York: The Century Co., 1898), 75–76.

15. Ibid., 284–85. The decidedly mixed character of the American intervention in Cuba was reflected by the subsequent adoption of the so-called "Platt Amendment," which effectively reduced Cuba to the status of an economic dependency of the United States.

16. Stephen Krasner, "Sovereignty and Intervention," in Lyons and Mastanduno, *Beyond Westphalia?* 240–42. See also Leslie Bethell, *The Abolition of the Brazilian Slave Trade* (Cambridge: Cambridge University Press, 1970). Sir Frederick Rogers, a prominent British political figure of the day, summarized the basis for British policy on the question of slavery: "The English nation, while its own interests are not very visibly and gravely concerned, has a strong vein of philanthropy, but it is in regard to negro slavery that this feeling has so taken hold of the people, and is so powerfully organized as to become a political influence." Quoted in Stowell, *Intervention in International Law*, 197.

17. Ann Thomas and A. J. Thomas, *Non-Intervention* (Dallas: Southern Methodist University Press, 1956), 9.

18. J. Leurdijk, *Intervention in International Politics* (Leeuwarden, Netherlands: Eismas BV, 1986), Appendix 1.

19. Franck and Rodley, "After Bangladesh: The Law of Humanitarian Intervention by Force," 276.

20. Thus we have the following mocking description from President Eisenhower about being asked by the British to consider a joint military inter-

vention in Iran against the Mossadegh regime in 1953: "I received a lecture on the might, the power, the majesty of the two great nations of the United States and the United Kingdom marching in before these little trembling dictators and announcing our decision—which of course is always based upon justice, reason and consideration, to say nothing for a very deep concern for all humanity." Quoted in Marc Trachtenberg, "Intervention in Historical Perspective," in *Emerging Norms of Justified Intervention*, eds. Carl Kaysen and Laura W. Reed (Cambridge, MA: American Academy of Arts and Sciences, 1993), 26.

21. 11 United Nations SCOR, 746th Meeting 27 (1956).

22. Franck and Rodley, "After Bangladesh: The Law of Humanitarian Intervention by Force," 286.

23. Sean D. Murphy, *Humanitarian Intervention* (Philadelphia: University of Pennsylvania Press, 1996), 60–61.

24. Franck and Rodley, "After Bangladesh: The Law of Humanitarian Intervention by Force," 286.

25. R. J. Vincent, *Nonintervention and International Order* (Princeton, NJ: Princeton University Press, 1974), 202–3.

26. Ibid.

CHAPTER 2

The Realm of Philosophy

In discussing the philosophical debate over humanitarian intervention, it is a given here that what might be considered relatively abstract philosophical propositions do have a distinct effect on human behavior. As the noted British economist John Maynard Keynes once said with respect to the supposed difference between theory and practice, "Practical men, who believe themselves to be quite exempt from any intellectual influences, are usually the slaves of some defunct economist. Madmen in authority, who hear voices in the air, are distilling their frenzy from some academic scribbler of a few years back."[1] The point is that some type of theory—in this instance a set of ethical first principles—does have a significant, perhaps ultimately even a controlling, force in shaping our actions, including (or perhaps especially) our political actions even if they remain unstated. What are the first principles that may be identified as central to the debate over humanitarian intervention?

Perhaps the most basic of these concerns the whole issue of one political community's responsibility for the fate and welfare of other such communities. The Hobbesian tradition in Western political thought dismisses the idea that one society or culture has a humanitarian obligation to any other. Proclaiming that "man is a wolf toward man" (*homo homini lupus*), Hobbes describes nations as living in a state of nature in which their government's only true obligation is to maintain domestic tranquillity and to secure the safety of the nation from the inherently predatory threats of others. In this respect, he argues, sovereigns may legitimately use any means available in dealing with other states, even to the extent of harming "innocents," if this should prove useful in gaining their interests. The point is that since states live in an environment in which there is a war of all against all, there can be no true concern for humanity in state relations.[2] Followers of the Hobbesian tradition assert, then, that the very idea of an "international community" is essentially a contradiction in terms. To the extent that community is an important concept in our lives, it can only be understood in local and parochial terms; it is hardly applicable to the whole range of human society. The practical policy implication of such a stance is that the concept of humanitarian intervention is itself a contradiction in terms: No particular nation will, or can be expected to, expend its resources of blood and treasure in service to others not of that nation.

In sharp contrast to the Hobbesian school of thought, there is a countervailing philosophical tradition that emphasizes not the inherent conflict and incompatibility among political communities; rather, it cites their mutual bonds as well as the possibility—and the duty—of collective action for humanitarian ends. We have referred to this position briefly in our earlier discussion, but it is well to recognize that this tradition, too, has a lengthy historical pedigree. Indeed, it can be traced back to some of the earliest formulations of classical "Just War" doctrine. The traditional version of bellum justum held that a Prince not only had a right, but even an obligation, to intervene in the territory of others if there were injustices that remained unchecked by prevailing authority.[3] This grant of the right of intervention was tied closely to the concept of the *Respublica Christiana*, articulated most notably by Saint Thomas Aquinas, and it combined both political and religious elements. It was accepted that there were separate sovereignties, but at the same time, there was a religious order connecting these sovereignties that produced its own rules and rights, and that, in turn, emanated out of "natural law." The theory of natural law held that there were certain enduring principles that governed the operations of Nature and man that emanated essentially from God Himself, and that man had sufficient resources of reason to identify these principles. A resort to humanitarian intervention inherently constituted, then, an "Appeal to Heaven," or to Heaven's Laws as they were interpreted through right reason.[4]

As the notion of the *Respublica Christiana* began to fade in the sixteenth century, it became necessary to address the question of humanitarian intervention against a background of rising state power and centralization. The Spanish moral theorist Francis de Vitoria argued for the continued legitimacy of such intervention by stressing the idea of a "human community" in which shared obligations were paramount. Quoting from the book of Ecclesiastes, to the effect that "God has laid a charge on every individual concerning his neighbor," he went on to add, "and they are all our neighbors." Vitoria then drew up a list of eight specific situations in which humanitarian intervention would be legitimate. The noted Dutch jurist and philosopher, Hugo Grotius, writing almost a hundred years later, also faced the problem of the diminishing sense of religious cohesion among the European states. In its place, he established the notion of a community of states nevertheless bound by the precepts of natural law (as well as by what he saw as an emerging body of positive law). Grotius was particularly concerned with "whether a war for the subjects of another be just, for the purpose of defending them from injuries inflicted by their ruler." His conclusion was that "kings and those who are possessed of sovereign power have a right to exact punishment not only for injuries affecting immediately themselves or their own subjects, but for gross violations of the law of nature and of nations, done to other states and subjects."[5]

In the contemporary philosophical debate over humanitarian intervention, the influence of Hobbes and the "Just War" theory may lie quietly in the background, but the debate also has its own character and terms of reference. An assertion, for example, that the fate and condition of others should properly be (and indeed is) a concern of the separate national societies that make up the international system does not, in itself, provide a definitive answer to the various questions surrounding the current implementation of humanitarian intervention. This is especially the case if we define humanitarian intervention in terms of the coercive injection of outside power into a state without the consent of political authority in that state. On this more restrictive question, there are specific arguments, both normative and utilitarian, that are offered by proponents and opponents of humanitarian intervention in the contemporary era.

THE CASE AGAINST INTERVENTION

A central theme among those who take a position against such interventions deals with their acceptance of the inherent legitimacy and moral standing of the sovereign state within the international system—and thus their rightful claim not to be interfered with by other sovereignties. Not incidentally, this so-called statist approach insists that international relations continue to be first and foremost relations among states and not individuals. The latter have a voice in international affairs only through the intermediary of the state (in practical terms, the recognized government of that state). Individual human beings, in this formulation, are the *objects* of international politics, but not the subjects. The protection and assertion of basic human rights can only be pursued within the framework of a state—indeed, it is the existence of one's own state that provides the fundamental basis for individuals achieving such rights. As Michael Walzer, often identified as one of the principal statist theoreticians, has put it:

> Against foreigners, individuals have a right to a state of their own. Against state officials, they have a right to political and civil liberty. Without the first of these rights, the second is meaningless: as individuals need a home, so rights require a location. . . . Rights are only enforceable within political communities where they have been collectively recognized, and the process by which they come to be recognized is a political process which requires a political arena. The globe is not, or not yet, such an arena.[6]

Walzer says that individuals have a right to "political and civil liberty" from their own governments, but even if this is not forthcoming (as clearly it is not in many contemporary states), this still does not produce a license for humanitarian intervention by foreigners. Statist philosophers place great stress on the fact that "rights" can only be understood in terms of specific sociopolitical circumstances; that is to say, they can only be discussed with reference to the cultural peculiarities of different societies. What may seem to be retrograde human-rights standards from the perspective of foreigners have to be seen as reflections of the fundamental social, communal, and historical experience of the given society. As Walzer further says, "the history, culture, and religion of the community may be such that authoritarian regimes come, as it were, naturally, reflecting a widely shared world view or way of life."[7] Outsiders must not impose their own abstract conception of rights in such situations. This smacks, on one hand, of a kind of moral imperialism, and, on the other hand, of a kind of intellectual arrogance that implies that a foreigner has a better understanding of the society in question than those who live within it.

The statists also typically offer a utilitarian assertion in this connection: Even if human-rights conditions in a given state may seem self-evidently repulsive, an enduring remedy to this situation requires a fundamental reordering of the whole society and its values. This is a task not likely to be accomplished by the injection of an outside force in the service of humanitarian goals: The complexity of such a task is inherently self-defeating. In a somewhat cynical sense, then, the argument here is that people always get the government they deserve. On a less captious note, the assumption is that the pursuit of liberty ultimately must depend primarily on the efforts of those most immediately affected, the citizenry themselves. John Stuart Mill offered the basic argument a long time ago in his essay "A Few Words on Nonintervention." Mill's essential proposition was that a people could not be saved from themselves, and if the requisite thirst for liberty was lacking, once a humanitarian intervention had been concluded, "it is only a question in how few years or months that people will [again] be enslaved."[8] Another utilitarian argument offered by the statists, that is often paired with this one, is the likelihood that widespread acceptance of the concept of humanitarian intervention will lead to all sorts of abuse by aggressive governments that will use it as a fig leaf for their expansionist designs. From this perspective, most if not all humanitarian intervention is either unavailing or cynical, and in both instances can hardly be expected to produce any tangible humanitarian return.

Other, more purely normative, considerations also figure as well in the statists' skepticism about humanitarian intervention. They point to the high probability that a country or countries that intervene on behalf of human rights may well violate the principle of proportionality; that is, they will contribute more to the deaths of innocents than to the aid of the oppressed. "Innocents" in this formulation means those who are not the direct agents of oppression, but who become the hapless victims of a violent effort by outsiders to end this oppression at quite a disproportionate cost. Combining this concern for proportionality with the likelihood of abuse deriving out of a general regime of humanitarian intervention, statists frequently settle on a "rule-utilitarian" philosophical position. The rule-utilitarian is not focused so much on the consequences of a particular action as on the *overall* benefit to humanity of adopting or rejecting certain standards of conduct. Thus, a rule-utilitarian approach to humanitarian intervention can accept that in certain isolated instances such an intervention might do more good than harm, but that in the broader perspective an acceptance of the general notion of humanitarian intervention will have the opposite effect. A particular achievement of justice, in other words, may have to be sacrificed in the interest of avoiding injustice in a number of other circumstances.[9]

At the very core of the statist philosophy is an assumption that states can, in a real sense, be regarded as "individuals" with a right of autonomy and a moral personality similar to individuals within civil society. A well-known treatise on international law in 1895 offered the basic proposition: "Independent states . . . have a moral nature identical with that of individuals . . . and with respect to one another they are in the same relation as that in which individuals stand to each other."[10] Just as we ought not curtail the individual's right to pursue his or her self-interest and moral ends so long as he or she does not impair the rights of others to do the same, states have (or should have) a freedom to define their own destiny providing that they do not threaten the equivalent claims of other states to do so as well.[11] As the British theorist R. J. Vincent put it,

> Those who first expounded the doctrine of nonintervention thought of it as primarily a principle of justice either arising from or being part of the doctrine of the fundamental rights of states. The rights of states to equality, liberty and independence, and thus the duty of nonintervention, were the expression in international life of the natural rights and duties of individual men.[12]

From this perspective, humanitarian intervention represents a denial of the rightful autonomy of the state *qua* individual.

Some statists, in developing the concept of political sovereignties as "individuals," style the relationship between government and people as analogous to that between parent and child. The well-known British philosopher G. F. Elfstrom, for example, asserts that "in the eyes of the larger world community, the government of a nation-state stands in a special relationship somewhat similar to the special relationship between parent and offspring."[13] Just as in domestic society our standard expectation is that the parent will shape—and has the right to shape—the moral universe of the child without interference from outside authority, so governments must have a similar leave in their relationship with their citizenry. This position is obviously connected to the notion that the state is the ultimate repository of individual rights, and that if the state abuses these rights, a resolution must be sought within the confines of the state itself, just as a child growing older has to work out an acceptable framework of values and actions with his or her parents.[14]

A further normative argument advanced by statists that is once again connected to the "parent-child" analogy is that outside interference by other powers in a society's affairs represents an abridgment of the right of free choice of those citizens, and in many cases perhaps the majority, who have no particular objection to their government's authoritarian practices or who may be left relatively untouched by them. Elfstrom addresses this issue as well: "In most cases of human rights violations by governments, the rights of all citizens are usually not directly affected. The most serious violations of rights are rarely directed at an entire population, but rather at a small minority. . . . If the majority is complacent . . . then intervention will constitute a violation of their right of autonomy."[15]

Yet another ingredient in the statist philosophy is that the *legitimacy* of a particular government (or, for that matter, a state) is essentially a matter of objective and non-normative criteria. This so-called representation theory is a staple of classical international law, and it suggests that any government (state) that meets certain standards should be considered an equal participant in the international system, with all the accompanying rights and duties of such participation. The traditional requirements for a "state" to be considered sovereign and thus a "legal person" under international law are that it must occupy a fixed (and populated) territory over which it exercises exclusive jurisdiction, that there must be a stability of organization and administration, and that it must be able to fulfill its international obligations.[16] The latter two stipulations are as equally relevant to governments as they are to states, and are generally supplemented by a requirement that there be no substantial opposition to the government's writ within the state's boundaries. What this comes down to, then, is that a state and its government are accepted as full, legitimate members of the international system if they are demonstrably *independent* and not beholden to the control of any other state or regime. There is no suggestion here that the character of the government in place is in any essential way relevant to its being accepted as legitimate.

THE CASE FOR INTERVENTION

Quite in contrast to statist thinking on the question of humanitarian intervention is the position taken by those we may style as the "cosmopolitans." The crux of their debate with the statists revolves around whether even a state admittedly established on the basis of self-determination, and meeting the traditional requirements for recognition detailed above, should be accorded any inherent legitimacy by the international community. Michael Walzer suggests that "the international standing of governments derives only indirectly from their standing with their own citizens. . . . Hence states can be presumptively legitimate in international society and actually illegitimate at home."[17] From the cosmopolitans' point of view, this is not only patently false, but borders on being a *non sequitur*.

Their argument is that legitimacy can or should only be granted to a political entity if a further set of conditions beyond the "objective" ones are met, which essentially have to do with the state's record of observing basic human rights and promoting social justice. Given an absence of social justice, the mere fact that a state has been established on the basis of self-determination and traditional legal norms hardly has any redeeming political value. Fernando Tesón admirably summarizes the basic position:

> The rights of states under international law are properly derived from individual rights. I therefore reject the notion that states have any autonomous moral standing—that they have international rights that are independent from the rights of individuals who populate the state. Because the ultimate justification of the existence of states is the protection and enforcement of the natural rights of the citizens, a government that engages in substantial violations of human rights betrays the very purpose for which it exists and so forfeits not only its domestic legitimacy, but its international legitimacy as well.[18]

The cosmopolitan theorist David Luban emphasizes that we have to "distinguish mere de facto exercise of sovereign power from legitimate exercise of it . . . the duty of non-intervention exists only toward states which are legitimate (in the sense of the term employed in normative political theory)."[19] Cosmopolitans, in short, argue that individual states have to "earn" their legitimacy within the international system. For those who fail the test, no putative assertion of the principle of self-determination or objective criteria of statehood can substitute for their lack of achievement in this respect. More to the point of this book, such states lay themselves open to rightful humanitarian intervention. As Luban concludes, a war in defense of what he calls "socially basic human rights" (subject to proportionality) is just.[20]

Cosmopolitans place great stress on such rights. Henry Shue describes these as being "everyone's minimum reasonable demands upon the rest of humanity," and they are basic in the sense that their enjoyment is necessary to the attainment of any other rights. They include what are sometimes called "negative" rights, that is, freedom from physical oppression, torture, even killing, and "positive rights," such as a claim to minimal standards of food, clothing and shelter.[21] The effect of identifying a core set of basic human rights at the same time establishes a justification for humanitarian intervention but also implicitly (and perhaps paradoxically) places some limits on such a practice. There are rights that, while important (such as the right of workers to organize themselves into unions), are not so basic as to legitimize foreign intervention. These are rights that are derivative of more basic claims and thus may vary from society to society and may require some tolerance by outsiders in the diversity of their application.

As to the rationale for attending to or caring about the socially basic human rights of others, the philosopher Robert Phillips suggests that in defending what he calls "basic human goods" for everyone, we are, in effect, serving a dual purpose. These goods are, in Phillips' formulation, "open-ended and, therefore not the possession of anyone. They are common goods that are the condition of human flourishing. Hence, if life or integrity are goods for me, they are also goods for others. Moreover, in the exercise of charity toward those who are suffering lies my own fulfillment, not in some sense of 'enlightened self-interest,' but in the sense that the fulfillment of self can only come through the forgetfulness of self."[22] By setting out to do good, then, we also wind up doing well in terms of establishing our own moral identity.

Cosmopolitans are particularly impatient with the argument that, in their view, conflates the rights of an identifiable political community with that of a state. Any intervention against that state becomes an intervention against that community, since the state *is* in a very real sense the community or at least its international representative. Tesón casts scorn on such a proposition, saying that it is "impossible to articulate a concept of the state as morally being analogous to a person. . . . states are not persons, and although governments are made of persons, their moral rights *qua* governments are not grounded in any mystical quality of the state . . . but in the consent of their subjects. The rulers are agents of the people; therefore they do not hold, *qua* government, any independent right of autonomy."[23]

What we are dealing with here really lies within the realm of social contract theory, and in this regard, Luban distinguishes between "horizontal" and "vertical" contracts. The horizontal contract represents an implicit decision by a large group of people to associate together, whether on the grounds of race, language, common history, or some combination of these and other criteria. The vertical contract suggests a decision by that community to grant limited powers to central governmental authority in order to serve the interests of the community. The point is that the community, or the nation, *precedes* the state, and the state has legitimacy only if it can be shown that the "vertical contract" has been willingly agreed to and that its terms are being upheld by state authority. Such an approach stands in vivid contrast to, say, contemporary fascist totalitarian theory, which argued that the state in fact creates the nation and that the nation has no identity or meaning without it. The Italian philosopher Giovanni Gentile, for example, intoned that "it is not nationality that creates the State, but the State which creates nationality, by setting the seal of actual existence on it."[24]

Given the cosmopolitans' attitude toward the social contract, it is hardly surprising that they rather contemptuously dismiss the metaphor of "parent and child" to describe the relationship between the governors and the governed. Actually, they say the relationship is almost the reverse: It is the nation that is the parent and the government that is the child, and if the latter misbehaves or abuses its authority, it becomes ipso facto a delinquent within the international community and, presumably, in the eyes of its own people. This inevitably leads to the question of the "right" of a political community to remedy injustice within its own state borders without interference from the outside. As we have already discussed, such a right supposedly has both a normative and a utilitarian dimension—normative in the sense that a community has a right to settle its own affairs without dictate from foreigners, and utilitarian in the sense that it's only through self-help that genuine humanitarian progress can be achieved.

This Millsian position is vigorously dismissed by the cosmopolitans, who question whether a community's "right" to settle its own affairs has any real meaning when in fact it is subject to a tyrannical regime that systematically denies it any real opportunity for doing so. In this connection, the shibboleth that it is only through "self-help" that progress in human rights within a given society can be achieved, and that, absent some tangible effort by the people to oppose oppression from above, they in effect "deserve" the government they have ignores the awesome and depressing range of instruments that tyrannies can utilize to maintain themselves in power. Simply because the people are silent or passive in the face of oppression, therefore, doesn't mean that they tacitly accept or even approve of their circumstances. On the contrary, they may have an understandable concern with simply avoiding the torture chambers and the firing squads of the despot. In such a situation, it is only through outside intervention that they have a realistic prospect of ameliorating their condition.

The essence of the cosmopolitan philosophy may be summarized in terms of the universality of human rights and their place within a world of sovereignties. This posits that each and every individual has an *inherent* claim to certain rights, and that these are not dependent on a particular grant of such rights from a given political authority. Thus, the individual has (or should have) a personal realm of autonomy and legitimate aspiration that necessarily places limits on the powers of government. Luban summarizes the basic argument rather effectively:

> Human rights accrue to people no matter what country they live in and regardless of history and traditions. If human rights exist at all, they set a moral limit to pluralism. . . . making pluralism the overriding value is incompatible from the outset with a theory that grants universal human rights.[25]

An integral corollary of Luban's theory of universal human rights is a firm rejection of moral or cultural relativism, the notion advanced by the statists that each society has its own particular vision of human rights and the social condition, and that these should not lightly be tampered with. As the cosmopolitans would argue, why should the treatment of women as inferiors in certain societies be accepted simply because it accords with "tradition" or "history"? Unless it can be shown that women in these countries voluntarily and actively accepted their inferior status—a proposition somewhat incredible on its face—their rights as individuals to appropriate treatment must take precedence over the prevailing norms of the community in which they dwell. To say otherwise is to surrender to a type of elitism in which "advanced" human-rights standards are to be expected and need be defended only in relatively "sophisticated" (read "Western") societies. In this connection, cosmopolitans are notably unsympathetic to the claims sometimes advanced by non-Western critics of humanitarian intervention that such actions represent "cultural imperialism." To insist that a country observe basic standards of treatment of individuals is not imperialism; rather, it is a reflection of the shared rights of humanity.

DISPUTE AND RECONCILIATION

In assessing the debate between the statists and the cosmopolitans concerning humanitarian intervention, we might begin by focusing on the question of consent: whether the majority of those living in a country subject to possible intervention have to give either tacit or even explicit agreement to the introduction of outside forces to "relieve" their suffering. Not surprisingly, Walzer feels that such consent is a primary requirement for just humanitarian intervention, and that it must be exceedingly explicit. He states categorically that outsiders

> are not to intervene unless the absence of "fit" between the government and community is radically apparent. Intervention in any other case usurps the rights of subjects and citizens. . . . When invasions are launched by foreign armies . . . it is entirely plausible to say that the rights of subjects and citizens have been violated. Their "slowness" has been artificially speeded up, their "aversion" has been repudiated, their loyalties have been ignored, their prudential calculations have been rejected—all in favor of someone else's conceptions of political justice and political prudence.[26]

Cosmopolitans such as Fernando Tesón, on the other hand, question whether it is really possible in the majority of circumstances to determine whether a local population actively desires foreign intervention. The penalties of open opposition to a tyrannical government are such that the will of the "silent majority" is extremely difficult to divine. In situations of manifest oppression, then, Tesón seems to suggest that a reasonable assumption—justifying humanitarian intervention—can be made that the citizenry of that country *would* revolt if given a reasonable chance of success. Thus, they can implicitly be said to be welcoming of outsiders coming to their rescue. At the very least, given their oppression, it is facile to argue that they are taking any sort of stand about their right to "self-determination."

Tesón goes further than this, however. He suggests that even if the majority of those living in a tyrannical society *are* reasonably content with their lot, it does not rule out the possibility of legitimate humanitarian intervention to protect the rights of a minority who are decidedly not content. As Tesón argues, "It is morally unacceptable to condone human rights violations just because the majority wants it. Therefore, oppressed minorities are entitled to receive outside help, even if a majority of citizens oppose the intervention."[27] Tesón even maintains that if a majority within a society is willing to fight for their tyrannical regime against an incursion by outsiders—whether from motives of patriotism, self-interest, or ignorance—they then must accept a share of moral culpability for the oppression that does exist.

> Those citizens who support the tyrants in the repression of a segment of the population do not have any moral claim to defend that government against foreigners. To some extent they are accomplices of the government in its criminal enterprise. If they decide to take arms to defend the dictators against foreign humanitarian intervention, they are guilty of, and have to take the responsibility for, fighting an unjust war.[28]

This sort of argument seems to equate with the "collective guilt" thesis sometimes offered about the German people's general responsibility for the Holocaust. The suggestion in this instance is that even though the majority of Germans may not have actively approved of a program for the physical destruction of the Jews, their relative silence in the face of extreme Nazi anti-Semitism placed a heavy burden of responsibility on them as being essentially complicit in this great atrocity (even assuming they did not know of its specific details).[29]

The debate between the cosmopolitans and the statists over a society's consent for a humanitarian intervention would seem to indicate an almost irreconcilable conflict between their respective positions. In reality, however, the divide may not be quite as extreme as would appear at first glance.[30] Even Tesón, for example, accepts that one of the basic criteria in identifying a truly legitimate humanitarian intervention is subsequent evidence that those it was designed to help—whether they were the majority or the minority—welcomed this intervention on their behalf, even if they were unable to make their wishes clearly known prior to the action. Despite his general reluctance to admit the possibility of legitimate humanitarian intervention, Walzer allows for the occasional exceptional case "when the violation of human rights within a set of boundaries is so terrible that it makes talk of community or self-determination . . . seem cynical and irrelevant, that is, in cases of enslavement or massacre."[31] Aside from purely physical oppression taking place, Walzer seems to suggest that in such situations, the "fit" between the regime and its people has essentially been shattered, and in these circumstances, the very notion of self-determination itself comes into question. Thus, the interventions that removed Pol Pot from power in Cambodia and Idi Amin from power in Uganda were theoretically justified in service *to* the principle of self-determination.[32]

Given the exceptions that Walzer establishes for rightful humanitarian intervention, the differences between him and the cosmopolitans become, in many instances, not those of theory but of definition: Just what is "enslavement and massacre," both quantitatively and qualitatively? To a surprising degree, there may be (or at least can be) some community of agreement here. There are exceedingly few cosmopolitans who argue for intervening all over the world to remedy every sort of derogation of human rights principles, even if such violations may, in the abstract, undermine the claim of the offending state to full legitimacy in the international system. On the contrary, the cosmopolitan ethos tends to focus on the most extreme cases of human suffering, the very ones that would also give Walzer pause. Moreover, most cosmopolitans are sensitive to the perennial problem of proportionality, the danger that even a well-meant intervention may produce more evil effects than good and thus prove indefensible. This danger is, of course, a staple of statist thinking.

Consider as well Mill's belief that interventions in support of self-determination frequently carried the risk of escalation and war among the major powers. Even more to the point, a people could not be saved from themselves. In other words, violations of democratic principles could only rarely, if ever, be ascribed solely to the evil of a particular regime or leader; instead, they were at least partial reflections of a whole political culture and historical tradition. At least implicitly, many if not most cosmopolitans accept that local societal factors, as well as relations among the most powerful states, have to be seriously considered when a specific humanitarian intervention is being contemplated. Their theoretical arguments may disguise this utilitarianism, but perhaps we ought to take some comfort in the fact that at least a working consensus between the statists and the cosmopolitans on when humanitarian intervention is justified may be more within reach than their often-contentious rhetoric would suggest.

That such an outcome is possible was suggested by the well-known legal philosopher, Tom Farer, following what was perhaps the first major scholarly conference in the post-war era to deal specifically with humanitarian intervention as a contemporary issue. Held at the University of Virginia one year after the Indian intervention in East Pakistan in 1971, the conference assembled an impressive range of academic and governmental luminaries. Despite two days of sometimes heated exchanges and obscure disputation concerning the merits of humanitarian intervention, Farer saw a reason for optimism:

> The salient fact is that almost every member of [the] group *agreed* on the desirability of humanitarian intervention to prevent large-scale abuse, on the appropriateness of exhausting multilateral remedies whenever time allowed, on the need to calculate the damage to the target society as well as to the imminent victims, and on the inadmissibility of interventions designed to safeguard commercial property or ideologically congenial regimes. What divided us, then, was a narrow point of strategy.[33]

Of course, even "narrow points of strategy" can sometimes arouse considerable disagreement. This is especially the case when the strategy involves relatively technical, or even relatively untechnical, questions that bear on the international legal system and indeed on the whole legal framework that surrounds humanitarian intervention.

NOTES

1. John Maynard Keynes, *The General Theory of Employment, Interest and Money* (New York: Harcourt, Brace and World, 1965).
2. Steven Forde, "Classical Realism," in *Traditions of International Ethics*, eds. Terry Nardin and David Mapel (Cambridge: Cambridge University Press, 1992), 75–77.
3. Robert L. Phillips, *War and Justice* (Norman, OK: University of Oklahoma Press, 1984), 20.
4. John Dunn, "The Dilemma of Humanitarian Intervention," *Government and Opposition* 29 (Spring, 1994), 252–54.
5. J. Bryan Hehir, "The Ethics of Intervention: Two Normative Traditions," in *Human Rights and U.S. Foreign Policy*, eds. Peter G. Brown and Douglas MacLean (Lexington, MA: Lexington Books, 1979), 125–28.
6. Michael Walzer, "The Moral Standing of States," in *International Ethics*, ed. Charles Beitz (Princeton, NJ: Princeton University Press, 1985), 234, 236.
7. Ibid., 224–25.
8. J. S. Mill, "A Few Words on Nonintervention," in *Essays on Politics and Culture* (New York: Doubleday, 1962), 174.
9. Fernando R. Tesón, *Humanitarian Intervention* (Irvington-on-Hudson, NY: Transnational Publishers, 1985), 103.
10. William Edward Hall, *A Treatise on International Law*, 4th ed. (Oxford: Clarendon Press, 1895), 18.
11. Tesón, *Humanitarian Intervention*, 53.
12. R. J. Vincent, *Nonintervention and International Order* (Princeton, NJ: Princeton University Press, 1974), 344.
13. G. F. Elfstrom, "On Dilemmas of Intervention," *Ethics* 93 (1982–83), 714.

14. A curious version of the "parent-child" analogy in the affairs of states could be found in Senator Albert Beveridge's (R-Indiana) "March of the Flag" speech defending American intervention against Cuba: "Cuba will finally be ours. . . . The Opposition tells us that we ought not to govern a people without their consent. . . . [W]e govern our children without their consent." Cited in Bill Kovach, "Do the News Media Make Foreign Policy?" *Foreign Policy* (Spring, 1996), 173.

15. Elfstrom, "On Dilemmas of Intervention," 717.

16. Gerhard Von Glahn, *Law Among Nations*, 3rd ed. (New York: Macmillan Publishing, 1976), 65.

17. Walzer, "The Moral Standing of States," 220, 222.

18. Tesón, *Humanitarian Intervention*, 15–16.

19. David Luban, "Just War and Human Rights," in *International Ethics*, 199.

20. Ibid., 210. For another expression of the cosmopolitan position, see Gerald Doppelt, "Statism Without Foundations," *Philosophy and Public Affairs* 9 (Summer, 1980), 398–403.

21. Henry Shue, *Basic Rights: Subsistence, Affluence and U.S. Foreign Policy* (Princeton, NJ: Princeton University Press, 1980), 3, 6–12.

22. Robert Phillips, "The Ethics of Humanitarian Intervention," in *Humanitarian Intervention*, Duane Cady and Robert Phillips, eds. (Lanham, MD: Rowman and Littlefield, 1996), 10.

23. Tesón, *Humanitarian Intervention*, 74.

24. Giovanni Gentile, *Genesis and the Structure of Society*, trans. H. S. Harris (Urbana: University of Illinois Press, 1966), 121.

25. David Luban, "The Romance of the Nation-State," in *International Ethics*, 242.

26. Walzer, "The Moral Standing of States," 222–23.

27. Tesón, *Humanitarian Intervention*, 87.

28. Ibid.

29. Daniel Goldhagen's *Hitler's Willing Executioners* (New York: Knopf, 1996) makes the even stronger argument that most Germans were *active* contributors to the persecution of the Jews, particularly given what he calls their long belief in "exterminationist anti-Semitism."

30. A good attempt to reconcile some of the opposing arguments here may be found in Michael Smith, "Ethics and Intervention," *Journal of Ethics and International Affairs* (1989), 12–16. See also Jack Donnelly, "State Sovereignty and International Intervention: The Case of Human Rights," in *Beyond Westphalia?* eds. Gene Lyons and Michael Mastanduno (Baltimore, MD: Johns Hopkins University Press, 1995), 120–22. Donnelly asserts an "internationalist model" of the world order, occupying a space somewhere between the statist and cosmopolitan paradigms, in which states continue to

be the primary actors in world affairs but normative constraints on their behavior are increasingly accepted.

31. Michael Walzer, *Just and Unjust Wars* (New York: Basic Books, 1977), 90.

32. In *Just and Unjust Wars*, Walzer does allow two other exceptions to the general rule of non-intervention: (1) When two separate and identifiable political communities are in conflict over *each* one's right to self-determination, that is, when it is a question of secession or a "national liberation" movement and (2) When a foreign power has already intervened in the domestic affairs of a state. Drawing on J. S. Mill's principle enunciated in "A Few Words on Nonintervention," what can simply be regarded as *counter-intervention* to balance the effect of the earlier intrusion may then be justified. In some of his more recent writings, Walzer goes beyond his earlier restrictive approach to humanitarian intervention and now accepts its justification in a somewhat wider variety of circumstances than just the three cited here. See, for example, "The Politics of Rescue," *Dissent* (Winter, 1995).

33. Tom J. Farer, "Humanitarian Intervention: The View From Charlottesville," in *Humanitarian Intervention and the United Nations*, ed. Richard Lillich (Charlottesville: University of Virginia Press, 1973), 164.

CHAPTER 3

The Realm of Law

If the question of humanitarian intervention has been in part a subject for the moral philosophers, a greater share of the debate over such interventions has rested—fortunately or unfortunately—in the hands of the international legal fraternity. Indeed, there has been a virtual cottage industry of discussion among legal scholars revolving around two basic points. Is the very concept of humanitarian intervention "legally" defensible or identifiable? If the answer is yes, is it, then, possible to codify a set of criteria for legally justified intervention on humanitarian grounds, including the methods by which it is decided on and what restrictions should apply in its use? In many ways, the discussion on these points has reflected, in its relative proportion of heat and light, an ongoing question about whether it is possible to define "aggression" in international law and what are the obligations of the international community in the face of such aggression.

In assessing the legal debate over humanitarian intervention, it is useful at the outset to address what are the generally accepted sources of international law. Clearly, legal attitudes toward intervention have to derive from a conception of how the relevant law is established and how it can be (hopefully) identified. In this connection, the statute that established the International Court of Justice, especially Article 38, is very often cited as the summary of the agreed-upon sources of international legal norms. These include

(a) international conventions [treaties], whether general or particular, establishing rules expressly recognized by the contesting states;
(b) international custom, as evidence of a general practice accepted as law;
(c) the general principles of law recognized by civilized nations;
(d) . . . judicial decisions and the teachings of the most highly qualified publicists of the various nations.[1]

The reliance on "international conventions" as a source of international law is self-explanatory, given that it represents the basic written (and formal) record to which nations have committed themselves. "International custom" simply means that the majority of states have indicated by their actual behavior that they accept a certain principle as binding, even if it hasn't been formally codified through treaty. The idea of "general principles of law" depends—at least in part—on an examination of commonalities in the municipal (domestic) legal systems of the majority of states. The last source, judicial decisions and the teaching of publicists, remains perhaps the most amorphous indication of what constitutes an international legal norm, especially since the statute for the International Court specifically states (in Article 59) that its decisions in a particular case apply only to that case and do not necessarily establish a binding legal precedent.

For those who argue that there is a legal right of humanitarian intervention, a typical theme is that such interventions have long been an accepted customary practice among nations and that there are numerous writings by various publicists identifying it as an acceptable action. In this connection, reference is sometimes made to the writings of early authorities on international law, such as Hugo Grotius. Later references are to the groundbreaking treatise in 1836 of Henry Wheaton, who argued for a customary legal right of humanitarian intervention "where the general interests of humanity are infringed by the excesses of a barbarous and despotic government."[2] The precedent in law that supposedly dates from this earlier period is often reinforced by citations of more contemporary authority, such as the well-known study on intervention undertaken by Ellery Stowell in 1921[3] and, most especially, the noted text on international law by Lassa Oppenheim, which first appeared in the early twentieth century and went through a number of subsequent editions. Oppenheim observed as follows:

> There is general agreement that, by virtue of its personal and territorial supremacy, a State can treat its own nationals according to discretion. But there is a substantial body of opinion and practice in support of the view that there are limits to that discretion; when a State renders itself guilty of cruelties against and persecution of its nationals in such a way as to deny their fundamental rights and to shock the conscience of mankind, intervention in the interests of humanity is legally permissible.[4]

The phrase "to shock the conscience of mankind" is a virtual mantra among those who argue for the legal right of humanitarian intervention, although the definition of which practices are likely to create such a shock and, for that matter, how we can determine whether the conscience of mankind is actually aroused over a particular situation is left unstated and ambiguous. What is important here is that defenders of the legality of humanitarian intervention tie their case to what they feel are significant legal precedents. More to the point, they assert that these precedents retain their force even given new legal regimes such as those established by, say, the United Nations Charter (about which more later). In the contemporary period, the writings of Richard Lillich, Julius Stone, Myres McDougal, and Michael Reisman have been prominent in their support of a legal right to humanitarian intervention in appropriate circumstances.[5]

There is an equally strong position held by other international legal scholars that humanitarian intervention has no foundation in the law of nations and, indeed, that such action is specifically proscribed by international legal norms. Not surprisingly, the emphasis in this case is on the absence of any general international convention allowing such intervention. Moreover, these scholars are quite unpersuaded that a customary right of humanitarian intervention has been or ever was established. The debate in this instance generally turns on very different interpretations of actual state practice with regard to humanitarian actions, which is essentially an empirical rather than a narrowly legal issue. Those who favor humanitarian intervention are confident that states have, in fact, often intervened on humanitarian grounds; those opposed suggest that such has rarely, if ever, been the case. These arguments are sometimes expressed in surprisingly fierce terms, with the skeptics sometimes implying, for example, that proponents of the right of humanitarian intervention are a threat to the very sanctity of the international legal system or at least to the effective restraint that that system has imposed on the behavior of states.

Take, for example, the position held by one of the leading British authorities on international law, Ian Brownlie. In reacting to the claim of one of his American colleagues, Professor Richard Lillich of the University of Virginia, that a presumptive legal right of humanitarian intervention may indeed be identified, Brownlie waxes indignant, and in places almost more than indignant. "It is clear to the present writer," he says, "that a jurist asserting a right of forcible humanitarian intervention has a very heavy burden of proof. Few writers familiar with the modern materials of state practice and legal opinion on the use of force would support such a view."[6] Brownlie offers his own rather numbing list of authorities who have questioned the legal basis for humanitarian intervention. He also suggests in the bargain that Lillich's stance on humanitarian intervention is "almost entirely devoid of any serious examination" of how customary and especially conventional international law (particularly as it involves the Charter of the United Nations) has regarded the practice of humanitarian intervention.[7] The most that Brownlie is willing to concede is that there may be very rare occasions in which a "euthanasia analogy" may be justified in international relations. The practice of euthanasia is legally proscribed almost everywhere—and, according to Brownlie, should remain so—but doctors do nonetheless occasionally assist in ending their patients' suffering. It is a little unclear here how nations, rather than individuals, can actually be put out of their suffering.

SORTING OUT THE LEGAL ISSUES

What to make of all the legal disputation concerning humanitarian intervention? First, it would appear that there have been three general phases in the attitude of most legal scholars toward the subject. Prior to 1945, there was a distinct, although hardly universally agreed, position that humanitarian intervention was a legally-defensible activity, particularly if custom was accepted as a source of international law. In the years after 1945, however, given the obligations of the United Nations Charter, opinion swung back toward the idea that humanitarian intervention was proscribed, given a positivist interpretation of the duties that treaty (convention) provided. More recently, a reinterpretation of both customary and conventional sources of international law has led many to the conclusion that humanitarian intervention *may* be legally defensible if certain circumstances obtain.

Even in the recent period, of course, there is hardly a legal consensus. As Tom Farer has suggested, the stance that one takes toward the legality of humanitarian intervention depends very largely on one's overall theory about how international legal principles come into existence. Farer distinguishes between the so-called classical and realist schools of thought in international law. The classical school emphasizes the traditional sources of that law, including formal texts, a narrow interpretation of intentions, and state practice itself. The realist school operates more from a policy oriented perspective and grants legitimacy to actions based on the effective exercise of power in support of community objectives, and that receive at least tacit acceptance. Farer concedes that it is not possible, even today, to support a contemporary right of humanitarian intervention if one takes the classical approach.[8]

For those who favor a right of humanitarian intervention chiefly on the basis of moral considerations, it is tempting to suggest that if international law doesn't allow for such interventions, so much the worse for international law. As the scholar D. W. Bowett has written, the presumed legal prescription against humanitarian intervention "is, because of its divorce from actual practice, rapidly degenerating to a stage where its normative character is in question."[9] Still, an attention to the legal framework by which humanitarian intervention can or should be conducted isn't just a matter of dueling academics or tiresome abstractions. The international legal system has sometimes acted to restrain the more brutal or anarchic instincts of states and is not to be disregarded lightly. More to the point, there are some substantive aspects of the legalistic debate concerning humanitarian intervention that ought to engage the attention even of those who don't normally spend much time pondering the latest pronouncements of the World Court.

The Influence of the United Nations Charter

The first of these has to do with the Charter of the United Nations and, more generally, with the original purpose of that organization in bringing a greater stability and progress to the functioning of international relations. One of the basic concepts of the United Nations was that sovereign states should have an overall freedom from "dictatorial interference," as one of the classic definitions of the right of sovereignty had it.[10] Those who drew up the Charter took special note of this principle in Article 2, Paragraph 4:

> All Members shall refrain in their international relations from the threat or use of force against the territorial integrity or political independence of any state, or in any other manner inconsistent with the Purposes of the United Nations.

Article 7, Paragraph 2 elaborated on this right of independence:

> Nothing contained in the present Charter shall authorize the United Nations to intervene in matters which are essentially within the domestic jurisdiction of any state or shall require the Members to submit such matters to settlement under the present Charter.

Some twenty years later, the UN General Assembly reaffirmed the centrality of state sovereignty in a resolution passed on December 21, 1965.

> No State has the right to intervene, directly or indirectly, for any reason whatever, in the internal or external affairs of any other State. Consequently, armed intervention and all other forms of interference or attempted threats against the personality of the State or against its political, economic, or cultural elements are condemned.[11]

The last sentence seems as definitive a statement ruling out humanitarian intervention as we are likely to get, particularly with its reference to the "personality of the State" and the sanctity of its political processes. It is precisely these items that tend to spur possible humanitarian interventions, particularly when they are seen as not measuring up to generally accepted international standards. The whole thrust of the provisions in the original Charter and in subsequent United Nations resolutions was, of course, to establish that all the types of direct and indirect aggression identified with the Nazi regime (and others as well) before World War II was now definitely proscribed under international law. The Charter was, after all, a formal treaty and was officially ratified by virtually all the states in the international system, and was thus undeniably a primary source of contemporary international law. The well-known legal scholar Louis Henkin has summarized the position of those who claim the Charter effectively rules out a legal right of humanitarian intervention:

> It was the original intent of the Charter to forbid the use of force even to promote human rights or to install authentic democracy. Nothing has happened to justify deviations from that commitment. . . . Surely the law cannot warrant any state's intervening by force against the political independence and territo-

rial integrity of another on the ground that human rights are being violated, as indeed they are everywhere.[12]

The last phrase is suggestive in its implication that since abuses of individuals by governments around the world are commonplace, it is fruitless to imagine a regime that could systematically deal with such a problem.

At the same time, proponents of the legality of humanitarian intervention have hardly abandoned their case in the face of supposed restrictions of the United Nations Charter. They point, for example, to other provisions of the Charter that list the protection and advancement of human rights as a *primary* purpose of the United Nations system. The preamble to the Charter cites some of the goals of the United Nations as the reaffirmation of a "faith in fundamental human rights, in the dignity and worth of the human person, in the equal rights of men and women and of nations large and small." Articles 55 and 56 specify that member nations agree to promote "universal respect for, and observance of, human rights and fundamental freedoms [and] to take joint and separate action in cooperation with the Organization for the achievement of [these] purposes."

Given the importance attached to human rights by the United Nations, then, is it credible to suggest that the Charter allows only moral suasion in achieving them? In this connection, it is suggested that the famous Article 2, Paragraph 4, which prohibits the "threat or use of force against the territorial integrity or political independence of any state," is hardly inconsistent with humanitarian intervention, since such interventions are not designed to challenge the territorial integrity or political independence of the state, but rather to compel the state to observe fundamental international norms of human rights. In Article 2, Paragraph 7, which proscribed United Nations intervention in matters "which are essentially within the domestic jurisdiction of any state," the further argument is that standards of human-rights conduct are *not* essentially a matter of domestic jurisdiction once the state has ratified international treaties governing such rights (for example, the original Helsinki Accords). At this point, issues of human rights should be regarded as part of a state's international obligations, and thus subject to the supervision and possible sanction of the international community. As one noted legal scholar said, "Once a human right appears in treaties it then acquires international status, and it is no intervention in the state's domestic affairs to criticize its performance in relation to that obligation."[13] This of course leaves unanswered the issue of whether "to criticize" may be legitimately translated into forceful intervention to secure such performance.

A more amorphous claim that proponents of humanitarian intervention advance in the context of the United Nations Charter refers to the provisions in Chapter VII that establish the UN's right to respond to situations that threaten "international peace and security," particularly under the aegis of Article 42, which provides for the use of armed force in such circumstances. The premise here is that widespread and unchecked violations of human rights constitute a prima facie threat to that peace and security, for example, in creating large numbers of refugees or in escalating domestic civil strife that may spill over into other countries. Moreover, much is made of the fact that Article 2, Paragraph 7, the so-called domestic jurisdiction clause, concludes with a sentence to the effect that "this principle shall not prejudice the application of enforcement measures under Chapter VII." To say that such a position on Chapter VII is "amorphous" refers basically to the (perhaps) problematical nature of the argument. As a practical matter, however, the legal basis on which most, if not all, contemporary United Nations activity, identifiable as being at least a modified form of humanitarian intervention, has been located within Chapter VII. Thus, the mandatory economic and arms embargoes leveled against the breakaway white supremacist regime in Southern Rhodesia in 1965, as well as equivalent sanctions against the apartheid government in South Africa, were both officially defended as being within the purview of Chapter VII. More recently, the United Nations intervention in Somalia drew from the same source. Security Council Resolution 794 of December 3, 1992, found that the "magnitude of human tragedy in Somalia" itself constituted a grave threat to international peace and security and thus justified forceful international action.[14] The program of protecting the Kurds of northern Iraq from Saddam Hussein's oppression also operated (even if only implicitly) under the same imprimatur.

In assessing the practice of humanitarian intervention within the context of the legal regime established under the aegis of the United Nations, two concluding reflections seem appropriate. In the first place, the United Nations has clearly operated in various circumstances to restrain instability and conflict in international affairs. While its more utopian supporters may be disappointed at its less than total success in this regard, the organization does act as a force for good and represents, in many ways, a distinct attempt to consolidate more acceptable standards of international behavior. To say that the impulse toward humanitarian intervention should take into account the principles of the United Nations Charter and subsequent resolutions is thus not just a tiresome quibbling over legal details. An unrestrained series of interventions by powerful states, even if in supposed service to humanitarian goals but undertaken with a blithe disregard for the obligations of the United Nations system, might do serious, even fatal, damage to the reputation of the organization. Under these circumstances, the cost of such interventions would be high indeed, perhaps unacceptably high.

At the same time, it is clear that the putative legal standards set down in the original United Nations Charter are hardly immutable. Even those who are most committed to a narrow, strict interpretation of the Charter have to accept that as a document, it must evolve and be subject to reevaluation in response to emerging international problems and values. It is almost a cliché that the U.S. Constitution has retained its vitality precisely because succeeding generations have read it in new and creative ways in order to deal with issues undreamt of by the original Framers. The same consideration applies to the Charter, if it is to maintain its own vitality as a guide to peace and justice in world affairs.

Sovereignty and Suffering

Discussions on the effect and role of the United Nations Charter in affirming or denying a legal right of humanitarian intervention have obviously taken place against a broader background of ideas about the principle of state sovereignty. We have previously referred to the classical definition of sovereignty as "freedom from dictatorial interference." Why this devotion to the concept of sovereignty? How should we weigh its claims against those for humanitarian action to ameliorate or correct gross abuses of human rights?

The answer to the first question has deep historical roots. With the development of the modern state system in the Western world (generally identified as coming in the early 17th century), as well as the increasing secularization of politics, there was a clear move away from theories of natural law and a single human community to a relatively unalloyed emphasis on the rights of sovereigns to complete authority within their own jurisdictions. Emmerich Vattel was a particularly important figure among the legal scholars in insisting on this new primacy of sovereignty. In his *Law of Nations*, published in 1758, Vattel offered this observation: "It clearly follows from the liberty and independence of Nations that each has the right to govern itself as it thinks proper, and that no one of them has the least right to interfere in the government of another."[15] What this meant in practice was that the benefit of the doubt in almost every situation went to the ruling regimes of the recognized European states, no matter how egregious their behavior might be. Thus, outside intervention into their affairs purely on humanitarian grounds was virtually set aside as beyond the pale in relations among "civilized" states.

Those beliefs might seem contradictory to our earlier statements that a customary right of humanitarian intervention was accepted by many writers of the time and that various such interventions were actually carried out. Actually, however, the discrepancy is more apparent than real. Aside from very brief anomalies such as the Holy Alliance, the only real exceptions to the rule of complete sovereignty came when the target countries were not considered members of the European state system, for example, the Ottoman Turks, or were at best only marginal members of that system, such as Portugal or some of the new-born East European states.[16] In these instances, the European powers might intervene without—at least in their view—compromising their right to virtually total freedom in conducting their own internal affairs.

As a concept, the notion of state sovereignty can actually be approached from a variety of angles. In our previous discussion, we referred to the philosophical arguments of the statists and the cosmopolitans about the moral significance of unfettered sovereignty. The international legal fraternity has its own (sometimes laborious) approach to the idea of sovereignty as well, which involves especially an interpretation of state practice and international conventions. It must be recognized, however, that the issue of sovereignty is more than just a matter of the favored abstractions of the philosophers and the legal scholars. Indeed, the whole concept of state sovereignty is embedded in some very practical issues of politics and foreign policy, which raise some legitimately differing national perspectives on the issue, particularly as it involves the question of humanitarian intervention.

As a historical matter, the primacy of the idea of state sovereignty, at least within the West, had a distinctly utilitarian rationale. Exhausted from the brutalities of the Thirty Years War—the population of Germany was reduced by an estimated one-third during the fighting—the signatories to the Treaty of Westphalia in 1648 recognized that a new theory of social and political rights had to be established in order to avoid a repeat of this catastrophe. The approximate cause of the war had been the efforts of various parties, notably the Hapsburgs, to impress their own religious-ideological systems on other countries in Europe. The principle of sovereignty that became enshrined at Westphalia virtually eliminated the (at least nominal) role of the Holy Roman Emperor as a final authority on religious and even political questions within Western Christendom. Henceforward, each ruler was granted virtually unchecked power to govern his domain as he chose, although there were provisions that some degree of religious tolerance should be extended to dissenters within this domain. The treaty, as one writer summarized it, "introduced the principle that *all* states, regardless of their size or power, were equal under international law and endowed with full and complete control over their territories and inhabitants."[17]

Ironically, when the Westphalian regime was first established, it could be morally applauded as providing a new order that (hopefully) would put an end to the atrocities inherent in wars for ideological and religious purposes. Certainly, it was greeted with a sigh of relief by many Europeans at the time precisely because it held out this prospect. Today, however, the Westphalian standard of unfettered sovereignty is seen by many as an *obstacle* to justice as well as to sustainable international order.

The Third World and Sovereign Rights

In the contemporary era, the countries of the developing world have been most rigorous in defending the continued political relevance of unfettered sovereignty. There is a certain paradox here, given the view of many of these states that "traditional" international law has often worked against their interests (for example, by insisting that their nationalization of foreign economic concerns seen as exploitative must follow stringent legal guidelines). There are, however, two commonsense ingredients in the Third World's position on the sovereignty question.

In the first place, the notion that the international community now has at least a qualified right to intervene in the domestic affairs of states carries a suspicious connotation of neocolonialism. The vast majority of developing countries were once colonial appendages of the European powers, and there are understandable fears that a new writ for intervention in world affairs would simply be a disguise for these powers' manipulation of their affairs as in the past. Thus, Farooq Hassan, in criticizing the Tanzanian invasion of Uganda in 1979 to topple Idi Amin (ironically, one developing country invading another), dismisses the very notion of humanitarian intervention as "simply a cloak of legality for the use of brute force by a powerful state against a weaker one, and experience has shown how readily more powerful states have used the pretext of a higher good to impose their will and values on weaker states."[18]

There is also the practical consideration that a dilution of the principle of sovereignty will in any case impact *them* (the Third World) far more than it will the countries of the Northern Hemisphere. It is germane to observe in this context that while a number of cases identified as justifying potential humanitarian intervention involve basically Islamic cultures (for example, the Sudan), about ninety percent of humanitarian-relief agencies continue to be based in the West. International humanitarian law is largely Western-derived as well. When the International Committee of the Red Cross asked a group of noted Islamic scholars to identify common themes between Islamic law and the Geneva Conventions, the Islamic scholarly community refused, saying that humanitarian conventions should originate with Islamic law and not the reverse.[19] The fact remains that even the most fervent supporters of humanitarian intervention rarely speak of intervening in Spain in order to protect the Basques from the "oppression" of Madrid, nor do they suggest a United Nations operation to secure the rights of the black minority in the United States. Inherently, then, a new consent for humanitarian intervention would seem to involve a series of intrusions into still very fragile developing countries in the supposed service of human rights. Not surprisingly, the regimes in these countries have a somewhat more jaundiced view about the "imperative" of protecting such rights than do their counterparts in the developed world.

Even while demonstrating some sympathy for this position, we have to recognize that it has certain problematical aspects as well. Without falling prey to excessive generalization, the fact remains that many of the most striking abuses of human rights today *are* taking place in the Third World. There may be a variety of explanations, including the dolorous effect of the formal colonial administrations, but this doesn't alter the basic reality. There is also an inconsistency, which at times amounts to an embrace of an obvious double standard, that characterizes the conduct of regimes in the developing world. One is struck by the fact, for example, that some of the most repulsive regimes in black Africa led the way in denouncing the abuses of apartheid in South Africa. Apartheid certainly represented a genuine stain on the conscience of mankind; at the same time, though, the old admonition about "physician, heal thyself" carries at least some weight. There was also the depressing absence of any real effort by the Organization of African Unity to deal with the catastrophe in Somalia. Instead of recognizing the situation there for what it was—a human tragedy caused largely by the selfish interests of the local political elites—the response of the OAU was mostly to disparage efforts by outside powers to use force in assisting the most affected among the Somali people.

It must also be said that the Third World's general aversion to the concept of humanitarian intervention, and its corresponding devotion to the notion of state sovereignty, has hardly followed a straight line. Ironically, in fact, the position taken by the black African states toward South Africa in earlier years effectively undermined their claims that sovereignty was sacrosanct. The justifiable criticism of apartheid was that it violated the collective right to self-determination of black South Africans and denied them fair treatment as a community. More to the point, such behavior rightly laid Pretoria open to measures, including coercion, by outside powers to remedy the situation. In a classic case of whose ox was being gored, such a stance logically led to the black African states themselves being legitimately subject to outside scrutiny concerning their own human-rights performance.[20]

Another situation that involved apparent African inconsistency concerned the so-called Unilateral Declaration of Independence of the white minority government of Ian Smith in Southern Rhodesia in 1965. Black Africa's outrage at this step was so overwhelming that the Organization of African Unity passed a resolution that called upon its members to appeal to the Security Council to pressure the United Kingdom to use force to rescue the people of Zimbabwe from a tyrannical white minority regime. If the UK refused, the United Nations would be asked to take action itself under Article 42 (which authorized the UN to use military force to deal with threats to international peace and security).[21] The Algerian delegate at the United Nations expressed strong support for the OAU's position and used language that proponents of humanitarian intervention could hardly improve on. He suggested that "in every organized society there existed elementary general principles which made it a duty to limit the legislative and even constitutional powers of the State, in particular whenever it was a question of ensuring respect for and the integrity of the human person."[22]

It is also striking, in this connection, how many in the Moslem world stridently denounced what they saw as the indifference of the Western nations to the suffering in the former Yugoslavia, particularly as it affected the Moslem community in Bosnia. There were repeated calls as well for a humanitarian intervention that would aid their co-religionists, and that vividly contrasted with their resistance to similar efforts in other areas. Several Moslem countries, in fact, among them Iran and Turkey, evidently decided on unilateral intervention themselves, and provided the Sarajevo regime with considerable quantities of financial assistance, military equipment, and even volunteers.

All this suggests that the abstract commitment to the norm of sovereignty, even within the developing world, may wax or wane depending on the circumstances of individual cases. Yet this hardly needs to be regarded as necessarily objectionable or invariably hypocritical. The spectacle of massive human suffering may rightly cause one to rethink certain legal principles, at least as they apply to particular situations. This seems to have been the case in the instance of Godfrey Binaisa, the successor to one of the worst tyrants of modern times, Idi Amin of Uganda. Following Amin's ouster by an invading Tanzanian force, Binaisa chided the United Nations for its past inaction in the face of the barbarities that had taken place in Uganda: "Our people naturally looked to the United Nations for solidarity and support in their struggle against the fascist dictatorship; unfortunately, their cries seemed to have fallen on deaf ears . . . somehow, it is thought to be in bad taste or contrary to diplomatic etiquette to raise matters of violations of human rights by member states within the forums of the United Nations."[23]

It would be unwise simply to ignore the Third World's concerns about the doctrine of humanitarian intervention as merely self-interested and inconsistent. There is ample opportunity for this doctrine to be abused in various ways. At the same time, it is apparent that the whole notion of sovereignty is in the process of being significantly revised, with an increasing emphasis on the rights of sovereignty applicable to a *people* rather than to a regime. As Michael Reisman forcefully observes, "In modern international law, sovereignty can be violated as effectively and ruthlessly by an indigenous as by an outside force, in much the same way that the wealth and natural resources of a country can be spoliated as thoroughly and efficiently by a native as by a foreigner."[24] From this perspective, leaders such as Castro, Ceausescu, Marcos, Mobutu, and a host of others have done far more to violate their countries' "sovereignty" than have any outsiders.

The move toward an altered definition of sovereignty was actually anticipated as long ago as 1923, when the Permanent Court of International Justice offered the dictum that "the question of whether a certain matter is or is not solely within the jurisdiction of a state is an essentially relative question; it depends on the development of international relations."[25] The former Secretary-General of the United Nations, Boutros Boutros-Ghali, summarized more recent developments when he suggested that "the centuries-old doctrine of absolute and exclusive sovereignty no longer stands, and was in fact never so absolute as it was conceived to be in theory. A major intellectual requirement of our time is to rethink the question of sovereignty."[26] In recent years, the United Nations has in fact moved toward a more elastic definition of sovereignty than its earlier pronouncements would have suggested. In 1988, for example, the General Assembly adopted Resolution 43/131, which recognized the rights of civilians to international aid in certain emergencies and the legitimate role of Non-Governmental Organizations (NGOs) in offering such assistance. Two years later, Resolution 45/100 reaffirmed these rights and endorsed the concept of "corridors of tranquillity" by which international aid could successfully reach suffering peoples. In 1991, Resolution 46/182 asked the Secretary-General to create the post of emergency-assistance coordinator to work with governments and local insurgents to ensure effective humanitarian relief. That resolution made no distinction between natural and man-made disasters, and established that only the "tacit" consent of local authorities was needed rather than their formal "request" in order for the United Nations to act.[27] A United Nations Department of Humanitarian Affairs was subsequently established in 1992 in order to carry out the mandate of Resolution 46/182.

A process has clearly been taking place wherein the perennial conflict between "sovereignty and suffering" has increasingly been resolved in favor of the latter rather than the former. One wry reflection on the new approach to the issue of sovereignty could be seen in the United Nations decision to intervene in Somalia. In order to mollify lingering concerns about violations of Somalia "sovereignty," the Somali chargé d'affaires in New York, who effectively represented no one, agreed to write a letter to United Nations authorities "requesting" international assistance for his country. This legal fiction persuaded the remaining holdouts within the UN membership that they could now, in good conscience, support what was in effect a UN receivership over Somalia.

A Code for Humanitarian Intervention

Another important issue in the legal debate over humanitarian intervention, especially among those who feel that such interventions can at times be legitimate, is whether it is possible, or even desirable, to develop a formal set of standards that would control the future use of humanitarian interventions.[28] Former United Nations Secretary-General, Perez de Cuellar, urged that work indeed begin on such a project. Needless to say, those who are dubious about the whole notion of humanitarian intervention have scorned the idea of such a code. In their view, establishing a set of "objective" legal parameters for humanitarian intervention would lead powerful states, citing conventional legal rights for such intervention, to engage in even more abusive behavior toward weaker states than in the past. This time it would be under a rubric of humanitarianism. In the process, such legal protection as Article 2 (4) of the United Nations Charter affords to states against outside interference would become almost moot. Brownlie's euthanasia metaphor is particularly to the point here: While we might not want totally to rule out any kind of humanitarian intervention, the practice should remain a rare exception to the rule of non-intervention and certainly not to be encouraged.

Even among those who generally support humanitarian intervention, however, there has been a relatively contentious discussion about the utility or even attainability of an agreed-on code of humanitarian intervention. In contrast to the argument presented by Brownlie and others, some argue that such a code would help *limit* potential interventionary abuses by powerful states, since they would to have to satisfy objective criteria before being granted a right of legitimate humanitarian intervention. In a curious sense, then, a code would actually reinforce the general prohibitions contained in Article 2 (4), particularly if it were drawn as narrowly as possible. Clearly, there is also a (sometimes unstated) political rationale to the argument of these individuals: Governments facing difficult domestic problems of political persuasion concerning a commitment of national resources to a particular humanitarian intervention could point to the code as a justification for such action.

Various writers have suggested a range of items that ought to be included in any code establishing criteria for legitimate humanitarian intervention. Common among these is the existence of an immediate human-rights crisis of very substantial scope, the lack of other alternatives for dealing with it, and an attention to questions of proportionality, that is, will the intervention do more good than harm? Other stipulations sometimes found in these proposed codes include the requirement (in the case of unilateral interventions) for a prompt report to the United Nations or other regional bodies on the rationale for the action and its expected duration, and a clear indication that the intervening state or states does not intend to threaten the right of sovereign self-determination of the affected society.[29]

The idea of a standard code of conduct governing the recourse to humanitarian intervention has a certain appeal and might help in many instances to defuse some of the controversy that inevitably is attendant on such an action. At the same time, it is hard not to agree with the skeptics that the difficulties in developing such a code are formidable and perhaps even insuperable. Some of these have to do with the substantive circumstances that would have to be present before a legitimate humanitarian intervention could be undertaken. It seems almost impossible to envision a single code—or even broad statement of principles—that would be of much use in influencing specific decisions on a specific intervention. The combination of circumstances that might give rise to such an intervention seems almost indefinitely elastic and broad. There is a very wide range of human-rights abuses taking place in the world today, but only a small number of them may rightfully be regarded as requiring potential intervention by outside powers. Such decisions are, by the nature of things, likely to be ad hoc judgments that depend on the analysis, as well as the values, of particular governments at the time. Moreover, the political rationale for a code of humanitarian intervention seems dubious at best. Few governments would be willing to commit themselves in advance to intervening on behalf of human rights if a situation supposedly fell within the technical parameters of such a code. Nor is their citizenry likely to be persuaded to support a given humanitarian intervention simply because it is "justified" under the criteria established. Inevitably, each case will have to be argued on its own merits, and political support would have to be developed by the force of the arguments bearing on a particular situation.

One of the supposed rationales for developing a code of humanitarian intervention is that it will help separate the sheep from the goats, that is, it will deter certain interventions that are really only self-interested and not humanitarian, while at the same time, it encourages truly altruistic interventions on behalf of human rights. It is hard to see, however, how a code would be of much use in this regard. States will inevitably have a mix of motives in undertaking any major foreign policy enterprise, and their calculations on this score are not likely to be significantly affected by some abstract stipulation that they take action only if their motives are entirely pure. In any event, the real case against attempting to develop some formal code of humanitarian intervention is that it is essentially a diversion of energy from the actual task at hand, which is to convince an increasing number of governments that they have significant responsibility for the well-being of others beyond their borders. There is virtually no evidence that the international community is at all interested, at least for the foreseeable future, in developing a code of humanitarian intervention. If they are pressed on the matter, many states might even become more reluctant to commit themselves to humanitarian enterprises because they resent the pressure being applied.[30] In this instance, as in many other matters in international affairs, the best seems likely to wind up being the enemy of the good.

AN OVERVIEW

In summarizing the range of legal questions that continue to bear on the notion of humanitarian intervention, several conclusions seem appropriate.[31] A key factor in the legal debate clearly remains to determine how we can or ought to identify the legal framework governing state conduct. In the Brownlie-Lillich dialogue referred to earlier, Professor Brownlie clearly takes a very strong positivist (or "classical") approach. In concluding his attack on Lillich, he says that "what I find depressing is the absence of evidence that proponents of humanitarian intervention and other very plastic doctrines have spent much time examining state practice in detail."[32] From this perspective, international law is based—and should be based—on what states actually *do* and not on what they ought to be doing or may potentially do in the future. Richard Lillich, on the other hand, regards the international legal system as being in a constant state of flux, and his task—and that of others—is to identify emerging trends in that system that may produce new rules or principles of international law. As he forthrightly says, "This writer prefers a *doctrinal* approach which forthrightly sanctions . . . humanitarian interventions when they meet detailed criteria."[33] Clearly, this is a more creative—some would say speculative—way of looking at legal practice, and it is easy to see why it should make his writings vulnerable to the critiques of the legal traditionalists.

Then there is the continuing issue of unilateralism versus multilateralism (to be discussed in greater detail later). Brownlie may be dubious of humanitarian intervention in general, but he is especially adamant that *unilateral* interventions on behalf of human rights are quite without legal foundation. On the other hand, he at least seems open to persuasion that multilateral efforts on behalf of oppressed groups, particularly when they receive formal imprimatur from the United Nations under Chapter VII ("threats to international peace and security"), might be considered as prima facie legal in exceptional circumstances. If Lillich's position means anything, however, it is that unilateralism in humanitarian intervention has to be accepted not necessarily as the preferred course, but at least as a last resort if the international community has failed collectively to take any action. Thus, he argues strongly for the legitimacy of the Indian move into East Pakistan in 1971 precisely on these grounds: "The abject inability of the United Nations to take effective action to terminate the genocidal conduct and alleviate the mass suffering in Bangladesh necessitates a fundamental reassessment . . . of the role of . . . humanitarian intervention in international affairs today."[34]

In this instance, a review of developments since the original Lillich-Brownlie debate does suggest that Brownlie's assertion—that there was no formal legal sanction for *unilateral* interventions on behalf of human rights—continues to be the prevailing position. It is striking, for example, that in the three most famous examples of putative humanitarian intervention cited in the post-1945 period—East Pakistan in 1971 and Cambodia and Uganda in 1979—*none* of the intervenors actually defended their actions primarily in terms of a doctrine of humanitarian intervention, although India and Tanzania made a few nods in this direction. It is difficult, if not impossible, to identify any convention or treaty law that provides legal cover for such interventions, and it is unlikely that there will be any appreciable change in this situation in the foreseeable future, for a variety of reasons.[35]

As to customary international law, that is to say, international practice that is widely accepted but not yet enscribed in formal conventions, the right of humanitarian intervention is murkier. As detailed above, some authorities assert that there is at least an implicit or nascent trend in the actual behavior of states that amounts to their sometimes grudging acceptance of certain unilateral interventions to protect human rights. If such behavior becomes established practice, then we are well on our way toward a new customary rule of law. It is only fair to recognize, however, that this continues to be a minority position. At the same time, as we have also discussed, there does seem to be a growing consensus that multilateral humanitarian intervention, notably by the United Nations but also possibly by regional organizations such as the Organization of American States or the Organization of African Unity, may be legally sanctioned, not only as a matter of customary but even treaty law. In the case of the United Nations, the provisions of Chapter VII, particularly those in Article 39, are particularly apt; they are now widely taken to mean that a collective intervention in response to gross human-rights violations that threaten international peace and security are legitimate (the action to protect the Kurds of Iraq being a prime example).[36]

Returning to the more general question of the relationship between formal legal norms and humanitarian intervention, there is a certain bleakness in taking a strictly positivist approach to this matter, especially since doing so hardly speeds the process by which standards of international law can take increasingly progressive forms. Because states have behaved in certain ways in the past doesn't make that behavior intuitively defensible or something to be enshrined as embodying an acceptable principle of international law. Why not press the community of nations to examine their standards of behavior with renewed rigor and, in so doing, create the possibility of establishing a more morally just international legal system? On the other hand, the arguments of those who favor a right of humanitarian intervention also have to be subjected to some fairly rigorous evaluation, involving, in particular, an empirical analysis of their supposed instances of actual intervention in support of human rights. For example, the Stanleyville, Zaire, operation in 1964 to rescue Europeans trapped by the civil war there is sometimes cited as a good example of a humanitarian intervention, as are the American interventions in the Dominican Republic in 1965 and in Grenada in 1982.[37] Few historians of international relations would likely consider them as such. The British scholar R. J. Vincent was eloquent in suggesting a way out of this impasse: "Between a naturalism careless of state practice and a positivism that would simply render any and all state conduct as the law, international law has to find a middle way."[38] The challenge, then, is clearly to marry the normative theory to a more rigorous examination of what actual humanitarian interventions have taken place, what their practical effects have been, and what legal criteria can be justly applied in their future implementation.

NOTES

1. Herbert W. Briggs, ed., *The Law of Nations*, 2nd ed. (New York: Appleton-Century-Crofts, 1952), 24.

2. H. Wheaton, *Elements of International Law* (London: B. Fellowes, 1836).

3. Ellery Stowell, *Intervention in International Law* (Washington, DC: John Byrne and Company, 1921).

4. L. Oppenheim, *International Law,* 7th ed., ed. H. Lauterpacht (London: Longmans, Green, 1948), 279–80.

5. See, for example, Richard Lillich, "Forcible Self-Help by States to Protect Human Rights," *Iowa Law Review* 53 (1967); Julius Stone, *Aggression and World Order* (London: Stevens, 1958); Myres Smith McDougal, *Law and Minimum World Public Order* (New Haven, CT: Yale University Press, 1961); and Michael Reisman, "Sovereignty and Human Rights in Contemporary International Law," *American Journal of International Law* 84 (October, 1990), as well as his "Humanitarian Intervention to Protect the Ibos," in *Humanitarian Intervention and the United Nations*, ed. Richard Lillich (Charlottesville: University of Virginia Press, 1973).

6. Ian Brownlie, "Thoughts on Kind-Hearted Gunmen," in *Humanitarian Intervention and the United Nations*, ed. Richard Lillich (Charlottesville: University of Virginia Press, 1973), 218.

7. Ibid., 220.

8. Tom Farer, "An Inquiry into the Legitimacy of Humanitarian Intervention," in *Law and Force in the New International Order*, eds. Lori Fisler Damrosch and David Scheffer (Boulder, CO: Westview Press, 1991), 188–96.

9. D. W. Bowett, "Reprisals Involving Recourse to Armed Force," *American Journal of International Law* 66 (1972).

10. Lassa Oppenheim, *International Law: A Treatise* (New York: Longmans, Green and Co., 1905), 305.

11. Cited in Kelly Kate Pease and David P. Forsythe, "Human Rights, Humanitarian Intervention, and World Politics," *Human Rights Quarterly* 15 (May, 1993), 292.

12. Louis Henkin, "The Use of Force: Law and U.S. Policy," in *Right v. Might*, eds. Louis Henkin et al. (New York: Council on Foreign Relations Press, 1989), 61.

13. Rosalyn Higgins, "Intervention and International Law," in *Intervention in World Politics*, ed. Hedley Bull (Oxford: Clarendon Press, 1984), 34.

14. Damrosch, "Introduction," in *Enforcing Restraint*, ed. Lori Fisler Damrosch (New York: Council on Foreign Relations Press, 1993), 10.

15. *The Law of Nations or the Principles of Natural Law*, edited and translated by Charles Fenwick (Washington, DC: Carnegie Institute, 1916), II, 54, 131.

16. F. H. Hinsley's *Power and the Pursuit of Peace* (London: Cambridge University Press, 1967) is still one of the best treatments of the diplomatic mores of the period.

17. Edward McNall Burns and Philip Lee Ralph, *World Civilizations*, vol. II, 5th ed. (New York: W. W. Norton and Company, 1974), 641.

18. Farooq Hassan, "Realpolitik in International Law: After Tanzanian-Ugandan Conflict 'Humanitarian Intervention' Reexamined" *Willamette Law Review* 17 (1981), 860.

19. Frederick C. Cuny, "Humanitarian Assistance in the Post-Cold War Era," in *Humanitarianism Across Borders*, eds. Larry Minear and Thomas G. Weiss (Boulder, CO: Lynne Rienner Publishers, 1993), 158.

20. Cristopher Clapham, *Africa and the International System* (Cambridge: Cambridge University Press, 1996), 189.

21. Igor I. Lukashuk, "The United Nations and Illegitimate Regimes: When to Intervene to Protect Human Rights," in *Law and Force in the New International Order*, eds. Lori Fisler Damrosch and David Scheffer (Boulder, CO: Westview Press, 1991), 150. The Security Council did institute a mandatory economic embargo of Southern Rhodesia, but this was not an Article 42 action.

22. Jean-Pierre L. Fonteyne, "Forcible Self-Help by States to Protect Human Rights: Recent Views from the United Nations," in *Humanitarian Intervention and the United Nations*, 208.

23. Thomas M. Franck, "Intervention Against Illegitimate Regimes," in *Law and Force in the New International Order*, 162.

24. Michael Reisman, "Sovereignty and Human Rights in Contemporary International Law," *American Journal of International Law* 84 (October, 1990), 872.

25. Cited in Pease and Forsythe, "Human Rights, Humanitarian Intervention, and World Politics," 293.

26. Boutros Boutros-Ghali, "Empowering the United Nations," *Foreign Affairs* (Winter, 1992/93).

27. Thomas G. Weiss and Larry Minear, "Commentary," in *Humanitarianism Across Borders*, eds. Larry Minear and Thomas G. Weiss (Boulder, CO: Lynne Rienner Publishers, 1993), 119.

28. Jarat Chopra and Thomas Weiss, "Sovereignty Is No Longer Sancrosanct," *Ethics and International Affairs* (1992), 99–101.

29. See, for example, Tom Farer, "A Paradigm of Legitimate Intervention," in *Enforcing Restraint*, 327; John Norton Moore, "The Control of Foreign Intervention in Internal Conflict," *Virginia Journal of International Law* 9 (1969); and Richard Lillich, "Forcible Self-Help by States to Protect Human Rights," *Iowa Law Review* 53 (1967).

30. Professor Akehurst makes the convincing point that "a desire to develop more effective sanctions for breaches of international law should not blind us to the possibility that a legal system may be brought into disrepute if sanctions are *too* severe." Michael Akehurst, "Humanitarian Intervention,"

in *Intervention in World Politics*, ed. Hedley Bull (Oxford: Clarendon Press, 1984), 111.

31. For recent assessments of the legal status of humanitarian intervention within the purviews of international law, see Michael J. Reppas, "The Lawfulness of Humanitarian Intervention," *St. Thomas Law Review* 9 (Winter, 1997); David Bills, "International Human Rights and Humanitarian Intervention: The Ramifications of Reform on the United Nations' Security Council," *Texas International Law Journal* 31 (Winter, 1996); Richard Falk, "The Complexities of Humanitarian Intervention: A New World Order Challenge," *Michigan Journal of International Law* 17 (Winter, 1996); and Michael L. Burton, "Legalizing the Sublegal: A Proposal for Codifying a Doctrine of Unilateral Humanitarian Intervention," *The Georgetown Law Journal* 85 (December, 1996).

32. Brownlie, "Thoughts on Kind-Hearted Gunmen," 228.

33. Richard B. Lillich, "Humanitarian Intervention," in *Law and Civil War in the Modern World*, ed. John Norton Moore (Baltimore, MD: Johns Hopkins University Press, 1974), 250. Emphasis supplied.

34. Ibid., 230.

35. Michael Akehurst, "Humanitarian Intervention," in *Intervention in World Politics*, 95–99. Akehurst takes note of the fact that in 1971 the Indian representative at the United Nations initially referred to the Indian move into East Pakistan as an example of humanitarian intervention, but in the final edited version of the debate on the matter in the Security Council, this defense had been dropped, and it was now claimed to be an act of self-defense since Pakistan had attacked first.

36. Pease and Forsythe, "Human Rights, Humanitarian Intervention, and World Politics," 302.

37. Professor Lillich, for example, cites both the Stanleyville and Dominican Republic affairs in his list of postwar humanitarian interventions.

38. R. J. Vincent, *Nonintervention and International Order* (Princeton, NJ: Princeton University Press, 1974), 348.

CHAPTER 4

Issues and Ambiguities

The material covered so far in this book has been at a fairly high level of generality. Rather abstract questions of definition, philosophy, and legality have been addressed, and in discussing a matter as contentious as humanitarian intervention, there is no doubt a need to clear away certain intellectual underbrush. At the same time, an analysis of humanitarian intervention—if it is to be truly useful or relevant—almost inevitably has to descend from the cloud of theory to consider some specific matters of policy and implementation. We begin in this chapter with an assessment of certain issues at the core of humanitarian intervention as a special type of political action. The next chapter will address in some detail the actual factors that seem to move states to intervene or not to do so. Finally, there will be a discussion of the elements necessary for successful humanitarian interventions and that logically govern as well our judgment about their legitimacy, given the circumstances of the particular case.

SOVEREIGNTY AND HUMANITARIAN ACTION

Humanitarian intervention has been defined here as the use—or the threat—of force by one or more outside states into the affairs of a sovereign country in response to a pattern of systematic human rights violations that are the result either of the conscious policies of the regime in power or that arise out of the general breakdown of any central-regime authority in the targeted country. Attention has been given to the legal disputation concerning the idea of humanitarian intervention, but this discussion has, in important ways, been overtaken by events. Although there is no generally accepted legal theory setting out the formal right of, and the proper parameters for, such intervention, it is unmistakable that there is, in practice, a growing *tolerance* for various forms of humanitarian intervention.[1] This suggests, in turn, that the basic structure of the international system, and even—ultimately—its legal character may be changing in ways that are so profound as to represent a fundamental reordering of the classical Westphalian model of relations among states.

A crucial factor here has to do with what is generally called "the internationalization of human rights." Under the traditional theory of sovereignty, individuals, basically, had no way of remedying abuses of their persons or their lives by their own governments other than to appeal to these very same governments. Such a principle has been increasingly consigned to the dustbin of history, and it is now widely accepted that human-rights outrages are properly the concern of the international community as a whole.[2] Michael Reisman makes the point with his usual directness: "No serious scholar still supports the contention that internal human rights are 'essentially within the domestic jurisdiction' of any state and hence insulated from international law."[3] Articles 55 and 56 of the United Nations Charter, as we have already discussed, impose a formal duty on member states to assist in and to accept a system of respect for basic standards of human rights. At a summit meeting of Security Council states in 1992, the new principle was clearly stated that the world community "no longer can allow advancement of fundamental rights to stop at national borders."[4] Even from a narrow or positivist legal viewpoint, the fact that a state formally accepts legal norms that govern standards of human rights converts such rights into something outside their traditional "domestic jurisdiction" and are thus subject to outside enforcement.

There has been a wide range of agreements that have fleshed out the notion of the internationalization of human rights: from the famous Universal Declaration of Human Rights adopted by the UN General Assembly in 1948 to a number of subsequent UN covenants on civil, political, economic, social, and cultural rights, including specific issues such as genocide, racial discrimination, torture, and even matters as specific as freedom of association and collective bargaining. Three world regions—Western Europe, the Western Hemisphere, and Africa—have established their own treaties governing human rights: the European Convention on Human Rights and Fundamental Freedoms (1953), the American Convention on Human Rights (1978), and the African Charter on Human and Peoples' Rights (1986).[5] In Europe, a particularly notable development was a protocol in 1991 to the European Convention that gave legal standing to individuals to bring cases against their own governments before the European Court of Human Rights.[6]

The whole course of events since 1945, in essence, has been in the direction of establishing the general idea that every human being has certain inalienable rights, and that the international community has a valid, collective interest in seeing that these rights are observed. The negotiations that led to the 1975 establishment of the Convention on Security and Cooperation in Europe (CSCE) were yet another piece of evidence of the new trend. Under so-called Basket Three principles, it was accepted that the CSCE had a legitimate right to inquire into member governments' treatment of their own nationals. While the CSCE had little in the way of enforcement powers, the subsequent review conferences, held concerning the implementation of the Helsinki Accords, provided a forum by which considerable moral pressure could be brought to bear on recalcitrant governments—and not without effect.[7] At a CSCE meeting in Geneva in 1991, there was unanimous agreement that "issues concerning national minorities, as well as compliance with international obligations and commitments concerning the rights of persons belonging to them, are matters of legitimate international concern and consequently do not constitute exclusively an internal affair of the respective state."[8]

The development of the CSCE system of rules and principles has also been accompanied by more general developments in what is usually called international humanitarian law. The four Geneva conventions on the protection of war victims, agreed to in 1949, and the subsequent Additional Protocols, signed in 1977, are notable in this regard. Other related documents include the Genocide Convention of 1948 and the still-binding Hague Convention of 1907, which represented perhaps the most important early attempt to place restraints on governmental violence. There was a fundamental commonality in all of these measures: They were not dependent on the principle of reciprocity; potential victims of violence had certain basic rights that could not be derogated; and the agreements were "consistent" in that they all applied to *all* parties regardless of ideology or politics. It might be noted that a number of regional organizations have adopted those same provisions of international humanitarian law into their own charters. Aside from the CSCE, the Arab League, the Organization of American States, the Organization of African Unity, and the Organization of the Islamic Conference are notable in also having done so.[9]

SELECTION AND PRIORITIZATION

To define humanitarian intervention as the use or threat of force to remedy systematic deprivations being directed against a population leaves open some rather sticky questions about how one specifically *identifies* a situation in which such "deprivation" is said to be present. In the spring and summer of 1992, for example, UN Secretary-General Boutros Boutros-Ghali became increasingly agitated about the relative attention the international community gave to the situation of the former Yugoslavia compared to that unfolding in Somalia. There was far more dying in the latter, he suggested, yet the Security Council seemed almost fixated on the problems of Croatia, Serbia, and Bosnia while it remained relatively oblivious to the travails of Somalia.[10] The sad, inescapable fact, however, is that there are numerous examples of unsavory regimes in the world today that hardly extend to their citizens the full range of privileges enunciated in, for example, the UN's General Declaration on Human Rights, or where the collapse of central government produces great suffering for a country's citizenry. To suggest that each of these cases is a suitable occasion for humanitarian intervention would be to expand the range of such interventions in an impossibly ambitious way.

The difficulty inherent in defining which human-rights cases properly qualify for possible forceful action is symbolized by the rather loose use of the term "genocide" in the debate over humanitarian interventions. Even for those who are generally convinced of the potential legitimacy of such interventions, the frequent invocation of this term to justify strong action must give one pause. Ernst Haas has argued in this connection that "the task facing the ethicist is to keep the losing party [in civil wars] from yelling 'genocide' merely because its civilian population is suffering heavy casualties."[11] Though this may be an unduly harsh way of putting it, Haas's argument does have some merit.

Charges of "genocide" have indeed entered into the public dialogue in a manner perhaps leading to a debasement of the term and to a vitiation of much of its moral force.

The controversy over a Spanish court's attempt to have former Chilean dictator Augusto Pinochet extradited to Spain to stand trial for human-rights violations is a case in point. Spain claimed jurisdiction partly on the basis that Pinochet had been complicit in genocide, and under the UN's Convention on Genocide, any signatory could undertake an action against the individuals involved.[12] Now the generally accepted estimate is that under Pinochet's rule in Chile, approximately three thousand people may have been killed or simply "disappeared." Grievous statistics indeed and ample evidence of Pinochet's brutality, but did this rise to the level of a genocide? Michael Radu, among others, was unequivocal in his response. "It has indeed become a habit in the media and the Left everywhere to qualify as 'genocide' any real or alleged large-scale abuse of human rights. . . . But just as most murderers are not Stalin or Hitler, most killings in wartime are not genocide." Radu concludes that "to call [such] actions 'genocide' is worse than bizarre—it is an insult to the victims of real genocide—Jews, Gypsies, Armenians, Tutsis."[13] It is interesting in this connection that shortly after the Spanish National Court's decision, a Cuban exile group from Miami filed a suit in the Madrid courts charging President Fidel Castro with genocide.[14]

The difficulties in establishing when a true genocide has actually taken place—or is taking place—have been especially prominent in the debate over the failure of the international community to react more strongly to the crisis in Bosnia. One of the most acerbic critics of Western policy toward Bosnia, David Rieff, has asserted that a quarter of a million Bosnian Muslims have been killed in the struggle and that this has constituted the "third genocide" of a small European people in the twentieth century (the others being the Holocaust and the massacre of the Armenians). His conclusion, then, based on this data, is that Western policy toward Bosnia was essentially one of moral bankruptcy: "The story of Bosnian defeat is the story of Western European and North American disgrace."[15]

The suffering of the Bosnian people certainly has constituted a grave humanitarian challenge to the world community, and there are disturbing questions about the relative ineffectiveness, or lack of will, of various parties in dealing with the challenge. At the same time, to say that others stood by while a "genocide" was undertaken in Bosnia is not a proposition without its own controversy. There is no question that Rieff's figure of 250,000 has been accepted in many quarters as a realistic accounting of the casualties in the Bosnian war, and it has become almost a piece of boilerplate in press accounts of the Bosnian crisis. Other prominent analysts of that crisis, however, have concluded that such a figure is, at the least, greatly exaggerated. Some put the real number at around 25,000, others suggest something in the 70,000 to 100,000 range.[16] Terrible enough, but hardly reaching the level of a "genocide." Moreover, there has been a steady confusion in the 250,000 figure. Rieff states specifically that these were the number of *Bosnian Moslem dead* in the struggle, whereas many others cite a quarter-million killed and *missing* and don't distinguish between Moslem, Serb, or Croatian casualties. Given the widespread dispersal of population caused by the Bosnian fighting—notably in the form of "ethnic cleansing"—it is not a small matter to determine as precisely as possible what percentage of the quarter-million are "missing" (e.g., refugees) but not, in fact, dead.

There is some evidence that the regime in Sarajevo may have intentionally floated the inflated figure of Moslem fatalities for its own purposes, and Rieff may have said more than he intended when he commented that "the Bosnians initially believed that if they could make the case that the Serbs were committing genocide, the signatories to the Genocide Convention of 1949 would come to their aid, as they were obliged to do by this treaty."[17] It is significant that the Bosnian authorities eventually offered (in April 1995) a revised figure of about 140,000 killed and missing, just over 3 percent of the prewar population. The intellectual odyssey of one George Kenney is still another interesting item in the debate over whether a true genocide took place in Bosnia. Kenney resigned from the State Department in 1992 to protest what he saw as his government's indifference to what he specifically described as the *genocide* taking place in the former Yugoslavia. In a series of newspaper op-eds and public appearances, he subsequently drummed away on his theme of American culpability in the committing of a massacre. For whatever reason, however, Kenney now says that, in fact, no genocide ever occurred in Bosnia, and that the quarter-million figure was simply cooked up by the Bosnian government, the international media, and certain United Nations officials. "Bosnia is not the Holocaust," he says today, "or Rwanda. It's Lebanon."[18]

Whatever the true numbers of dead, wounded, and missing in the Bosnian crisis, the debate over Western policy toward that war stands out as an almost perfect example of the complications and ambiguities of terminology in determining valid circumstances for a humanitarian intervention. At the very least, the confusion over whether a "genocide" actually took place in Bosnia makes it all the more difficult to judge what a morally appropriate (and productive) approach to the conflict would actually have entailed (even assuming, as I do, that a more forceful Western response was certainly warranted).

If terminology often makes the debate over humanitarian intervention extremely heated, the temperature of the discussion about which situations provide just cause for humanitarian action is raised even more by the perennial issue of "cultural relativism," to which we already briefly referred earlier. The notion here, of course, is that what may be seen as repugnant by one society may be generally accepted by another. If this be the case, on what grounds does one country (or several countries) set themselves up as moral arbiter of the world, whether it be Marxist Russia, Wilsonian America, or even the very select membership of the United Nations Security Council? Again, such a position cannot be simply set aside in any serious consideration of the core legitimacy of humanitarian intervention. There are indeed a variety of circumstances in which supposedly offensive practices by a particular regime may actually be in accord with the traditional norms of that society, and the world community should proceed with caution when it insists on the "adjustment" of those norms (by force, if necessary) to accord with more "advanced" standards.

The argument that all values are relative is, of course, a central tenet of the "realist" (or statist) school of political thought. Their position is that the effort to establish universally accepted standards of human rights founders on the conflict between the socialist or Third World countries, which tend to regard social and economic values—full employment, guaranteed health, housing, and old-age benefits—as the essence of human rights, and the position of the Western industrial democracies, which may place more emphasis on political, religious, and civil liberties.[19] Whatever one's attitude toward the statist position in this regard—which gives special emphasis to differing stages of political-economic development—there is a wider issue to be addressed in the debate over cultural relativism that goes well beyond this type of argument, and it concerns differing attitudes toward the "public" and "private" realms within various cultures. The stance adopted in particular by various Asian countries is that there is a sphere of private life that is properly beyond the control of political authority (or at least *outside* authority) and whose norms, in many instances, are rightly determined by sacred rather than secular influence. Among the components of this private realm are standards of marriage and divorce, the protection of children, decisions on family planning, and various other elements of traditional religious and cultural practice.[20]

The tension between the notion of cultural relativism and an insistence on a universal code of human rights that would be binding on all was seen in particular at the second United Nations World Conference on Human Rights held in Vienna in 1993. The Western participants in that conference were particularly concerned with avoiding any appearance of moving away from a commitment to universal standards of human rights. American Secretary of State Warren Christopher offered the reasoning behind this position with unusual directness: "We cannot let cultural relativism become the last refuge of repression."[21] As it happened, the theory of the universality of human rights was strongly incorporated in the final Declaration and Programme of Action that emerged from the conference. A typical passage stated that "all human rights are universal, indivisible and interdependent and interrelated. . . . It is the duty of States, regardless of their political, economic and cultural systems, to promote and protect all human rights and fundamental freedoms."[22]

The outcome of the Vienna Conference may be applauded as the reaffirmation of an ideal or cooly analyzed as simply a reflection of the dominant political forces obtaining at the time. What can we make of the argument of cultural relativism, however, in its own terms, and particularly as it influences our judgment on rightful humanitarian interventions? There is a lot to be said for the notion that the cultural relativist position is, on final analysis, more of a denial of reality than an interpretation of it. Any reasonable examination of the world's cultures and main religious movements reveals a set of core values that seems to transcend place and time. There is a need to give meaning to individual existence, pleasure (and sometimes sorrow) at family life, striving for security and freedom from want, and, perhaps above all, a sense of anticipated "proportionality" in which suffering will eventually produce some commensurate reward. From a somewhat different perspective, because a certain culture may regard a given practice as "ethical" does not make it so. Female infanticide was at one time regarded—and to a limited extent is still regarded today—by some cultures as an appropriate response to unwanted female births. That such a principle is or has been accepted does not make it worthy of equal moral weight compared to more enlightened behavior. The point is that ethical judgment that bears on humanitarian intervention is not merely a matter of subjective assessment. In the final analysis, it receives at least part of its definition from certain enduring, and intuitively identifiable, standards of conduct.

In any case, there is considerable reason to question whether the very idea of humanitarian intervention is as culturally biased as is often assumed. One well-known commentator advances the typical argument that "the concept of nations interacting under rules of international law and principles of humanitarian service does not always translate well in the Muslim world."[23] As Sohail Hashmi argues, however, there is "an a priori assumption in Islamic thought for the legitimacy of humanitarian intervention in collective action which has to be disproved rather than proved."[24] The basis for this assertion is that Islam has traditionally been antagonistic to the very idea of full state sovereignty; instead it has placed emphasis on the idea of one *umma* (or community), and that members of that community have a basic obligation to react to injustice anywhere within it. In this sense, the sometimes notorious concept of *jihad* can be understood only as an early formulation of a more general doctrine of humanitarian intervention.

Islamic doctrine even deals with the oppression of non-Muslims by members of the faith. The basic thrust of the Koran is that principles of justice are universal, and do not just apply within the *umma*, and by implication, cooperation with non-Muslims in dealing with assaults on these principles is, at least theoretically, permissible. The more typical focus is, of course, on outrages perpetrated by heretics against Muslims, and in this case the Koran dictates, "And why should you not fight in the cause of God and of those who being weak are ill-treated and oppressed." The two practical alternatives in this regard suggest either the relocation of those oppressed, but if this is not availing, the use of arms to correct the prevailing injustice. In the interesting case of Muslims being oppressed by other Muslims, the Koran says that attempts at peace should first be attempted, but if necessary, force can be employed to deal with especially severe outrages—but only to cause their cessation rather than the replacement of the regime responsible.[25]

Whatever one's attitude about the subtleties of Islamic theology and the concept of humanitarian intervention, it is not easy to set aside Julius Nyerere's response to the criticism of his invasion of Uganda in 1979 to topple Idi Amin. In an obvious state of exasperation, Nyerere proclaimed that "there is a strange habit in Africa: an African leader, as long as he is African, can kill Africans just as he pleases."[26] This is about as effective a response to the "situational ethics" premise behind so much of the cultural relativism rhetoric as one can imagine. Even so, this hardly settles the issue completely. In establishing proper criteria for rightful humanitarian intervention, Michael Walzer is surely right in emphasizing that such interventions cannot be justified simply "for the sake of democracy or free enterprise or economic justice or voluntary association or any other of the social practices and arrangements that we might hope for or even call for in other people's countries."[27]

In sorting out this matter—that is, what *types* of human-rights violations can justly occasion humanitarian intervention—it is well to summarize the standard categories of human rights that are contained, for example, in the International Covenants on Economic, Social and Cultural Rights, and on Civil and Political Rights. The first covenants include the right to an adequate standard of living, to physical and mental health, to just and favorable working conditions, to access to educational opportunity, and to participation in cultural life. The latter covenants address prohibitions against torture, arbitrary imprisonment, and unfair trial, as well as a right to liberty of movement, to freedom of opinion, assembly, and political participation.[28] There is controversy among commentators on human rights about whether all these rights are essentially indivisible, with each one, in fact, *dependent* on the achievement of the others. From the perspective of ethical theory, it is hard to argue against this proposition, and this was the stance to which the final declaration of the Vienna Conference strongly adhered.

When it becomes a matter of legitimate humanitarian intervention, however, things are not quite so simple, and the position taken here is that, at least under present circumstances, it is necessary to focus on a more restrictive definition of human rights deprivations that may rightly warrant such intervention. In the best of all (possibly future) worlds, the existence of, say, widespread economic inequality in a society might invite outside action, but this possibility lies well over the horizon. For the immediate future, the emphasis should be on what Rhoda Howard has referred to as "gross human rights violations," that is, the most egregious types of physical oppression and overt mistreatment by governmental authority (or from similar suffering caused by the breakdown of such authority).[29] The idea here is to focus on a minimal and universal code of human rights that involves protection from politically inspired murder, slavery, torture, and, in the most extreme cases, true genocide.

The rationale for establishing a core group of rights, the violation of which may justly vindicate outside intervention, is twofold. On the one hand, it establishes a more practical regime under which true forceful humanitarian action may be accepted by the international community. The point has already been made that to argue for potential humanitarian intervention in order to remedy every conceivable type of human-rights derogation is to effectively reduce the possibility that humanitarian intervention itself will be taken very seriously as a basic concept. R. J. Vincent argues convincingly that "the attraction of the idea of basic rights . . . [is that] it seeks to put a floor under the societies of the world and not a ceiling over them. From the floor up is the business of the several societies."[30] On the other hand, an emphasis on a basic and universal standard of human-rights obligations goes a long way toward reducing the contentious aspects of the debate over "cultural relativism." Even those most attuned to the relativist position seem prepared to accept the notion of a minimalist code of conduct binding on all societies. Consider, for example, these comments from Kishore Mahbubani, Deputy Secretary of the Ministry of Foreign Affairs of Singapore, at the Vienna Conference. Mahbubani was quite critical of the efforts of the Western parties at the conference to push a wide range of "indivisible and interdependent" rights, but he did offer the following:

> Both Asians and Westerners are human beings. They can agree on minimal standards of civilized behavior that both would like to live under. For example, there should be no torture, no slavery, no arbitrary killings, no disappearances in the middle of the night, no shooting down of innocent demonstrators, no imprisonment without careful review. These rights should be upheld not only for moral reasons. There are sound functional reasons. Any society which is at odds with its best and brightest and shoots them down when they demonstrate peacefully . . . is headed for trouble.[31]

Even if one takes an approach to human-rights violations based simply on "moral reasons," particularly for purposes of identifying which situations provide just cause for humanitarian intervention, there are some further observations that may be offered in this connection. It is important in the first place to make a distinction between essentially discrete acts of violence or repression toward people in their *individual* capacities that, while repugnant, have some "logical" connection to, say, their threatening political activities and situations in which violence and repression are visited on a large number of people not because of what they individually have done, but because of their identity as members of a group. The anti-Semitic policies of the Nazis clearly fell into this second category. Anti-Semitism had always been a "feature" of German life, and even before Adolf Hitler's rise to power, certain German Jews had suffered various disabilities (for example, those aspiring to the German officer corps). At the same time, the prevailing belief within the German-Jewish community was that as they became more thoroughly assimilated into mainstream German life, their putative Jewish identity would become less and less a factor in their treatment. Indeed, there was a certain amount of evidence that this was or would be the case, and ironically, this experience contributed in part to the failure of many Jews to escape from Germany in the 1930s when there was still time to avoid what became the Holocaust. The prevailing belief among many was that if they only showed their full loyalty as Germans first and Jews second, they would be spared mistreatment. Jewish war veterans in particular saw themselves as being in a special category because of their past service. What was inconceivable to the German Jewry was that they were *all* subject to persecution simply because they *were* Jews—because their heritage imposed a collective guilt on all of them.

The point is that while individual mistreatment must always be condemned, it has to be regarded as a less pressing case for humanitarian intervention than when whole collectives are targeted for repression. The term "collective" can (and typically does) encompass a particular ethnic, racial, or religious group within a given society, but sometimes it can embrace the entire society itself. In this instance, the regime is in effect at war with one and all within its jurisdiction. Perhaps the best contemporary example was the horrendous reign of the Khmer Rouge in Cambodia. Certainly, the Pol Pot regime had a special antipathy toward the substantial Vietnamese population living within its borders, but this antipathy was only slightly less manifest in its treatment of the native Khmer population, who were basically regarded as retrograde and inherently "counter-revolutionary" in their character and attitudes and deserved the harshest measures to "reeducate" them along lines congenial to Khmer Rouge philosophy.

In identifying those special situations in which humanitarian intervention is not only legitimate, but perhaps even a necessity, it is not entirely facile to suggest that Supreme Court Justice William Potter's famous approach to identifying obscene material can serve as something of a model. "I may not be able to define it [obscenity]," he said, "but I know it when I see it." Along the same lines, the noted dramatist

Ben Jonson once commented that "the fact of twilight doesn't mean you can't tell night from day." The triggering mechanism for rightful humanitarian intervention (rising to the level of a duty) inevitably has to involve matters of both target and degree: Is a whole community, for example, under threat because of the conscious actions of a regime or the absence of any central order? Is the nature of that threat so fundamental that the very existence of the community—or at least its prospects for a minimally tolerable existence—is at risk?[32] Approached in this way, the number of cases that would qualify for humanitarian intervention would seem to be relatively limited and, to a surprising extent, not a matter of controversy. In the contemporary era, for example, the plight of the Kurds in northern Iraq at the hands of the Saddam Hussein regime and the suffering of the peoples of Somalia and Liberia because of the lack of any central authority in those countries are almost self-evident examples of appropriate targets for humanitarian intervention.

Still, a number of vexing issues remain. One of them has to do with the question of sheer numbers. To make a comparison between relative suffering is, of course, always invidious, but in a world of limited resources and finite political will, it seems inevitable that some sort of quantitative calculation will enter into decisions on humanitarian intervention. In each of the three cases just cited, we are talking about literally millions of people. There are a number of other instances in which the two criteria for humanitarian intervention that we have established may be formally present, but where the relative obscurity of the groups involved or their meager numbers may deflect the world's attention. Some would cite as a good example the plight of the Mayan Indian population in Guatemala. There is ample evidence that the military-dominated regime in that country was, for a long time, embarked on a program of systematic repression of the Mayans, which involved not just their cultural and social heritage, but considerable infliction of death and injury as well. Few, indeed, were the voices calling for a foreign military intervention to remedy this situation (although the United States did intervene in Guatemala in 1954 in the interests of Cold War anti-Communism).[33]

It is also not easy to define precisely what we may mean when we say that a community is fundamentally "at risk." Does this refer to their actual physical extermination (as with the Jews in Nazi Germany) or "simply" to their being subjected to a continual program of oppression and arbitrary treatment? Any meaningful argument for the legitimacy of humanitarian intervention would seem to mandate that we go beyond the first (and relatively rare) type of case. Certainly, large groups of people may be able to survive physically in onerous circumstances, but this hardly implies the bare minimum of human dignity and opportunity that they may rightfully claim. Still, the concept of a community being at risk will continue to provoke heated argument, especially where serious consideration of intervention by outside powers is involved. The position taken here is that as a concept, it has to be very rigorously interpreted, and in the process, a number of possibly doubtful claims for intervention may justly be set aside.

Having said this, there is a final issue that presents itself in trying to establish a modus operandi for rightful (and successful) humanitarian intervention: this has to do with duration and ultimate intention. In the strict sense, all humanitarian interventions have as their central purpose the relieving or redressing of grave human suffering, but this begs the question of whether the object should simply be to deal with the immediate manifestations of such suffering or whether it should also include a more fundamental reshaping of the political process that gave rise to this suffering in the first place. Stanley Hoffmann puts the issue with his usual eloquence:

> If the humanitarian crisis is . . . 'structural', provoked either by the disintegration of a state or by the deliberate evil policies of a government, it becomes extremely difficult for the intervenors to remedy the humanitarian disaster without addressing the causes that produced it. If they do not consider the causes, in order to stick to a narrow, humanitarian mandate—helping victims—they may well be doomed to playing Sisyphus. . . . If the political causes are not removed, victims will remain in danger and the intervention will risk, at best, being no more than a band-aid, and at worst, becoming part of the problem.[34]

This is indeed one of the most vexatious problems that has always burdened the concept of humanitarian intervention and that has provided a central frame of reference for those who question the very notion of such action. As Hoffmann says, a humanitarian intervention to correct wrongs being inflicted on a particular group may prove unavailing in the broader scheme of things unless there is a will and the resources to engage in a wholesale restructuring of the system that gave rise to these wrongs. Since remaking whole social and political systems is an enterprise almost always beyond the capacity or the energy of outside powers, the critics would suggest, any short-term success of a given humanitarian intervention must prove ephemeral. *A fortiori*, then, it is best not to engage in them in the first place.

This is a query not easily set aside, and it must be frankly admitted that an argument for an expanding regime of humanitarian intervention must accept that the tasks imposed will likely be of long, rather than short duration. This will present all sorts of difficulties as is suggested by the international community's experience in Somalia. What started out as a classic case of humanitarian intervention to help the starving Somalis because of the chaos in that country was (albeit rather briefly) transformed into an attempt to shape the domestic constellation of forces in Somalia by a direct assault on the forces of Mohammed Aideed, who came to be identified as the main obstacle to stability in Somalia. The resulting casualties that the UN's contingent suffered led to a general collapse of public support for the Somalia mission—particularly in the United States—and to its effective termination. In general, it would seem that the prospects for genuine systemic transformation in order to forestall future human suffering in a target country must rest on a close calculation of the balance of forces that is likely to exist there following the intervention. Will the international community, in other words, have such a preponderance of power that it can reasonably expect to be able to dictate fundamental changes in the local political structures? The historical record suggests that such situations are normally found mainly in the aftermath of a country's decisive defeat in major war, for instance, the Japanese and the Germans after World War II.

We can go too far here, however, in insisting that all humanitarian interventions must involve very broad political tasks and that, unless these are achievable, there is no rationale for attempting the intervention in the first place. The fact is that the massive suffering of large groups of people is not a spectacle that we can or should simply set aside just because it is doubtful that we will be able to transform the environment that gave rise to this suffering. The travails of the Iraqi Kurds are a case in point. To assert that no assistance should have been given to the Kurds unless there was a reasonable prospect that the Saddam Hussein regime could itself be brought down and, more than this, that a reasonably functioning democratic system with firm protections for minorities could take its place in Iraq, sets an impossibly high standard for legitimate humanitarian intervention. To do even partial good is better than to do no good at all, as we have attempted to argue earlier. According to the old saying, it is better to light even one candle than to curse the darkness.

THE CNN EFFECT

In lighting those candles or, more to the point, in choosing where to light them, this is as good a place as any to consider the famous—or fabled—"CNN effect." The jaundiced commentary that is sometimes directed toward the notion of humanitarian intervention, and specifically the American role in such intervention, almost always includes a brief, usually cynical reference to this supposed "phenomenon." The argument is that the technical capabilities of the electronic media in covering disasters around the world—symbolized in particular by the international coverage of CNN—have created a situation in which the emotions of the mass public can easily be aroused by terrible pictures. This, in turn, puts great pressure on their leaders to do something about the suffering on display. The implicit, and sometimes not so implicit, suggestion seems to be that CNN is actually doing a disservice to a rational and ordered foreign policy by diverting decision makers from attending to traditional needs dictated by the national interest.

Consider, for example, this analysis from the well-known political commentator Charles Krauthammer. Following a mortar attack on a marketplace in Sarajevo on February 5, 1994, resulting in 68 deaths—an event covered by the international media—the United States issued an ultimatum designed to prevent such future attacks. Krauthammer observed that this decision owed relatively little to "history," that is, an "objective" calculation of American interests in Bosnia. "The decision was made on the basis of TV pictures. What changed American policy was coverage of the massacre at the market. Foreign policy 'made by CNN' may be psychologically satisfying, but it is very dangerous."[35] An equally jaundiced assessment of the media's coverage of the atrocity in Sarajevo by Representative Jessica Matthews (D-CA) was that the West was currently unable . . .

> to harness its humanitarian impulse and its traditionally defined interests into a coherent approach to crises. . . . Televised events that stir emotions have an unprecedented ability to manipulate policy. . . . The process by which a particular human tragedy becomes a crisis demanding a response is less the result of a rational weighing of needs or what is remediable than it is of what gets on nightly news shows.[36]

It might be observed, in passing, that analyzing the CNN effect this way involves some distinctly curious propositions. In the first place, it seems to be based on an approving version of the old saw that "if a tree falls in the forest, and there is no one to hear it, does it really make a sound?" The notion seems to be that trees may indeed be falling all over the world—that is, human catastrophes are steadily taking place—but if CNN is not there to "hear" them, then we don't have to notice, indeed *won't* notice, and we can be comfortable in our ignorance. Criticisms of the CNN effect also have a condescending, not to say elitist, character to them. The idea is that the general public is basically immature and hopelessly sentimental, easily swayed by the latest evidence of human suffering, and unable to make any really sensible decisions about the commitment of the country's resources in international relations. Such decisions ought to be left to those who are "tough-minded" enough to set aside whatever natural human feelings they may have and focus instead strictly on the national self-interest narrowly defined.[37]

It happens that we have a good deal of evidence that the alarums about the CNN effect are considerably overdrawn. One ironic point here is that in recent years, there has been a substantial *decline* in international reporting by the Western media, especially by the American media, particularly by television. The reasons for the drop-off in international media coverage are typically cited as resulting from financial constraints as well as the general public's supposed lack of interest in foreign affairs. The point for present purposes is that in a great many cases, the public is not being alerted to humanitarian crises around the world, and thus can hardly be putting much pressure on their governments to take action in response to such disasters.

The lack of reporting about some major humanitarian disasters isn't always just a matter of resources or indifference by the editors in New York or the public itself. In many areas where such crises are unfolding, there are a formidable number of factors that discourage media scrutiny. Simply getting to these trouble spots may involve daunting transportation problems, and once reporters find their way there, the logistics of moving around what may be a very large area can also be quite difficult. A good example is the relative paucity of coverage about the ongoing problems of the Sudan, where civil war and famine have resulted in at least 300,000 deaths, compared to the attention given to Somalia. A major factor in this case, as Reid Miller, AP bureau chief in Nairobi, has said, is that "Sudan is a very, very difficult place to cover. Somalia was easy."[38] Aside from being a huge country with a very limited internal transportation system, the difficulties of covering the Sudanese tragedy also included the resistance of the authorities in Khartoum to granting visas to journalists as well as the reluctance of local officials from international aid organizations to jeopardize their relations with these authorities by cooperating with visiting media.

Even when reporters cover some ongoing humanitarian crisis, the real concern we might have with the CNN effect is that this coverage often does little to educate the public about the issues involved. Much of the reporting that takes place is of the "fireman" variety, characterized mainly by its superficiality. As a producer for ABC has said, "If it can't be done in three days, it hasn't happened."[39] Another perennial accusation is that reporters may have only the haziest idea of the true roots of the conflict they are covering. One good example was media coverage of the mass killings in Rwanda, which were largely depicted as another example of primordial tribal killings, primitive Africans once again on the rampage. In actuality, as close students of Rwanda argued from the outset, the crisis was really a *political* one, in which extremist Hutu political and military figures were determined to block all reforms in the Rwandan political system, and were willing to kill numbers of Tutsis and many of their own people, if necessary. As Roger Winter, director of the United States Committee for Refugees, said, the Hutu perpetrators of the slaughter in Rwanda "manage to survive and succeed time after time by duping foreign journalists and world leaders into believing that Rwanda's spasms of butchery are little more than the unavoidable by-product of Africa's hot ethnic passions. Don't believe it."[40]

Whatever the quality of media coverage of international humanitarian disasters, the evidence suggests that the basic premises behind the so-called CNN effect are actually quite shaky, especially in its assumptions about the decision-making process itself. As Bill Kovach has observed, those bewailing the ill effects of the CNN effect generally promote one or the other of two contradictory notions: "The media either take foreign policy out of the hands of the elite and open the process to an ill-informed public or they are indentured servants of the foreign policy elite."[41] To the extent that there is any truth in these propositions, the evidence (ironically) is that the second holds a good deal more water than the first. A close analysis of some recent cases of American participation in humanitarian intervention—or in certain instances, non-intervention—reveals that the decisions taken were in fact generated basically "within the Beltway" and could hardly be attributed to any mass public groundswell or demand that the American government act in response to a particular humanitarian emergency.

To be sure, extensive media coverage of a particular event can sometimes move an issue higher up on the policymaker's agenda in the sense of creating a "constituency" for action within the broader public to some extent but even more within the government itself. As a former USAID official has said, however, officials get relatively little of their information from the public media and hardly establish their priorities as a result of their exposure to it. "The truth is that most complex emergencies receive little media coverage at any stage. Usually it is when the disaster response is unsuccessful and people die that serious coverage occurs."[42] Ironically, officials often attempt to persuade the media to *focus* on a particular crisis in order to arouse public concern and support for governmental action. These efforts are not always successful, but it does appear that in establishing their agenda of potential stories, reporters tend to reflect the foreign policy concerns of their government far more than they shape those concerns themselves.

The case of Somalia provides some interesting support for these propositions. As of mid-summer 1992, various international agencies estimated that between 300,000 and 500,000 people had already died in Somalia as a result of the civil war raging there and the wide-ranging famine that accompanied it.[43] Up to that point, media coverage of the Somali crisis had been meager indeed, but various American governmental agencies, particularly the Office for Foreign Disaster Assistance (OFDA) at AID, had for some time been engaged in laying the groundwork for a program of assistance to the distressed Somali people. As part of this effort, key officials at AID, particularly Andrew Natsios, head of OFDA, embarked on a campaign to interest the media in more extensive coverage of events in Somalia. As news reports of the Somali disaster began to surface with greater regularity, top officials in the Bush administration, notably the president himself, began to focus on the issue more directly, but even before this, OFDA had been working through internal governmental channels to engage the attention of the White House about the needs of the Somalis. A fair conclusion is that even though the developing media coverage of Somalia helped move the issue to a prominent place on President Bush's policy agenda, he was already moving in that direction. The terrible pictures that showed the starving people in Somalia facilitated his decision to order help for the Somalis by arousing public support for such a course of action.

Haiti was another example of a decision to intervene that basically derived out of the values and the concerns of policymakers themselves. It is especially significant in this regard because media coverage of Haiti had definitely *not* led to any noticeable public pressure for a move against the Cedras regime. Public-opinion polls consistently showed majority *opposition* to the United States becoming involved in the travails of Haiti (despite fairly widespread television coverage of the suffering there). It was, presumably, not a coincidence that a clear majority in Congress were themselves on record as opposing any American attempt to oust Cedras. That was obviously the reason the Clinton administration declined the opportunity to submit its plans to Congress for prior approval before moving against the Haitian dictator.[44] At the same time, President Clinton was evidently sensitive to criticism he was receiving from members of the Congressional Black Caucus about his Haiti policy, particularly as the president needed the caucus's support for his emerging healthcare plan. Moreover, prominent members of the administration, particularly then National Security Adviser Tony Lake and his deputy, Samuel Berger, were privately arguing strongly for American intervention against Cedras.[45] In this instance, as in others, the putative impact of the CNN effect proved more a chimera than a reality. A fair conclusion is that media coverage can sometimes prove effective in garnering public support for a course of action that policymakers have already decided on, but this coverage is rarely decisive in causing them to adopt a particular stance in the first place.

If fears about the CNN effect can be shown to have some basic analytical flaws, there is the paradox that many of those who express concern about this supposed phenomenon are themselves journalists or at least commentators on public affairs. How can they square their bewailing of the effects of CNN news coverage with their traditional commitment to as wide-ranging a media attention to the issues of the day as possible? There seems no easy answer to this apparent contradiction. On the one hand, an increasingly informed public is regarded as the basic *mantra* of responsible contemporary journalism, particularly in terms of its contribution to a more sophisticated public dialogue about alternative governmental policies. On the other hand, there seems to be a belief that the public is not yet—and perhaps never will be—ready for a truly unvarnished coverage of all the brutalities and sins of the human condition. It is hard to argue that you can have it both ways: a (generally) rigorous search for reality and the truth, but only in measured doses that will not arouse uncomfortable and awkward public pressures to pursue certain policies.

The assumptions about an immature public unable to make reasonable judgments about the application of American power and influence—touched on several times in this discussion—actually deserves a little more attention. Most Americans may be relatively untutored about the specifics of foreign affairs, but there are also a number of indications that a rudimentary common sense guides the citizenry in its approach to many international questions.[46] A good example was the widespread uneasiness about the Reagan administration's fervent support of the Contras in Central America and its more general policy of aiding and abetting the overthrow of the Sandinista regime in Nicaragua. Perhaps chastened by the American experience in Vietnam, about two-thirds of those questioned in public-opinion polls consistently said they felt this was a lost cause or at least an inappropriate one. It is interesting that many, if not most, academic experts on Central America arrived at exactly the same conclusion as did the "lay public," even if the public may have done so intuitively.

For present purposes, in any case, one of the real objections to all the hand-wringing about the CNN effect is the way in which it implies quite a dubious normative argument. If we accept, for the sake of argument, that there may have been at least some cases in which the public became aroused (as a result of media reports) about an unfolding tragedy and demanded that their officials do something about it, is this necessarily to be condemned? The national interest, particularly when it involves questions of intervention or non-intervention, is hardly some cold-blooded abstraction whose definition can or should lie only in the hands of a small group of foreign-policy experts. Although they sometimes seem to be forgetful on this score, government officials are ultimately in office only to serve the interests—and the values—of their constituents. If the voters should be moved by pictures of human suffering and, as a consequence, pressure their representatives to take steps to ameliorate this suffering, who is to say that this is somehow a "false" interpretation of the nation's "interests"?

Take, for example, the situation in Ethiopia in the early 1980s. Partly because of natural disasters but even more because of the ill-advised economic policies of the Marxist regime in Addis Ababa, the people of Ethiopia were confronted with widespread famine. Although there were a number of accounts of this calamity in the print media, it wasn't until a BBC film crew managed to gain access to the most affected areas that the crisis implanted itself strongly on the public consciousness. In fact, the BBC produced a documentary of such power that it fundamentally altered the Western attitude about giving food relief even to this rather repulsive regime, which at the time was a virtual international pariah. The BBC film, first shown in the United Kingdom, eventually made its way to the United States and appeared on an NBC program. Shortly after its appearance, there was a quadrupling of food aid by the stridently anti-Marxist Reagan administration to those suffering in Ethiopia.[47] The decision to move in this direction seems to have been the result of twin pressures. Individual administration officials were appalled by what they had seen, and the general public was aroused as well; the combination of the two led to a change in policy. Given the hundreds of thousands of Ethiopian lives saved by the subsequent food shipments, is the BBC to be condemned or praised for having used grim pictures to bring the Ethiopian famine to everyone's attention?[48]

Aside from the putative effect of media coverage in persuading states to contemplate humanitarian interventions (or, in the absence of such coverage, to reject them), there clearly are a number of other elements that enter into the equation as well. Among these are particular societal value systems, calculations of self-interest versus the claims of altruism, concerns about disorder, relatively obtuse or devious behavior by potential target regimes, and, perhaps most interesting, the impact of personality. Each of these is considered in the next chapter.

NOTES

1. Adam Roberts, "Humanitarian war: military intervention and human rights," *International Affairs* 69 (July, 1993). The status of humanitarian intervention as an accepted feature of international relations was paradoxically accepted almost twenty-five years ago in a very influential article that *attacked* the idea that such intervention was *legally* allowed under current international norms. Thus, Thomas Franck and Nigel Rodley argued that "it seems clear that the drafters of human rights covenants did not intend to create rights that could be enforced unilaterally by the military force of the strong nations." Thomas Franck and Nigel Rodley, "After Bangladesh: The Law of Humanitarian Intervention by Force," *American Journal of International Law* 67 (April, 1973), 300. At the same time, they agreed that humanitarian interventions could at times be not only necessary but even desirable, and that in such situations there was unlikely to be any real international sanction or even disapproval by the community of states. Their point was that humanitarian intervention should lie not in the realm of law but in that of overwhelming moral conviction.

2. On this point, see David Forsythe, *The Internationalization of Human Rights* (Lexington, MA: Lexington Books, 1991).

3. Michael Reisman, "Sovereignty and Human Rights in Contemporary International Law," *American Journal of International Law* 84 (October, 1990), 869.

4. "Excerpts from Speeches by Leaders of Permament Members of U.N. Council," *New York Times* (February 1, 1992), A5.

5. David Forsythe and Kelly Pease, "Human Rights, Humanitarian Intervention, and World Politics," in *Human Rights Quarterly* (May, 1993), 294–96.

6. Gerhard von Glahn, *Law Among Nations*, 3rd ed. (New York: Macmillan Publishing, 1976), 194.

7. I examine this matter in much greater detail in *From Potsdam to Poland* (New York: Praeger, 1986), especially Part II.

8. Conference on Security and Cooperation in Europe, "Report of the CSCE Meeting of the Experts on National Minorities" (Geneva, 1991), 4.

9. Michael Veutey, "Assessing Humanitarian Law," in Larry Minear and Thomas G. Weiss, *Humanitarianism and War* (Boulder, CO: Lynne Rienner, 1994), 126.

10. Lori Fisler Damrosch, "Changing Conceptions of Intervention in International Law," in *Emerging Norms of Justified Intervention*, eds. Carl Kaysen and Laura W. Reed (Cambridge, MA: American Academy of Arts and Sciences, 1993), 105.

11. Ernst B. Haas, "Beware the Slippery Slope," in Ibid., 72.

12. Marlise Simons, "Judges in Spain Assert Pinochet Can Face Trial," *New York Times* (October 31, 1998).

13. Michael Radu, "The Pinochet Case: Anti-Communism on Trial," (Philadelphia: Foreign Policy Research Institute E-Note, October 30, 1998).

14. "Exiles Sue Castro in Spain," *New York Times* (November 6, 1998).

15. David Rieff, "The Lessons of Bosnia," *World Policy Journal* 12 (Spring, 1995), 88; David Rieff, *Slaughterhouse: Bosnia and the Failure of the West* (New York: Simon and Schuster, 1994).

16. Charles G. Boyd, "Making Peace with the Guilty," *Foreign Affairs* (September/October, 1995), 27. Boyd was the Deputy Commander in Chief of the U.S. European Command from November, 1992 to July, 1995.

17. Rieff, "The Lessons of Bosnia," 77.

18. George Kenney, "The Bosnian Calculation," *New York Times Magazine* (April 23, 1995), 42.

19. For an interesting discussion of this distinction, see Adamantia Pollis, "Cultural Relativism Revisited: Through a State Prism," *Human Rights Quarterly* 18 (1996), 318–19 ff.

20. Christina Cerna, "Universality of Human Rights and Cultural Diversity: Implementation of Human Rights in Different Socio-Cultural Contexts," *Human Rights Quarterly* 16 (November, 1994), 746.

21. Quoted in David P. Forsythe, "The UN and Human Rights at Fifty: An Incremental but Incomplete Revolution," in *Global Governance* 1 (1995), 301.

22. Cerna, "Universality of Human Rights," 741.

23. Frederick C. Cuny, "Humanitarian Assistance in the Post-Cold War Era," in *Humanitarianism across Borders*, eds. Larry Minear and Thomas G. Weiss (Boulder, CO: Lynne Rienner Publishe.s, 1993), 157.

24. Sohail H. Hashmi, "Is There an Islamic Ethic of Humanitarian Intervention?" *Ethics and International Affairs* 7 (1993), 55.

25. Ibid., 63–65.

26. Cited in Fernando R. Tesón, *Humanitarian Intervention* (Irvington-on-Hudson, NY: Transnational Publishers, 1985), 161.

27. Michael Walzer, "The Politics of Rescue," *Dissent* (Winter, 1995), 36.

28. Rolf Künnemann offers a very useful summary of the different types of human rights in his "A Coherent Approach to Human Rights," *Human Rights Quarterly* 17 (1995), 324–25. See also Jack Donnelly, *International Human Rights* (Boulder, CO: Westview Press, 1993), 24–28.

29. Rhoda Howard, *Human Rights and the Search for Community* (Boulder, CO: Westview Press, 1995), 14.

30. R. J. Vincent, *Human Rights and International Relations* (Cambridge: Cambridge University Press, 1986), 126–27.

31. Cited in Cerna, "Universality of Human Rights," 745.

32. This formula bears a resemblance to Michael Walzer's concept of the "supreme emergency," which he identifies as a situation in which (in wartime) a nation fighting in a just cause faces imminent defeat and the results of such defeat would be catastrophic for the whole society (e.g., the Nazi threat to Britain in 1940). In such circumstances, Walzer suggests, the nation involved may *temporarily* be allowed to set aside some of the standard moral strictures of the "War Convention" governing legitimate conduct in wartime. Our application of a variety of the supreme emergency construct, of course, has to do not with what states are *allowed* to do in the midst of a conflict (*jus in bello)*, but with what they may (should) feel compelled to do in *initiating* such a conflict in the form of an intervention (*jus ad bellum).* See Michael Walzer, *Just and Unjust Wars*, 2nd ed. (New York: Basic Books, 1992), 252.

33. Richard Immerman, *The CIA in Guatemala* (Austin: University of Texas Press, 1982).

34. Stanley Hoffmann, "Out of the Cold: Humanitarian Intervention in the 1990's," *Harvard International Review* (Fall, 1993), 9.

35. Charles Krauthammer, "Intervention Lite: Foreign Policy by CNN," *The Washington Post* (February 18, 1994), A25.

36. Jessica Matthews, "Policy Vs. TV," *The Washington Post* (March 8, 1994), A19.

37. Perhaps one of the most unvarnished statements reflecting this view was offered by Walter Lippmann in *The Public Philosophy* (New York: Mentor Books, 1955). Lippmann suggested that public opinion had consistently

been wrong on the major issues of war and peace in the twentieth century, that its reaction to major new ventures in foreign policy was invariably "no," and that in particular anything that was likely to be costly or lengthy in execution was subject to denunciation (23–24). Given the fact that Lippmann was himself a longtime journalist, supposedly committed to educating the public, these views are rather striking.

38. Steven Livingston, "Suffering in Silence," in *From Massacres to Genocide*, eds. Robert I. Robert and Thomas Weiss (Washington, DC: Brookings Institution, 1996), 76.

39. Edward Girardet, "Public Opinion, the Media, and Humanitarianism," in *Humanitarianism Across Borders*, 51.

40. John C. Hammock and Joel R. Charny, "Emergency Response as Morality Play," in *From Massacres to Genocide*, 121.

41. Bill Kovach, "Do the News Media Make Foreign Policy?" *Foreign Policy* (Spring, 1996), 171.

42. Andrew Natsios, "Illusions of Influence," in *From Massacres to Genocide*, 150.

43. I draw most of the following details of the Somali issue and the media from Todd Eachus and Steven Livingston, "Famine, Floodlights and U.S. Foreign Policy: Reconsidering the CNN Effect in the Case of Somalia" (Annual meeting of the International Studies Association, February, 1995).

44. Most polls suggested that opposition to intervention in Haiti simply to restore democracy there ran in the high 60 percent range. An interesting poll from *Newsweek*, however, said that 32 percent of those questioned felt President Clinton would go ahead anyway because he "will have political problems if he doesn't carry out his threat to invade." Andrew Kohut and Robert C. Toth, "Arms and the People," *Foreign Affairs* (November/December, 1994), 60–61.

45. Peter Viggo Jakobsen, "National Interest, Humanitarianism or CNN: What Triggers UN Peace Enforcement After the Cold War?" *Journal of Peace Research* 33 (May, 1996), 211.

46. Edward Girardet in fact argues that the mass public may actually be thirsting for somewhat wider and more sophisticated coverage of international affairs than is generally assumed. "Once you provide viewers with continuous intelligent coverage, their interest is reawakened. [Editors] say television has to give people what they want. But the discrepancy between what network directors think their audiences want, and what the audiences themselves want, may be enormous." Edward Girardet, "Public Opinion, the Media, and Humanitarianism," in Weiss and Minear, *Humanitarianism Across Borders*, 48–49.

47. Johanna Neuman, *Lights, Camera, War* (New York: St. Martin's Press, 1996), 21–22.

48. An interesting assessment of the whole BBC documentary episode may be found in Peter Boyer, "Famine in Ethiopia, the TV Accident That Exploded" *Washington Journalism Review* (January, 1985).

CHAPTER 5

How Governments Decide

Anyone who sets out to examine the history of, and the issues involved in, humanitarian intervention has to be struck early on by one central fact: There are far more "claimants" to such intervention than those that receive serious consideration, let alone action. The list of historical and more contemporary cases in which a humanitarian intervention would seem to have been amply justified, but which for one reason or another was never attempted indeed stretches out in depressing fashion.

One distant example that may be used as illustration concerns the alleged massacre of the Armenians by Turkish authorities in 1915. Perhaps one million Armenians died from various causes at the time, but the reaction of the international community was distinctly muted. In the more recent period, there was the civil war in Mozambique, in which more than one million are estimated to have been killed, with another four million as internal refugees, and still another one million fleeing abroad (mostly to Malawi but also to Tanzania, South Africa, Zambia, Zimbabwe, Swaziland). A United Nations mission ultimately played a role in persuading the warring parties to accept a political compromise to end the fighting, but there was never any serious consideration of a true humanitarian intervention to aid the people of

Mozambique. Then there are the cases of East Timor (in which almost 10 percent of the population may have fallen prey to Indonesian oppression); the repeated ethnic killings in Burundi; and (to mention only one other instance) the death and injury of hundreds of thousands in the Sudan at the hands of the regime in Khartoum.[1]

From a different perspective, however, the really surprising thing may not be how many legitimate human-rights crises have gone unaddressed, but how many *have* been addressed—far fewer, to be sure, than should have been the case but still, given the rather anarchic character of the international system, not totally unimpressive. The puzzle that presents itself here, then, is how to identify the factors, or combination of factors, that seemingly have to be present for states actually to commit to a given humanitarian intervention.[2] In addressing this matter, it seems cumbersome to go through a full case-by-case analysis of all the possible instances of such interventions. Instead, I want to engage in a *comparative* analysis in which certain key themes are extracted from the body of historical evidence on humanitarian intervention. Some of the cases considered here are rich in illustrative points while others may be relatively less useful in arriving at generalizations. The point, in any event, is to develop a set of propositions concerning humanitarian intervention that are based on an examination of actual state practice.

SELF-INTEREST AND ALTRUISM

Early on in this study we remarked that it is expecting a lot to assume that states will take steps involving the expenditure of treasure and (possibly) blood solely on the basis of altruistic motives. This doesn't mean that humanitarian intervention has not been a sometime feature of international relations. It is simply that in such instances, states have almost invariably had mixed motives of doing good and doing well, and that this should not be an occasion for surprise or condemnation. This argument can be seen simply as an empirical conclusion about the character of humanitarian intervention, but it has another aspect as well. In gauging those conditions under which humanitarian intervention may rightly be considered appropriate or feasible by a nation's leaders, it is manifest that in gaining support from their constituents for such an enterprise, they must present a case for action that combines both ideals and self-interest.

Operation Just Cause, the American invasion of Panama that resulted in the ouster of Manuel Noriega, provides a good example of this desideratum in operation. The domestic political criticism of Just Cause was surprisingly muted, particularly given the widespread unease within the American public about the Reagan administration's earlier aggressive policy toward the Sandinistas in Nicaragua. Opinion polls consistently showed that about two-thirds of those questioned doubted the wisdom of that policy. In the case of the Bush administration's launching of Just Cause, however, political leaders as disparate as Senators Jesse Helms and John Kerry both expressed their approval, and the polls revealed overwhelming public support for the operation. How to account for this level of acceptance?

Some may question whether Just Cause should actually be described as a humanitarian intervention, at least in terms of meeting the criteria set out earlier for rightful resort to such action. Even if there was no genocide taking place in Panama, it seems clear that a powerful motivating force for the United States to move against Noriega was the grotesque violation of democratic principles and basic human rights by his regime.[3] Elections were cynically manipulated, political opponents of the government were beaten up by the thugs of the "Dignity Battalions," and there was a systematic crushing of all types of free political expression. These depredations were viewed with increasing disgust by members of the Bush administration, and their influence on American decision making was touched on by former Secretary of State James Baker. "If ever a military endeavor were aptly named, this was it. At its core, Just Cause was an exercise in supporting democracy and the rule of law in the hemisphere."[4] Certainly this rationale for the invasion was given wide play by administration spokesmen in the period during and after the event.

At the same time, in garnering public support for Just Cause, President Bush and others were careful to suggest the other interests that were involved as well. After all, there had been repeated violation of "democracy and the rule of law" in other areas of Latin America over the years that had occasioned no American military action. What made Panama so special? There were, in fact, a series of more pragmatic considerations that ultimately played a significant role in the intervention. Noriega was seen as a prime conspirator in the drug traffic to the United States; he had developed increasing contacts with the Cuban, Sandinista, and even Libyan regimes; he was thought to be supplying weapons to Marxist rebels in El Salvador; and under the terms of the 1977 Panama Canal Treaty, a Panamanian was to be appointed chairman of the Panama Canal Commission by January 1, 1990. This impending appointment, it was said, could threaten American use of a strategic maritime passageway if the nominee was simply a Noriega stooge. Finally, American personnel stationed in the Panama Canal Zone were being increasingly harassed by Noriega's security forces, and one American serviceman was killed under mysterious circumstances. Given all these challenges to American interests, and American honor, it was not hard for the Bush administration to convince the public that the removal of Noriega was a consummation devoutly to be wished, even aside from the benefits his removal would have for the Panamanian people themselves.[5]

The Clinton administration's policy toward Haiti in the fall of 1994 provides a somewhat different perspective on the necessity of combining arguments both of self-interest and altruism to attract public support for a humanitarian intervention. The main difference between the Panama operation and the invasion of Haiti was that President Clinton found it far more difficult to present a package containing both elements that appealed to the American people (a point that we have already addressed). Just prior to the dispatch of American troops to Haiti in September, 1994, an ABC News poll showed that 73 percent of Americans were opposed to the use of force to remove the Cedras regime from power. Even after the president went on national television to plead his case for intervention in Haiti, a full 60 percent still registered their disapproval.[6]

How to account for the differences between Haiti and Panama? Certainly, President Clinton had at least as compelling a humanitarian case to make for toppling Cedras as the Bush administration had offered for deposing Noriega—and by any fair reckoning, a rather more powerful one. In his nationwide address on September 15, 1994, the president painted a devastating picture of current conditions in Haiti. "Cedras and his armed thugs have conducted a reign of terror. Executing children. Raping women. Killing priests. As the dictators have grown more desperate, the atrocities have grown ever more brutal." Clinton detailed cases in which the Haitian police executed Haitian orphans simply because of their "suspected sympathies" for the former Aristide regime. He recounted how the body parts of slain dissidents were left in full view in order to quell other potential political opponents, and how children were forced to watch as their mothers' faces were slashed with machetes.[7]

The president went beyond this grim account of conditions in Haiti, however, to suggest that American intervention was justified on narrower grounds of self-interest as well. He stressed that the United States was not acting as a unilateral "world policeman" but was instead supporting the United Nations and its position on Haiti reflected in numerous resolutions, and that some twenty countries would be involved in the military move against Cedras. Even more to the point, the United States had a "particular interest in stopping brutality when it occurs so close to our shores. Thousands of Haitians have already escaped to the United States, risking their lives to escape the reign of terror." The "refugee issue" was indeed the main practical reason Clinton gave for American intervention against Cedras. He emphasized that in the last two months, more than 21,000 Haitians had been picked up at sea by the Navy and the Coast Guard, and that some 14,000 were currently being sheltered at the American base at Guantanamo in Cuba. He made ominous references to some 300,000 Haitians who were hiding in their own country and who could constitute the next huge wave of migration to the United States. He even presented the specific financial costs of this situation; $177 million had already been spent to provide for the refugees and further substantial outlays on the horizon if the exodus continued. The president summarized the challenge that all this presented to the American people: "If we do not act . . . we will continue to face a mass exodus of refugees and a constant threat to stability in our region and control of our borders."[8]

As noted earlier, neither these appeals to the American conscience nor to American fears about an unrestrained flood of refugees resulted in a clear public mandate for intervention against the Cedras regime. The basic reality here seems to have been that the threat Cedras and his cronies posed to the self-interest of the United States hardly seemed to match the threat that Noriega presented (or was claimed to present): a participant in the drug traffic into the United States, a consortant of American enemies such as Castro and even Khadaffi, a threat to free American use of the Panama Canal, and so forth. The refugee issue may have resonated in some quarters of the United States, but as one comment had it at the time, Haiti was basically "a dagger pointed at the heart of Dade Country," the region around Miami, Florida, where the threat of a potential uncontrolled Haitian emigration was felt most strongly. Aside from this, as even an American diplomat stationed in Port-au-Prince admitted, Haiti hardly constituted a traditional "vital interest" for the United States, either in strategic or economic terms.[9]

Despite his failure to secure the support of the American people for a military solution to the Haitian crisis, President Clinton did, of course, go ahead with planning for the dispatch of American troops to that island, and only a last-minute negotiated settlement with Cedras removed the spectre of a forcible entry into Haiti by American forces. Several observations seem appropriate on this outcome. One is that a determined leadership can sometimes prove willing to—or be able to—overcome domestic resistance in committing their countries to a broadly humanitarian mission. There is no question that if Clinton had waited, for example, for formal Congressional approval for the overthrow of Cedras, he would have waited in vain. Even in the absence of such approval, he was willing to proceed. One well-known scholar on Haiti regards this act of courage as "the rare jewel in President Bill Clinton's foreign policy crown."[10] Whether or not one agrees with this general assessment of Clinton's foreign policy, it does seem unmistakable that the outcome in this instance was broadly beneficial. The democratically elected Aristide was restored to power (and eventually handed over power to a democratically elected successor), the human-rights situation greatly improved, and "overall, Haiti is a much better and more livable place than it was [previously]," as the above scholar suggests.[11]

At the same time, it is only fair to recognize that Clinton's willingness to hang tough on Haiti involved more than his compassion for the suffering of the Haitian people. As one critical assessment of his intervention in Haiti rightly asserts, the pressures of the Congressional Black Caucus, and more generally the appeals of other prominent African-American spokespersons—both of whom were important to his political power base—certainly played a part in forcing his hand on the Cedras issue. Moreover, Clinton was laboring in the fall of 1994 under an impression that he was a weak and vacillating president in international relations, an image that had been reinforced by his seeming indecision over Haiti in the preceding months.[12] By taking a decisive stand against Cedras, he could present himself as a leader willing to take risks, attracting the admiration even of those who might have doubts about the merits of this particular case. The point seems to be that in asserting the necessity of combining ideals and self-interest in moving nations toward humanitarian intervention, the rule applies just as much to leaders as to the led.

A final case in which an obvious admixture of ideals and self-interest has led to a willingness to intervene concerns French policy in Africa. France has had a prominent history of intervening on the African continent, and has enjoyed a significant degree of domestic support for such actions. For purposes of this discussion, at least two of these rank high on the list of what can legitimately be called humanitarian intervention: the toppling of the despised dictator Jean Bedel Bokassa of the Central African Republic in 1979 and the later dispatch of French troops to Rwanda in June 1994. Both of these steps clearly had significant humanitarian benefits, first, in removing a loathsome individual who had a grim record of brutalizing his own people, and second, in protecting large numbers of refugees from the ravages of the Rwandan killing fields. At the same time, both events clearly were part and parcel of a more general French policy toward Africa that was based on a special vision of French interests in that area.

Some of these interests have certainly been economic, with Africa serving as a source of vital raw materials as well as a market for French manufactures and as an outlet for capital investment. Over time, however, the economic factor in French policy seems to have steadily decreased, and other elements have been at the forefront. Certainly, in the days of the Cold War, Africa was a sort of *domaine reservé* in which France could carve out something of an independent role for herself outside the constraints of superpower hegemony. From a different perspective, France also saw herself serving as a guardian of Western interests in the region against attempts by Moscow or Beijing to penetrate weak African states. Aside from political and even economic considerations, however, French policy toward Africa has always had certain less tangible qualities to it. The notion of a *mission civilisatrice*, in which the blessings of French culture would be extended and sustained in present or past French colonies, has played a role here as elsewhere. Paris has also demonstrated a sense of moral responsibility—perhaps characterized best as a type of modified noblesse oblige—for regime development in Francophone Africa.[13]

It has been a rather complex picture, and one admirably summarized by Dominique Moïsi as "a mixture of idealism and cynicism, of a sense of duty and outright exploitation of the weaknesses of others."[14] It is also significant that French policy could be served at relatively little cost. A former French foreign minister, Louis de Guiringuad, admitted frankly that "Africa is the only continent that is still to the measure of France, within its reach. It is the only one where it can still, with 500 men, change the course of history."[15] The fact that France has always maintained a significant military presence in various African countries, in terms of troops and advisers, has also facilitated its role.

The relative ease with which France has been able to intervene in Africa has been a function as well of the fact that decision making on such interventions has been very closely held. A special ministry of cooperation was set up to regulate French relations with Africa outside the normal political and military chain of command, and policy on the use of force has typically been an ad hoc affair decided on within narrow presidential circles, formally legal in character (e.g., based on mutual defense treaties), and quite limited in size and timing.[16] Despite the general lack of public input in decisions on intervention, there has been very considerable domestic support for such decisions, as noted earlier. Either through luck or skill, successive French governments have evidently been able to convince their constituents that France has an opportunity to serve both her own interests as well as a wider set of values in pursuing an active diplomacy on the African continent.

EMPATHY AND INDIFFERENCE

In analyzing past instances of humanitarian intervention, it seems evident that the intervening state's basic societal system has often, although not invariably, been a key variable in the willingness of both the leaders and the led to commit resources to aid the oppressed. By "societal system," I am referring here to the essential social, political, economic, and demographic components of the state and, more generally, to the overall set of values and traditions to which that state claims to adhere. To say that differences in such systems may lead to different decisions on humanitarian intervention is, in a sense, almost a self-evident proposition, but it presents some interesting issues for discussion and may lead either to relatively optimistic or relatively pessimistic conclusions about the future possibilities of a wider series of such interventions.

It may be asserted, for example, that the steady spread of democratic polities around the world has now established democratic governance as a basic norm of the international system and, thus, has contributed to a mindset in which the absence of such a norm will increasingly be viewed as unacceptable. This is the basic thesis of Francis Fukayama's well-known treatise on the "end of history," wherein he argues that the perennial dialectic in world history between authoritarianism and democracy, between command economies and free markets, has been decisively settled in favor of freedom and economic liberalism.[17] To be sure, Fukayama's thesis doesn't necessarily lead inevitably to support for humanitarian intervention, but there is a logical connection that can be made in this regard. The work of Joshua Muravchik goes some distance toward making that connection. Muravchik suggests that since democratic principles *are* increasingly the international norm—and since the United States stands as the leading exemplar of this norm—it is incumbent on this country to establish the spread of democracy as a principal item on its foreign-policy agenda. He goes on to assert that simply employing "diplomacy" to create democracy "is ordinarily to employ a means insufficient to the ends."[18]

To argue that the character of societal systems is an important predictor of humanitarian intervention may, on the other hand, lead to rather pessimistic conclusions about the willingness even of democracies to engage in future altruistic exercises. One of the criticisms of the Fukayama thesis is that it omits some important swaths of the world in which respect for democracy and basic human rights hardly seems to match his rosy vision: sub-Saharan Africa, parts of Asia, and various states emerging out of the former Soviet Union. The point is that the most likely candidates for humanitarian intervention in the future will increasingly lie in obscure parts of the world that have somehow escaped the democratization trend so evident in other regions. Yet these are areas relatively remote from at least the Western experience and, as such, are unlikely to arouse public sentiment for intervention to protect peoples of which little is known or comprehended. This doesn't imply that there is necessarily some sort of subtle racism operating here, in which strange peoples are considered beyond the realm of help. It does suggest that there is a natural human tendency to take the travails of similar cultures more seriously than other less-familiar ones.[19]

The Indian intervention in East Pakistan in 1971 is a good example of this proposition. There had been a steadily growing tension between India and Pakistan since March of that year about the atrocities being committed by the Pakistani army against the Bengalis in East Pakistan. The crisis in East Pakistan had its origins in the desire of the Bengalis in that part of Pakistan for a far greater degree of autonomy. Ever since the formation of Pakistan in 1947, the eastern part of the country had been systematically discriminated against politically and economically, and under the Awami League of Sheik Mujibur Rahman, a broad-based movement developed in response to this perceived injustice. In parliamentary elections in November 1970, the Awami League won 167 out of 169 seats allotted to East Pakistan and in the process acquired a comfortable majority in the Pakistani National Assembly. The central government immediately perceived this result as a fundamental threat to its position, and on March 25, Yayha Khan ordered his army to brutally repress Bengali political dissent. Over the next several months, at least one million people are estimated to have died, and millions more fled into neighboring India.[20] Dehli hesitated for some months before deciding to use military force to resolve the crisis. One of the elements that finally moved India to take action was a very large Bengali population in India itself, which in turn pressured Delhi to support their ethnic compatriots across the border (an appeal to which the Indian government was responsive, if for no other reason than to maintain political stability in the Indian state of Bengal itself).[21]

A contrasting—and depressing—situation in which political and cultural factors deterred a response to foreign oppression can be seen in the relative American passivity when confronted with the outrages of Nazi policy toward German Jews in the late 1930s. To be sure, military action to improve the plight of the Jews of Germany seems hardly to have been a realistic prospect, but how can we account for the indifference, even hostility, of the United States to accepting large numbers of Jews attempting to emigrate from Germany in order to escape the Nazi yoke? There was steady opposition to changing the immigration laws to allow a special one-time dispensation for German Jews who wanted to come to the United States. Even more bizarre was the fact that only 35 percent of the *regular* quota for German immigration was filled even during the worst periods of German anti-Semitism in the late 1930s.

The basic American position toward the travails of the Jews in Germany was expressed early on by Secretary of State Cordell Hull, who prided himself on not letting "sentimental" considerations get in the way of realpolitik. All that the State Department could do, said Hull, was to continue "to watch the situation confronting the Jews in Germany with careful and sympathetic [*sic*] interest."[22] This feckless attitude was matched by that of President Roosevelt himself, who allowed that the plight of the Jews was "not a governmental affair" and that the United States could take no official steps except where American nationals themselves were concerned.[23] To be sure, the president used his influence to arrange for an international conference on the problem of Jewish refugees at Evian (in France) in the summer of 1938. The meeting accomplished almost nothing, however, and the French Prime Minister, Eduard Daladier, was not far off the mark when he said that Roosevelt had pushed for the conference basically for political reasons and to deflect demands from some quarters for more drastic action.[24]

There were a myriad of factors that contributed to the United States's not taking a stronger stand in the face of Nazi repression of German Jews. The forces of isolationism were particularly strong at the time, and the difficulties resulting from the Depression convinced many, if not most, Americans that their attention should properly be focused on domestic rather than foreign concerns. Moreover, Hitler was seen by some people as a firm bulwark against the spread of Communism, and too much should perhaps not be made of his other, more doubtful, policies. American Jews, themselves, were concerned about making too much of the plight of their brethren in Germany lest this arouse unwelcome manifestations of anti-Semitism in the United States. American labor unions were also adamant in pressuring the administration not to agree to a large-scale emigration that, in their view, would take away jobs from American workers.[25]

The above elements in American policy toward German Jews could be regarded as having at least some "rational" basis, but there was definitely a darker and more indefensible factor in that policy. The widespread, if sometimes subtle, anti-Semitism in American life made it unlikely that a scheme for helping Jews would fall on receptive ears in the United States. One public-opinion poll taken in the middle 1930s, for example, identified "the Jews" as the third most dangerous "threat" to the United States only exceeded by that of the Germans and Japanese. Still another poll showed that 80 percent of those questioned opposed a revision of the immigration quota system in order to allow more (mostly Jewish) refugees into the United States.[26] Father Charles Coughlin of Michigan, in his weekly radio broadcasts, reached an audience of over three million with his overtly anti-Semitic message. President Roosevelt was always very cautious not to venture too far ahead of American public opinion in reacting to the European crisis, and his policy toward German oppression of Jews stands as a prime example.

The same pattern may perhaps be seen in the passivity of the United States, as well as other Western countries, to the developing massacre of the Tutsi people by the Hutus in Rwanda in 1994. Rwanda was, to repeat British Prime Minister Neville Chamberlain's phrase at the time of the Munich agreement in September 1938 (which sanctioned German annexation of a part of Czechoslovakia), a "faraway country of which we know nothing." Senator Robert Byrd, in announcing his opposition to any American intervention in Rwanda, commented that "to go now into Rwanda invites an expansion of the relief role . . . into a security mission and then 'nation-building.' We had enough of that in Somalia."[27] Aside from the remoteness of Rwanda, there was a prevailing sentiment that such tribal slaughter was a regular thing in this most "uncivilized" part of the world and was hardly subject to genuine remedy. Defense Secretary William Perry put it more bluntly than most: "My job is managing an army, not a salvation army."[28] Despite a growing media coverage of the Rwanda crisis, the Clinton administration refused requests from various non-governmental organizations to intervene. Even when a number of African countries offered troops for a rescue mission and asked to use American airlift capabilities to move them, along with armored personnel carriers, to Rwanda, the United States continued to dally for four months. Finally, a small group of Americans were sent to Zaire for essentially logistical purposes, but even these forces were prematurely withdrawn when the Defense Department's funds for the operation ran out.[29]

An equivalent psychological distancing from atrocity appears to have been an important factor in the failure of states other than Vietnam to take a stronger stand against the atrocious policies of the Khmer Rouge in Cambodia. Despite the fact that a true genocide seemed to be going on in that unhappy land during the late 1970s, outside powers offered little except verbal denunciations and the occasional diplomatic démarche. In January 1979, the Vietnamese put an end to the Khmer Rouge regime by occupying virtually the whole of Cambodia. Whatever may be said about the actual motivations for this intervention (a matter to be discussed shortly), it is striking how, after this event, the international community seemed to be focused almost not at all on the release of the Cambodian people from oppression, but on the formal violations of Cambodian "sovereignty" occasioned by the Vietnamese action. The UN General Assembly condemned the invasion by a vote of 91–21 (almost all the dissenting votes came from the pro-Soviet camp) and continued to regard the Khmer Rouge delegate at the UN as the sole "legitimate" representative of the Cambodian government. The American representative, Andrew Young, long known for his commitment to human-rights causes, said that the issue of conflicting claims on the Cambodian seat at the UN was an "interesting" one, but he also supported (on instructions, to be sure) the continuing presence of the Khmer Rouge representative since he was "a representative of a government recognized by the General Assembly."[30] Countries such as Thailand and China obviously had prudential reasons for taking such a position against the Vietnamese intervention, given their perennial tensions with Hanoi. As for other, more distant lands, however, Kampuchea indeed seems to have been a place of which they knew nothing, and had little motivation to learn more about, in the bargain.

THE FEAR OF DISORDER

If a society's relative sense of detachment from the suffering of another, generally very different group of people deters sentiments for humanitarian intervention, there is also the prevailing fear of what might be called "uncertainty" or instability in international relations. Certainly, most governments—and their citizenries—have a tendency toward embracing the status quo, at least if the latter is seen as basically friendly to their own interests. Perhaps foreign humanitarian ventures can be undertaken without threatening these interests; on the other hand, why take the chance if the consequences of doing so are basically unpredictable? A good example of this factor in operation may be seen in the policy of the United States and other countries toward Chile during the Pinochet regime.

After a period of growing instability in Chilean politics during the early 1970s under the presidency of Salvador Allende, the Chilean military undertook a coup on September 11, 1973, that resulted in the ouster of the Allende government (and Allende's own death) and the imposition of an authoritarian regime led by General Augusto Pinochet. Pinochet's coming to power raised a number of very troubling issues not only because Chile in the past had been one of the few consistent democracies in Latin America, but also because of the unusual brutality of the Pinochet government. In the immediate aftermath of the coup, there were estimates that between 3,000 and 10,000 individuals had died. A state of siege was declared in which all political party activity was banned, the Chilean Congress was dissolved, labor union activity was proscribed, and military courts virtually supplanted the civilian judiciary in meting out justice.[31] Arbitrary arrest and detention became the order of the day, and a later Chilean Truth and Reconciliation Commission report detailed the appalling conditions prevalent in the detention centers:

> Mistreatment and torture were an almost universal feature of detentions. . . . Beatings and humiliations were common. . . . Keeping prisoners lying face down on the ground or keeping them standing rigid for hours; keeping them many hours or days naked under constant light . . . keeping them in cubicles so narrow that they were unable to move. . . . It was also common to hang prisoners up by their arms with their feet off the ground for very long periods of time.

They might be held under water, foul smelling substances, or excrement to the brink of suffocation. There are many accusations of sexual degradation and rape. A common practice was a simulated firing squad.[32]

By the spring of 1974, the U.S. State Department announced that it could "accept" an estimate that some 20,000 people in all had been killed since the coup. A subsequent Amnesty International report said that the death toll of political victims in Chile was "unprecedented in Latin American history and there is little indication that the situation is improving or that a return to normality is intended."[33]

The level of human rights violations that were then taking place in Chile cannot truly be said to equal those that were shortly to emerge in Cambodia under the Khmer Rouge or that were soon to begin in East Timor following the Indonesian annexation of that area in 1975. In both instances, the number of victims amounted to hundreds of thousands. At the same time, as the Amnesty International report suggested, the brutalities of the Pinochet regime were virtually unprecedented in Latin America. Nevertheless, the reaction not only of the United States, but also of the broader international community to events in Chile was fairly muted. Undertaking a full-fledged humanitarian intervention, involving the use or at least the threat of force in order to remedy conditions in Chile, may have been expecting too much of that community, but what is striking is how, even in the absence of such an intervention, there were a number of other actions that could have been attempted but for the most part went unexplored.

There were, to be sure, various levels of denunciation directed toward the Pinochet regime by various states during the worst period of the repression in the years following the coup. The Scandinavian countries took the lead in such denunciations, to the extent that the Swedish ambassador to Santiago was formally declared persona non grata. The UN Economic and Social Council passed a resolution condemning human-rights violations in Chile with only two abstentions (the United States and Chile). The UN General Assembly also passed resolutions regularly condemning "Pinochet's policies, most of which passed with overwhelming majorities. Within the United States, certain members of Congress such as Representative Donald Fraser (D-Minn) and Senator Edward Kennedy (D-Mass) led the fight for a tougher American policy toward Chile, and the Congress voted to curtail sales of military equipment to the Pinochet government until the human-rights situation improved. As a general matter, however, neither the Congress nor other international bodies seemed prepared to take measures that would have put genuine pressure on the Chilean regime.

The most obvious of these measures would have been to do to Pinochet what had been done to Allende, that is, use the influence of American and international financial institutions to put an economic squeeze on Santiago until it agreed to a change in policies. The virtual economic embargo that had been directed at Allende contributed to a major crisis in Chile's finances and was one factor that contributed to the instability that eventually brought him down. Pinochet, in his early years in power, was in just as perilous a financial situation, but luckily the money began to flow in. Loans from the Inter-American Development Bank, for example, went from around $11 million for Allende to $238 million for Pinochet, those from the World Bank rose from nothing to $66 million. American economic aid of various types rose from about $56 million in the Allende years to $324 million in the period 1974–76.[34] On the non-economic front, another important step that could have been taken would have been to suspend Chile's membership in the Organization of American States, as had been done to Cuba in 1962. Cuba's ouster from the OAS has obviously not led to the downfall of the Castro government, but there is no question that it has seriously isolated Havana from the regional community. The Pinochet regime, which placed a high premium on maintaining its relationships with other governments in the Hemisphere, might well have been more seriously affected by the opprobrium of such a step.

Why was none of the above seriously contemplated? The main answer seems to be that, whatever his other unpleasant characteristics, Augusto Pinochet had brought considerable "order" to a Latin American country that was an important regional actor and whose destabilizing influence on the region, perhaps causing a potential "domino effect," had been a matter of great concern under the Allende regime. In the first instance, this involved the United States, but it affected a number of other countries as well. As Secretary of State Henry Kissinger recalled, Washington was "persuaded that [the Allende government] would soon be inciting anti-American policies, attacking hemisphere solidarity, making common cause with Cuba, and sooner or later, establishing close relations with the Soviet Union."[35] As noted, such views were not his alone. Argentina and Brazil were obviously far more comfortable with the stolid Pinochet than they ever had been with Allende, and Spain, Britain, and France, among others, felt constrained to accept the new Chilean regime as a reality with which it was only sensible to do business. This acceptance of the Pinochet regime as a force for stability was accentuated by the first glimmerings of the so-called economic miracle that was to lead to very high growth rates for Chile in the latter 1970s, an important development that was partly spurred by international financial assistance but that was in any case a supposed indication that a calming of the Chilean political waters would continue.

None of this suggests that, even for those countries that treated Pinochet as the established leader of Chile, there wasn't a widespread unease and in some cases revulsion about certain practices of his regime. Enough was said in criticism of these practices that the repression following the coup eased noticeably after the mid-1970s (the human rights emphasis of the Carter administration played a significant role here). Still, from the viewpoint of many, this was an almost classic case of the tension between order and justice, and in this instance, the appeal of order seems to have generally won out. That it did so may have been significantly influenced by the fact that the *scale* of abuses in Chile did not seem to approach the sort of "critical mass" that has spurred historical humanitarian intervention. This is, of course, a subjective analysis and personal values, and there are many who view the relative quiescence of the international community in the face of Pinochet's transgressions as a sad chapter in international relations. At the very least, the case of Chile under Pinochet does seem to provide some important insight into the ongoing conflict between the claims of conscience and the fear of uncertainty.[36]

THE QUALITY OF THE OPPOSITION

There is still another point that needs to be addressed in any analysis of the factors that contribute to a decision for or against humanitarian intervention. One is struck by the fact that a decision for intervention is frequently the result of an extraordinary display of ineptitude, arrogance, or just plain stupidity by the leadership of the targeted country. What this suggests, for better or for worse is that a regime may be guilty of considerable crimes but still escape retribution given at least a modicum of sensible—or devious—decision making on its part. This is not an especially encouraging conclusion. Wrong-doing is, after all, wrongdoing, and cleverness by those responsible should not exempt them from judgment. In the real world of affairs, however, it seems that for humanitarian intervention to take place, it is often necessary that the miscreants *really* become their own worst enemies.

Various cases can be cited to illustrate that point. Whatever one's views about the justification for Operation Just Cause against the Noriega regime in Panama in December 1989, the record reveals that it was taken only as a last measure after Noriega had repeatedly rejected a deal with the United States that would have spared him his subsequent ignominious fate (a life sentence in federal prison for drug trafficking). Against the objections of many in his administration, President Reagan offered to drop the existing drug indictments in the United States against Noriega if the Panamanian dictator agreed to go into exile. The offer also allowed him to transfer a very large share of his ill-gotten financial assets in order to make his exile suitably comfortable. Noriega at first seem inclined to accept this offer, but he ultimately decided against it. In October 1989, when American-Panamanian relations had reached their nadir, Washington once again suggested that it would accept the so-called Spanish option for Noriega in which he would agree to surrender power and decamp to Spain, which had already offered to grant him exile. Given Spain's very strict extradition laws, this meant, in effect, that Noriega would be permanently free from the risk of trial in the United States. Once again, however, Noriega rejected such a deal, and Secretary of State James Baker's description of his behavior as increasingly "erratic and irrational" seems amply justified. Some eight weeks later Operation Just Cause put an end to Noriega's options.[37]

There was also the bizarre decision by the Pakistani government under President Yahya Khan to launch a preemptive air strike against India on December 3, 1971. We have already discussed the background to the crisis in East Pakistan in that year that had resulted in growing tensions between Pakistan and India. Over a period of months, India increased her military presence along the East Pakistani border to some seven divisions. But she hesitated to take direct military action, even in the face of the enormous problems presented by eight million Bengali refugees on her side of the border and the pressures from her own Bengali population referred to earlier. Clearly, one of the factors that deterred such a move was the opposition of the United States and China to any unilateral Indian intervention in East Pakistan, as well as the unease of the international community at the prospective violation of Pakistani "sovereignty." The air strike from West Pakistan, however, involving targets as far as three hundred miles deep into India, gave Delhi a golden pretext for doing what she was inclined to do in any case. The subsequent rout of Pakistani forces in East Pakistan could now be painted, if necessary, as simply an exercise in self-defense.

A case in which the relatively rational judgments of an offending regime negated the necessity of a forcible humanitarian intervention was Haiti in September 1994. In the final hours before an American-led intervention force was scheduled to land in Haiti, a negotiating team dispatched from Washington, composed of former President Jimmy Carter, Senator Sam Nunn, and former Chairman of the Joint Chiefs of Staff, Colin Powell, were engaged in an intense dialogue with Haitian dictator Raoul Cedras and his cohorts. The results of these discussions were that Cedras and several other junta members agreed to depart peaceably from Haiti. The carrots held out to them included a willingness to let them take all their ill-gotten gains from plundering the Haitian economy, two American aircraft to transport their immediate entourages and their baggage to safe haven in Panama, and a guarantee that Washington would not attempt to extradite them to the United States for trial on various charges, including drug-trafficking. American officials even agreed to compensate members of the junta for the rental of their various properties in Port-au-Prince.[38] However unredeeming a spectacle this was from the point of view of many critics of the Cedras regime, in this instance a looming military confrontation between an intervening force and local units was avoided because of the self-interested and pragmatic calculations of an otherwise very unpleasant group of individuals.

The late Jean Bedel Bokassa of the Central African Republic is a final example of a figure whose brutality and total insensitivity to civilized standards—not to mention his political obtuseness—made him an almost ideal candidate for removal by a humanitarian intervention. The French government had long supported Bokassa after he came to power by a coup in 1966, but his increasingly erratic behavior and steady descent into savagery was almost calculated to wear out his welcome in Paris. In the latter 1970s, for example, he began to establish contacts with Libyan dictator Muammar Khadaffi, a bête noire to French foreign policy because of his attempt to undermine the French-supported regime in Chad. It was on the human-rights front, however, that Bokassa eventually took a step too far and almost compelled French action to remove him because of the d'Estaing government's embarassment at being so closely associated with him.

In January 1979, Bokassa ordered all lycée students to purchase uniforms made by a factory owned by his wife. In the face of widespread protests against this decree, Bokassa's security forces launched a campaign of oppression in which 150 to 200 people, mostly lycée students, were brutally killed. An uneasy period of calm followed, but in late April, there was a further roundup of students and at least 100 of them were beaten to death in Ngaragba prison, with Bokassa being present and likely participating in this atrocity. When Amnesty International made the massacre public, the international outcry was such that French troops were sent to the CAR capital, Bangui, in September 1979 to remove Bokassa from office, thus ending his thirteen years in power. If a suitably villainous target was needed to justify a humanitarian intervention to both domestic and foreign audiences, Bokassa seemed almost typecast for the part. As it was, protests against the French action, at home or abroad, were virtually nonexistent.[39]

THE IMPACT OF PERSONALITY

In anticipating when a country—or countries—may be willing to commit to a course of humanitarian intervention, one of the most obvious factors can sometimes get lost in a welter of discussion on the "larger issues" involved. This concerns the personal value systems and perceptions of the individual decision makers themselves. This is no place to revisit the hoary debate over whether great men make history or whether they are the tools of history. Suffice it to say that an examination of actual humanitarian interventions almost always reveals the influence of a particular individual or individuals who, for reasons perhaps special to themselves, committed their nation's resources to remedying evils abroad.

Consider the Bush administration's decision to use American forces to reverse the Iraqi conquest of Kuwait in 1991. While this was not strictly an exercise in humanitarian intervention, and while there were obviously large resource and strategic interests involved in the development, first, of Desert Shield and, later, Desert Storm, the imprint of President Bush's own personality seems to have weighed heavily on the decision. This was true particularly during the period when there was a good deal of pressure on Bush, from home and abroad, to commit to a policy of economic sanctions over an extended period rather than commit to immediate military action, in order to persuade Saddam Hussein to withdraw from Kuwait.

As it happens, on a helicopter flight from Camp David to the White House on December 16, 1991, the president had before him an Amnesty International report on Iraqi conduct in Kuwait. The report detailed the horrible atrocities being committed by the Iraqi occupation forces: widespread rape, torturing even the handicapped, shooting children in front of their parents, using electric shocks and broken glass to the body and its private parts. In a subsequent interview with British interviewer David Frost, Bush recalled that "it was so terrible, it's hard to describe. . . . [I]t is primeval. . . . I'm afraid I'd get very emotional if I described more of it." His wife, Bush said, couldn't read past page two of the report. According to the president, the Amnesty report reinforced his belief that the Gulf crisis was simply a "clear case of . . . good versus evil. We have such a clear moral case." The first coalition air strikes against Iraqi targets commenced exactly one month later.[40] Among those who have known George Bush for any period of time, there is virtual unanimity that an "old-fashioned" sense of honor and rectitude is one of his most pronounced qualities.[41] This didn't mean that he was incapable of cold political calculation, but at the same time, he tended to view at least some issues in terms of principle and parameters of right and wrong. The Gulf confrontation seems to have been one of these.

Another example of a personal value system that influenced a statesman toward a decision for intervention may be found in the attitude of President Julius Nyerere of Tanzania toward the persona of Idi Amin in Uganda. Throughout the 1970s, Amin had presided over the increasing brutalization of Ugandan society, and eventually Tanzanian forces moved into Uganda in January 1979 to topple his regime. The intervention was spurred by a variety of factors, but one especially important element was that Nyerere saw Amin as a particularly loathsome individual who, among his other crimes, had brought shame to the reputation of black African countries generally. The depth of Nyerere's feeling about Amin may be seen in a speech he gave on December 9, 1978, which, rather remarkably, contrasted black Africa's indifferent attitude toward Amin with its stance toward the apartheid regime in South Africa.

> Amin is a killer. Since he took over the leadership of Uganda . . . he has killed many more people than Vorster has done in South Africa. . . . If Amin was white, we would have passed many resolutions against him. But he is black, and blackness is a license to kill Africans. And therefore there is complete silence; no one speaks about what he does.[42]

The use of this type of language—on other occasions, Nyerere referred to the Amin regime as simply a "government of thugs"—goes well beyond simply an antipathy for a fellow statesman that is common in the affairs of nations. The record of the Tanzanian intervention in Uganda clearly suggests that Nyerere had concluded that nobody else was going to do anything about Amin despite his appalling record and that it was left to him to remove a tyrant responsible for so much misery. He did not shrink from this responsibility.

In suggesting that decisions for humanitarian intervention may owe a good deal to the existence of a particular leadership at a particular time, there is an interesting theory that leaders may be more prone to sanction such interventions when they are at the end of their political careers. Earlier calculations of self-interest as well as the need to balance various conflicting bureaucratic interests may fade in importance compared to the leader's surge of interest in establishing his or her final mark in history as a humanitarian devoted to the larger interests of mankind. Two such examples involve, respectively, French President François Mitterrand's dispatch of French troops to Rwanda in June 1994 and President Bush's decision to send American forces to Somalia in December 1992.

Once again, the French action could hardly be considered entirely altruistic. France had long had important economic and political interests in a part of Africa that has four times as many French speakers as in France itself. Moreover, Paris had been a strong supporter of the previous Hutu-led regime, a support that included substantial arms transfers; cynics questioned whether Operation Turquoise wasn't meant to protect the Hutus from Tutsi revenge even more than it was to save the Tutsis. At the same time, the French intervention had the effect of saving many thousands of lives—most of them Tutsi—and a genuine humanitarian impulse seemed to be at least one important factor in the French action. As Alain Lamassoure, the French minister for European affairs, said at the time, "There might be ten good reasons for not intervening. The one essential reason for doing so is that a whole people is in the course of dying." President Mitterrand evidently shared Lamassoure's sentiments, not least because he was approaching the end of his fourteen-year tenure as French president. One aide put it this way: "He wants to leave office on a high, and not be accused of doing nothing in the face of genocide."[43]

As far as President Bush and Somalia are concerned, American officials had long been wary about getting involved in the morass of Somalia. The Joint Chiefs of Staff in particular considered Somalia a "bottomless pit." The American Ambassador to Kenya, Smith Hempstone, also argued against intervention, opining that "if you liked Beirut, you'll love Mogadishu." He added that the effects of a major American presence in Somalia would be to "keep tens of thousands of Somalia kids from starving to death in 1993 who, in all probability, will starve to death in 1994."[44] The president, however, supported by acting Secretary of State Lawrence Eagleburger, decided to commit American forces to Somalia to insure the distribution of relief supplies. A senior official from the Defense Department reflected on Bush's thinking: "I had the feeling that no matter what was said [by his advisers], he would not want to leave office with 500,000 people starving that he could have saved."[45]

Whether or not the American president had his eye on history, it is unmistakable that even though Operation Restore Hope was an obviously risky enterprise, Bush presented the case for action in unusually emotional and even personal terms.

> The people of Somalia, especially the children of Somalia, need our help. We're able to erase their suffering. We must help them live. We must give them hope. America must act. . . . I understand the United States alone cannot right the world's wrongs, but we also know that some crises in the world cannot be resolved without American involvement. . . . When we see Somalia's children starving, all of American hurts.[46]

Andrew Natsios, an aid official in the Bush administration, recalls a meeting around the time of the Somali decision that he attended in the Oval Office and that offered some interesting insights into Bush's mindset about the crisis. Among those at the meeting was Phil Johnson, the president of CARE and the acting head of United Nations humanitarian operations in Somalia. Apparently spurred by Johnson's presence, the president recalled a visit that he, his wife Barbara, and Johnson had taken to a CARE feeding center for starving children during the Sahelian famine of the mid-1980s in the Sudan. Bush said that he and his wife would never forget the scenes of death they had witnessed there. Natsios, listening to all this, was convinced that this searing memory clearly paved the way for the president's decision to send troops to Somalia to protect food shipments there.[47] Six weeks later Bush handed over the reins of office to Bill Clinton.

NOTES

1. These examples of "non-intervention" have persuaded even so perceptive and feeling a writer as Jack Donnelly to question whether the very

idea of humanitarian intervention can be taken seriously. Among his various writings on this subject, see "Human Rights, Humanitarian Intervention and American Foreign Policy," *Journal of International Affairs* (1983).

2. Laura Neack discusses this issue, at least indirectly, in her analysis of states' willingness to commit to United Nations peacekeeping. She establishes two theoretical paradigms that can explain such a commitment—"a state's idealistic committment to the global community and international peace, or from the member's national interest"—and comes down firmly in favor of the member's national interest as typically the more important factor. Her discussion of Canada's participation in peacekeeping is of particular interest. See her "UN Peace-keeping: In The Interest of Community or Self?" *Journal of Peace Research* 32 (May, 1995).

3. Michael Reisman is one who defends the Panama intervention specifically as an effort to support democracy. "Sovereignty and Human Rights in Contemporary International Law," *American Journal of International Law* 84 (October, 1990), 866–76.

4. James A. Baker, *The Politics of Diplomacy* (New York: G. P. Putnam's Sons, 1995), 193.

5. A good general survey of the situation in Panama under Noriega and the American policy toward him may be found in Kevin Buckley, *Panama: The Whole Story* (New York: Simon and Schuster, 1991).

6. George Church, "Destination Haiti," *Time* (September 26, 1994).

7. White House Office of the Press Secretary, "Selected Remarks Prepared for Delivery by President William Jefferson Clinton on U.S. Policy Toward Haiti" (September 15, 1994).

8. Ibid.

9. Church, "Destination Haiti."

10. Robert I. Rotberg, "Clinton Was Right," *Foreign Policy* (Spring, 1996), 135.

11. Ibid., 136. These outcomes, it might be noted, seem to have persuaded many Americans ex post facto that the American intervention was not such a bad idea after all. A poll taken in April, 1995 showed that 63 percent now agreed that it was *right* to threaten the Cedras regime with forcible removal if it didn't leave voluntarily. This finding provides further evidence for our proposition that strong moral leadership by a president is necessary to a humanitarian intervention and that this will often be applauded, if only belatedly, by his constituents. Program on International Policy Attitudes, "United Nations Peacekeeping Survey" (College Park: University of Maryland, April 19–23, 1995).

12. John Sweeney, "Stuck in Haiti," *Foreign Policy* (Spring, 1996), 150.

13. Alain Rouvez, "French, British, and Belgian Military Involvement," in *Making War and Waging Peace*, ed. David R. Smock (Washington, DC: United States Institute of Peace Press, 1993), 31.

14. Dominique Moïsi, "Intervention in French Foreign Policy," in *Intervention in World Politics*, ed. Hedley Bull (Oxford: Clarendon Press, 1984), 69. Moïsi points out that one key to French policy has been the continuing links between African elites and the Metropole. Eighteen out of fifty members of the OAU are former French colonies or territories, and French is an official language in 22 countries of the OAU.

15. Rouvez, "French, British, and Belgian Military Involvement," 29.

16. Guy Martin, "France and Africa," in *France in World Politics*, eds. Robert Aldrich and John Connell (London and New York: Routledge, 1989), 111.

17. Francis Fukuyama, *The End of History and The Last Man* (New York: Free Press, 1992).

18. Joshua Muravchik, *Exporting Democracy* (Washington: The AEI Press, 1992), 147.

19. The notion that culture will be a central driving paradigm of future international relations has been expressed in particular by Samuel Huntington. See, for example, his "The Clash of Civilizations," *Foreign Affairs* (Summer, 1993).

20. An excellent survey of the background to the crisis in East Pakistan may be found in Golan Choudhury's *The Last Days of United Pakistan* (Bloomington, IN: Indiana University Press, 1974).

21. When the Sixth Committee of the General Assembly was debating the definition of "aggression" in 1954, the Greek and Dutch representatives argued for the right of humanitarian intervention in cases where there were ethnic ties between the intervenor and the racial minority in the other state that was suffering persecution. Michael Akehurst, "Humanitarian Intervention," in *Intervention in World Politics*, 95. It might be noted here as well that when the Vietnamese moved against the Khmer Rouge regime in Cambodia in 1979, their decision was motivated in substantial part by the fact that the large ethnic Vietnamese population in Kampuchea (Cambodia) was subject to an increasing regime of abuse by the authorities in Phnom Penh.

22. American Jewish Committee, *American Jewish Yearbook 1934–35* (Philadelphia: American Jewish Committee, 1936), 438.

23. William E. Dodd, Jr., *American Dodd's Diary 1933–38* (New York: Harcourt, Brace and Company, 1941), 5.

24. Henry Feingold, *The Politics of Rescue: The Roosevelt Administration and the Holocaust 1938–1945* (New Brunswick, NJ: Rutgers University Press, 1970), 29.

25. Tony Kishner, *The Holocaust and the Liberal Imagination* (Oxford: Blackwell, 1994).

26. Thomas Paterson, J. Garry Clifford and Kenneth J. Hagan, *American Foreign Policy* (Lexington, MA: D. C. Heath and Company, 1991), 402.

27. *Facts on File, World News Digest* (August 4, 1994), 542E2.

28. Jeffrey Smith, "U.S. Mission to Rwanda Criticized," *New York Times* (September 5, 1994), 1.

29. Andrew Natsios, "Illusions of Influence," in *From Massacres to Genocide*, eds. Robert I. Rotberg and Thomas G. Weiss (Washington, DC: Brookings Institution, 1996), 162.

30. Shawcross, *The Quality of Mercy*, 75.

31. *Report of the Chilean National Commission on Truth and Reconciliation*, trans. Philip E. Berryman (Notre Dame, IN: University of Notre Dame Press, 1993), 73–79.

32. Ibid., 133–34.

33. *Facts on File 1994*, March 20, 252; October 19, 859.

34. Carol Schimke, "Democracy from Within: Chile's Response to International Pressure on Human Rights," unpublished manuscript, April, 1995, 21.

35. Henry Kissinger, *The White House Years* (Boston: Little, Brown, 1979), 654.

36. Ironically, the second Reagan administration in the late 1980s evidently decided that in the interests of order in Chile, it should now put pressure on Pinochet to *relinquish* power. The fear was that without a peaceful transfer of authority to a civilian regime, there might well be massive demonstrations that would seriously destabilize the Chilean polity. See Paul Sigmund, *The United States and Democracy in Chile* (Baltimore, MD: Johns Hopkins University Press, 1993).

37. Baker, *The Politics of Diplomacy*, 179–88.

38. A good survey of the last days of the Cedras regime may be found in Roland Perusse, *Haitian Democracy Restored, 1991–1995* (Lanham, MD: University Press of America, 1995).

39. Thomas O'Toole, *The Central African Republic: The Continent's Hidden Heart* (Boulder, CO: Westview Press, 1986), 53–55.

40. Bob Woodward, *The Commanders* (New York: Simon and Schuster, 1991), 343–44.

41. Michael Duffy and Dan Goodgame, *Marching in Place* (New York: Simon and Schuster, 1992).

42. Cited in Caroline Thomas, *New States, Sovereignty and Intervention* (New York: St. Martin's Press, 1985), 98.

43. "The Horrific Scars of Rwanda's Civil War," *U.S. News and World Report* (July 4, 1994), 52.

44. Don Oberdorfer, "The Path to Intervention," *Washington Post* (December 6, 1992), A35.

45. Ibid.

46. *Washington Post* (December 2, 1992), A6.

47. Andrew Natsios, "Illusions of Influence," 168.

CHAPTER 6

Judging Decisions, Judging Results

We have examined various factors that seem to be important in persuading states either to turn away from an apparently humanitarian intervention or to commit to one. An equally important, though related, challenge is to develop a system by which we can judge the *legitimacy* of a given intervention, both in terms of the process by which a state or states decided to act and in terms of the results that their action produced. It should be clear enough by now that our position in this book favors the basic notion of humanitarian intervention. Indeed, the argument here is that, historically, there should have been more rather than fewer such interventions—and that this principle ought to apply in the future as well. Even so, we cannot escape the need to establish a set of criteria for assessing the moral defensibility of the decision itself to intervene as well as its outcomes.

The first of these tasks is important in sorting out two quite different types of situations. One has to do with cases where a state intervenes under a humanitarian garb but whose real motivation is basically self-interested and indifference to actual humanitarian concerns—that is, cases of "hypocrisy." More interesting and complex are cases in which a state may genuinely want to do good, but whose decision to use military force in a particular circumstance to accomplish such good can be questioned—that is, cases of inappropriate humanitarian intervention. Even if our verdict on the decision to intervene may be approving, there remains the second task referred to above: to assess the relative outcomes of the intervention from what is usually called a "consequentialist" perspective. In the tangled web of human affairs, there is what can be called the "rule of unintended consequences," the perennial tragedy of those who set out to do good and wind up doing evil. Good intentions, after all, are no shield against unexpected outcomes that may actually worsen rather than ameliorate a situation. Massive food-aid programs to the developing world, for example, are sometimes cited here: In the short term, these programs feed the starving, but they may also destroy, or at least greatly skew, the indigenous agricultural system that is critical to the long-term welfare of the people.[1]

In developing a set of standards for judging the "before and after" of interventions—that is, the decision to intervene itself as well as its ultimate effects—I want to rely here on some aspects of classical Just War doctrine. This set of principles seems particularly apt to our purposes since Just War theory has long been accepted as perhaps the most salient way of organizing moral judgments on the use of force.[2] The most important stipulations that this theory establishes for a rightful resort to arms is that it involve a just cause, that it be decided on by legitimate authority, that it be based on "right intention" (that is, the righting of a wrong, but not for the purposes simply of, say, revenge), that it be a last resort once other means have failed, that it produce an ultimate peace in which justice can prevail, and that it follow the canons of proportionality. The issue of just cause and humanitarian intervention was discussed in Chapter 4, and the idea of peace with justice in Chapter 1. Thus I want to focus here on the concepts of right intention, proportionality, and last resort, as well as two other concepts that seem particularly important in weighing humanitarian interventions having to do with the sometimes morally ambiguous character of both victims and intervenors.[3]

THE PRINCIPLE OF RIGHT INTENTION

The notion of "right intention" as established by Just War theory holds that sovereigns may only resort to arms if (among other stipulations) their purpose is the righting of a wrong and the "reestablishment of a just order."[4] Thus, wars simply for glory, expansion, or revenge are proscribed: The object of the fighting must be the restoration of a state of peace and one in which maximum justice may be achieved. As used in this study of humanitarian intervention, the requirement of right intention obviously has its greatest applicability when we are considering possible cases of hypocrisy (naked self-interest in a humanitarian disguise). It is necessary to proceed carefully here, however. No reasonable definition of legitimate humanitarian intervention would hold that there can be *no* other purposes for the action than the relief of the oppressed (the phenomenon of mixed motives to which we have already given attention). What we are saying is that a "just" humanitarian intervention must have as one of its *principal* goals the ending of gross human rights abuses.

There are more specific items in the application of right intention to humanitarian interventions that may be enumerated as well. Fernando Tesón offers his own list of the elements in a "bad" or illegitimate intervention: Did foreign troops occupy the invaded territory longer than necessary? Did the intervenor demand certain favors or advantages from a newly established government? Or even worse, did the intervenor actually seek to dominate the target country in a way unrelated to humanitarian concerns?[5] In essence, as another analysis has it, a rightful humanitarian intervention has to be directed not at an entire nation, but at those responsible for wrongdoing, and at the protection of the victims of such wrongdoing.[6]

The international community's activities in Somalia might seem, at first glance, to be a good example of the violation of the principle of right intention. A standard criticism of those activities is that what started out as a relatively straightforward famine-relief operation became transformed over time into an exercise in nation-building and political transformation. The United Nations contingent in the country—so it is said—became mired in the murky clan politics of Somalia, at one point clearly aligning itself with the forces opposed to Mohammed Aideed, with disastrous results. Now there is no question that the net effect of this shift in policy seriously eroded public support in the intervening countries for a continuation of the effort. The reaction in the United States, particularly after the death of eighteen Americans at the hands of Aideed's supporters, was especially harsh, and led directly to President Clinton's removing all American personnel from Somalia. It is also true that the success that was achieved in dealing with the Somali famine itself seems to have been largely obscured because of the subsequent course of events, and the generally negative public perception of that intervention has undoubtedly made it more difficult for

American presidents and leaders of other countries to undertake such humanitarian efforts in the future.[7]

Despite all the complications and difficulties in the Somalia situation, however, we can hardly advance a claim of lack of "right intention" in criticizing international operations there. There is no evidence whatsoever that any of the participating parties were interested in establishing their own dominion over Somalia or even in staying there longer than was absolutely necessary. From the very beginning, the whole point of the international community's efforts in Somalia was to deal with a "failed state" whose collapse was having a devastating effect on its people, particularly in mass starvation. The turn against Aideed was indeed taken only because he came to be seen as the primary obstacle to stabilizing the Somalia situation. This decision may be questioned on practical grounds, and perhaps the intervening forces overestimated their ability to engage in nation-building and peacemaking in a very difficult corner of the world, but we can hardly question their motives in striking out along this path.

A good example of an intervention that raises very troubling issues of right intention, however, was the Vietnamese invasion of Cambodia in December 1979. At first glance, this action seemed to have much humanitarian justification. Given the character of the Khmer Rouge regime in Phnom Penh, it was hard not to breathe a sigh of relief for the long-suffering Cambodian people and to provide the Hanoi authorities with at least a muted round of applause for at last doing what should have been done a long time ago: ridding the world of a genuinely loathsome government. The only problem here is that there is little, if any, evidence that the Vietnam forces actually were motivated by humanitarian concerns in moving against the Khmer Rouge. Some months before the invasion, Senator George McGovern told a hearing of the Senate Foreign Relations Committee that the record of the Khmer Rouge made the Nazis "look very tame by comparison," and he then asked the obvious question: "Do we sit on the sidelines and watch a population slaughtered or do we marshal military force and put an end to it?"[8] It might seem as if Vietnam's actions in December were intended as a response to McGovern's query, but in fact the Vietnamese Foreign Minister, Nguyen Co Thach, admitted to Congressman Stephen Solarz that "human rights was not a question; that was their problem. We didn't go along with the McGovern proposal. We were concerned only with security."[9]

The curious fact was that the Vietnamese communists had been instrumental in helping the Khmer Rouge gain power earlier in the decade, and for a long time, had made little, if any, comment about subsequent conditions in Cambodia. But the Pol Pot regime demonstrated a quite impressive ineptness in its subsequent policy toward its benefactor, and it began to adopt a confrontational stance on a range of bilateral issues, including border questions and the large ethnic Vietnamese presence within Cambodia. By the spring of 1977, the Khmer Rouge began destroying Vietnamese villages and killing substantial numbers of Vietnamese along the border and even in Vietnam itself; at one point penetrating more than four miles into the country. Some 100,000 Khmer troops were assembled on the border, and egged on by their Chinese sponsors, Phnom Penh issued a series of ever more drastic denunciations of Vietnamese "imperialism."[10]

Under these circumstances, it was not surprising that Vietnamese patience eventually ran out and that they decided to settle accounts with Pol Pot by using force (that they would not shrink from such an option was suggested by an earlier incursion into Cambodia in December 1977). If the subsequent intervention had confined itself to the border regions, the international reaction might have been relatively muted, but Hanoi evidently decided to end the Khmer challenge once and for all. Attacking with some 100,000 troops and using much of its air force, Vietnam occupied the Cambodian capital within fifteen days, and, as of January 12, 1979, with the capture of the main Khmer military base at Kompong Chnang, effectively controlled almost all the major towns and roads in Cambodia.[11]

Even given this very expansive military action, Hanoi might still have complied with the principle of right intention, at least in spirit, if it had then effectively "internationalized" the crisis and invited outside participation to form a new coalition regime in Phnom Penh comprising all the main anti–Khmer Rouge factions. The ASEAN states of Southeast Asia made precisely such a proposal. Instead, Hanoi set up a virtual puppet regime styled as the "People's Republic of Kampuchea" under the leadership of one Heng Samrin and later Hun Sen, both former Khmer Rouge commanders but now, effectively, mouthpieces for Vietnamese interests. The resistance that sprang up in Cambodia against this regime led to thousands of Vietnamese troops remaining in the country until the last units were withdrawn in September 1989.[12] Eventually, the Paris accords of October 1991 were signed and led to the formation of the sort of coalition regime that had been rejected in 1979.

At the United Nations and in other forums, Vietnam defended its invasion as a legitimate exercise of self-defense under Article 51 of the UN Charter. It was only when this appeal fell on deaf ears that Hanoi began to speak of the appalling human-rights conditions in Cambodia under the Khmer Rouge, which, implicitly, justified their actions. The Vietnamese representative at the UN, Ha Van Lau, bewailed the tribulations of the Cambodian people under the Khmer Rouge, calling life there "unique in living history, a living hell."[13] Given Vietnam's own dubious record on human rights, many found it hard to credit this concern. Ironically, the only other time in which the Vietnamese leadership seemed to have been concerned with the human rights policies of the Pol Pot regime came *before* its December 1978 intervention, but it had nothing to do with the welfare of the Cambodian people. In the fall of that year, the Khmer Rouge authorities, nervous about Vietnamese intentions, began a general public relations campaign to try to soften the brutal picture that world opinion had of them. At a press conference at the United Nations in mid-October, for example, Ieng Sary offered to open Cambodia's borders to Western observers (including journalists) in order to rebut charges of massive human rights violations. He also said that Secretary-General Kurt Waldheim had been invited to visit the country for the same purpose. Vietnam was greatly concerned with these developments since it had already completed plans for the December offensive and was counting on Pol Pot's genocidal image to quell international protests at its actions. In order to stem the Khmer Rouge's efforts to clean up its reputation, Hanoi, for the first time, began to speak of Cambodia as "a land of blood and tears, hell on earth," in which several million people had already been executed.[14]

Putting the best face on it, one might argue that Vietnam felt it had to install a "friendly" regime in Phnom Penh in order to prevent further Cambodian revanchism, which had significant historical roots, given the hundreds of years of tension between the Khmer and the Vietnamese over territory, peoples, and general influence in Southeast Asia. Moreover, the Vietnamese invasion *did* put an end to the worst abuses of the Khmer Rouge regime (a point to be considered in more detail shortly), and the People's Republic of Kampuchea itself pursued policies that were a good deal less draconian than its predecessor's. At the same time, even the most detached of observers could be forgiven for concluding that Vietnam was simply pursuing a policy of expansion and hegemony in the region (she had occupied virtually all of Cambodia in the early 19th century) and that to the extent that she spoke of the "humanitarian" benefits of her actions in Cambodia, it was simply a cover for far more practical concerns. Even if this wasn't the case, the general course of Vietnamese policy in Cambodia certainly gave it the appearance of reality and, to this extent, raised serious questions concerning what we have called the principle of right intention.

Certain of the same questions might be raised about the Tanzanian invasion of Uganda in 1978–79. When Idi Amin first seized power in Uganda in 1971, his new regime was widely welcomed by the Ugandan people as a promising alternative to the increasingly authoritarian and divisive rule of Milton Obote. Over the coming years, however, Amin systematically squandered this initial reservoir of good will. By 1978, Amnesty International characterized the Amin reign of terror as a

> structure of repression [that] can be said without fear of exaggeration to have transformed the whole society in a short period of time into a ruthless military dictatorship marked by arbitrary arrest, torture, murder, the removal of virtually all fundamental human rights, the terrorization of the population, the turning of tens of thousands of Ugandans into refugees.[15]

It was not for nothing that Idi Amin was frequently referred to as the "Hitler of Africa," and the Tanzanian intervention can be rightly applauded for bringing an end to all the horrors of his period in power. At the same time, the actions of Tanzanian President Julius Nyerere presented certain problems.

As Tanzanian forces moved toward Kampala, they gave official support to a Ugandan dissident group styled as the Ugandan National Liberation Front (UNLF), and eventually the Tanzanians were the main reason that the UNLF assumed power in Uganda. The record suggests, in fact, that there had been secret discussions between Neyrere and the UNLF and other Ugandan rebel elements well *before* the Tanzanian invasion of Uganda. Presumably because of his concern that these meetings might become public knowledge, President Nyerere attempted to emphasize that Tanzania was not actually intent on overthrowing Amin on its own: "I do not fight for others. . . . The Ugandans do have a reason to remove Amin, but we don't. It is not our business; we shall not send our troops into Uganda to remove Amin."[16] Nyerere adopted the "two wars" conceit in defending his actions. There were, he said, two conflicts taking place at the same time: a war of self-defense by Tanzania against Ugandan aggression, and a liberation struggle by Ugandans themselves against the Amin regime.

Once Idi Amin fled Uganda, a transitional government under Professor Yusuf Lule was established, and within a relatively short period of time, the former Ugandan leader Milton Obote resumed power. One problem during this period was that Tanzanian forces remained in force in Uganda as the months passed. Still, it seems difficult to argue that the new regime in Kampala was equivalent to the puppet government set up by the Vietnamese in Phnom Penh after its invasion of Cambodia in 1979. The temporary presence of Tanzanian troops was important in giving, first, the Lule and, later, the Obote regimes a chance to consolidate themselves and to develop a retrained Ugandan army and police. Moreover, Tanzania bore substantial costs in keeping its forces in Uganda (by some estimates amounting to over 500,000 pounds sterling per day), and this belies the notion that Tanzania was enjoying a profitable occupation of a neighboring country. Finally, Milton Obote, while undoubtedly beholden to Nyerere, commanded substantial support within Uganda—despite his checkered past—and from this perspective could hardly be considered a Tanzanian "puppet."[17]

The other issue bearing on the question of right intention in the Tanzanian invasion of Uganda concerns Nyerere's somewhat ambiguous rationale for his original intervention. In October 1978, Idi Amin sent his troops into the so-called Kagera Salient in Tanzania in pursuit of disloyal Ugandan troops and to reestablish what he considered the "rightful" border between Uganda and Tanzania.[18] This invasion of his country outraged President Nyerere and, not incidentally, gave him a legally comfortable basis on which finally to confront the Amin regime on the grounds of legitimate self-defense. The issue is whether Amin's aggression really gave leave to the Tanzanian forces to occupy all of Uganda rather than simply repelling the Ugandan forces within Tanzania itself. Doing so seemed to stretch the concept of self-defense to rather uncomfortable lengths. More to the point, as time passed, Nyerere began to give increasing emphasis to the *humanitarian* rationale for Tanzania's actions. This confusion in explaining his motives provided critics of Tanzania's behavior with some ammunition for charges of "hypocrisy" and violation of international standards against forceful intervention for self-interested purposes.[19] As with a number of our other cases here, the best judgment seems to be that Julius Nyerere was genuinely appalled by Amin's record of human rights abuses, but at the same time, he was concerned with defusing future Ugandan challenges to Tanzanian security interests. Perhaps one of the more compelling arguments that can be offered in defense of Tanzania's right intentions is that its intervention in Uganda received very little public criticism from other African states. Nigeria and Sudan were among the few who denounced the Tanzanian action, and it was widely assumed that the former did so because of its continuing resentment at Tanzania's support for Biafra in the Nigerian civil war of the late 1960s.

THE PRINCIPLE OF PROPORTIONALITY

The principle of proportionality, as taken from the classical theory of Just War, essentially means that a given action may be counted as ethical if the good it produces is greater than its (possible) evil side effects. The idea of proportionality actually applies both to the decision to use force (*jus ad bellum*) and to the ways in which it is employed once the fighting starts (*jus in bello*). States should not use the sword unless there is a strong probability that doing so will produce sufficient justice to outweigh the horrors that war always entails. In the conduct of war itself, the military measures taken must be sufficiently necessary to the achievement of victory in a just cause to counterbalance the destruction the measures entail, although there are certain measures that are always proscribed, particularly attacks on the innocent.

As used here in our discussion of humanitarian intervention, the concept of proportionality might also be taken to have an additional (if rather different) meaning, to which we might devote at least a few words. In this formulation, proportionality can refer to the reasonable balance between what a country *can* do and what it does or should do. It is tilting at windmills to argue that a state must mortgage its core interests—perhaps its very existence—to the service of humanitarian causes. At the same time, there is a limited arena of opportunity in which a state may be said to have a capacity to act and, perhaps, a duty to do so. In responding to criticism that he was prepared to help the innocent in Haiti whereas he had done little to aid the suffering of those in Bosnia or Rwanda, President Clinton defended himself (however convincingly or unconvincingly) by emphasizing that Haiti was easily accessible, that she could be rescued with relatively little effort, and that there was a workable international consensus on what to do.

There is also this interesting comment from Acting Secretary of State Lawrence Eagleburger in December 1992, concerning the American "national interest" in helping the starving people of Somalia.

> This debate [on Somalia] is around the issue of our national interest, and that's a legitimate issue. But the fact of the matter is that a thousand people are starving to death every day, and that is not going to get better if we don't do something about it, and it is in an area where we can affect events. There are other parts of the world where things are equally tragic, but where the cost of trying to change things would be monumental. In my view, Bosnia is one of those.[20]

Eagleburger generally took an unsentimental and "realistic" approach to matters of foreign policy, and the fact that he should accept the notion of opportunity equaling duty is a tribute to his sometime capacity for a broader vision of the American role in the world.

To return to the more traditional definition of proportionality, the balancing of the good and evil effects of a given action, a preliminary, although not necessarily decisive, indication that a given intervention has the stamp of "proportionality" involves the reaction of the people of the country against whom the intervention is targeted. Michael Levitin offers the vivid, if perhaps somewhat exaggerated, suggestion that an intervention is lawful "if the people throw flowers; if they do not throw flowers, and or if they throw anything else, the invasion is unlawful."[21] Substitute "proportionality" for "lawful" here and the point seems evident enough. Generally, people in a particular community, no matter how vexed by their government, are likely to be suspicious of foreigners coming in to settle their affairs. If in certain, rare instances they actually welcome such an intrusion, this seems prima facie evidence that their travails have reached such a level that they now welcome *any* method of rescue; to this degree, the intervention becomes legitimate.

In applying this standard, it would seem that various of the interventions considered here had at least a tentative claim to proportionality. In response to Operation Just Cause, the American invasion of Panama in late 1989, the evidence was that the overwhelming majority of the Panamanian people actually welcomed the Americans despite the fact that the Organization of American States roundly condemned the American action.[22] Similarly, when the Clinton administration moved against the Cedras regime in Haiti in 1994, there was almost no opposition from the local population, a major factor in the success of the operation. Most Ugandans also breathed a sigh of relief as invading Tanzanian forces moved on Kampala to depose Idi Amin in 1979. They were so relieved that Amin threatened to "punish" those who openly extended their hand to the intervening army.

Simply because a society seems to welcome an intervention by outsiders, of course, doesn't necessarily settle all the delicate questions involved in the demands of proportionality. For example, despite the Panamanians' initial approval of Operation Just Cause, the proportionality of that operation also has to be weighed in terms of the large number of civilian casualties that resulted from the invasion, on the order of at least 900 and perhaps a good deal higher. A more solid example of proportionality in a humanitarian intervention would be the Indian invasion of East Pakistan in 1971. A report from the International Commission of Jurists presented a horrifying picture of conditions at the time:

> The principal features of this ruthless [Pakistani] oppression were the indiscriminate killing of civilians, including women and children and the poorest and weakest members of the community; the attempt to exterminate or drive out of the country a large part of the Hindu population; the arrest, torture and killing of Awami League activists, students, professional and business men and other potential leaders . . . the raping of women; the destruction of villages and towns; and the looting of property. All this was done in a scale which is difficult to comprehend.[23]

The Indian military campaign that began on December 4, 1971, took hardly more than two weeks, with relatively limited casualties, and in the aftermath, millions of Bengali refugees were able to return from their exile along the Indian border. Not only was the Pakistani army's campaign of terror against the Bengali people ended, but there was also the establishment of a self-governing Bangladeshi state that could now hope to meet the legitimate political, social, and economic aspirations of its citizenry.

Of all the "hard cases" we can examine as far as intervention and proportionality are concerned, perhaps the most challenging is—once again—that of the Vietnamese invasion of Cambodia in December 1978. We have already suggested that at least in terms of the principle of right intention, it may be questioned whether the Vietnamese action even ought to be called a humanitarian intervention, no matter how broadly we define the term. At the same time, how can one forget the charnel house that Cambodia had become under the rule of the Khmer Rouge? The estimated figures of those killed are familiar enough, but no less depressing on repetition. The standard guess is that at least one million Cambodians perished in the Khmer Rouge's fanatical campaign to "remake" Cambodian society into a classless system based on pristine rural values and free of all foreign or "modern" influences. Some put the figure much higher, perhaps approaching two million. One survivor of this period described his experiences in terms that make all this suffering concrete:

> I remember a Charlie Chaplin film where he was so hungry, he ate his shoe; we all laughed when we saw it. If you'd been with us at that time [under the Khmer Rouge], you wouldn't have laughed at all—it was reality. We ate grass; there were even people who ate cadavers; they tried to dig down and just get a bit of the flesh. In one case, the Khmer Rouge took them by surprise and killed them.[24]

Earlier in our discussion, we established as one criterion of a "true" humanitarian intervention that it must result in a demonstrable release of suffering by the target society. It seems hard to deny that the Vietnamese intervention at the end of 1978 produced just such a result.

The international community, as noted, in an especially bizarre and depressing performance, seemed to be indifferent to this result and to the whole issue of proportionality that the overthrow of the Khmer Rouge by the Vietnamese raised. Certainly, there was reason to question what the Vietnamese invasion meant for the stability and security of other countries in Southeast Asia (a matter that necessarily shaped any judgment on the intervention's proportionality), given Hanoi's demonstrated fondness for power politics, indifference to minimal norms of restraint in interstate relations and the quasi-Stalinist character of its own regime. Moreover, the idea that one country should be allowed or even encouraged to invade another because of their differences was not exactly an attractive one. Even so, to style the Khmer Rouge as the "legitimate" representative of the Cambodian people, and to offer them support on the theory of rightful sovereignty, was itself riddled with contradictions. For example, the Khmer Rouge had hardly come to power through some clear expression of the political will of the Cambodians; it had essentially shot its way into authority. More generally, were rote references to the privileges of sovereignty really a sufficient basis on which to defend the "rights" of a regime that had rivaled Hitler and Stalin in its brutality? A clear case here indeed of the perennial tension between sovereignty and suffering.

The regime that Hanoi installed in Cambodia after the invasion was hardly an ideal example of Jeffersonian democracy, but it was also hardly so murderous in its attitude toward the Cambodian population as its predecessor. Most Cambodians seemed to have extended an initial welcome, even though it may have been an uneasy welcome, to the advancing Vietnamese troops, since their appearance signaled the end of the long Khmer Rouge nightmare. One early example of the Cambodians' relatively more favorable prospects was the fact that they could now leave the collectives into which they had been herded by the Khmer Rouge that had effectively reduced them to a status of serfdom. Indeed, the new regime actively encouraged this process, and hundred of thousands now began to trek back to their native villages.[25]

On the negative side of the proportionality ledger, the People's Republic of Kampuchea (PRK), as noted earlier, was not exactly a place where the citizenry had access to a full range of civil and political rights. One telling fact about the new regime was that a number of its top leaders had served the Khmer Rouge itself in an earlier period, which was hardly an encouraging sign of a commitment to liberty.[26] A fair verdict would be that in their individual lives, Cambodians had relatively free rein, but their opportunity for political participation—not to mention political dissent—was distinctly limited. Moreover, as a consequence of obtuse economic policies pursued by the Cambodian government—mirroring those followed in Vietnam—there was widespread economic deprivation and even periods of outright famine. A reasonable conclusion from all this is that the people of Cambodia were certainly better off under the PRK, but their suffering had hardly disappeared. Particularly telling here was the fact that a proud nation had effectively lost its full independence, although Hanoi's influence over Cambodian affairs subsided throughout the 1980s.

Arriving at a judgment about whether the Vietnamese invasion of Cambodia in December 1979 met the test of proportionality, then, is no easy matter. Various aspects of the PRK regime, and more especially the negative precedent of one country using unilateral forceful intervention to implant its influence in a neighboring country, clearly argue for a negative verdict. The fact that a great many Cambodian lives were undoubtedly saved in the long run by the Vietnamese action moves us to take a different position.[27] Considering the numbers—projected in terms of how many would have died if the Khmer Rouge had been allowed to continue in power—a decision to support the proportionality of the intervention seems ethically compelling. The real lesson of this whole affair is that in hard cases involving the concept of humanitarian intervention, we may have to be satisfied with the achievement of the relative rather than the absolute good.

THE PRINCIPLE OF LAST RESORT

In Just War doctrine, the notion of last resort requires that a state, before resorting to force, must exhaust every other alternative means of settling a dispute, even though justice is on its side in the conflict. In this discussion of last resort and humanitarian intervention, I want to expand the application of the principle to include certain practical as well as moral considerations. The concept of last resort can actually be seen to have two different rationales. For potential intervenor states or organizations, there is the need to avoid overextending one's resources in attempting to deal with a whole series of possibly manageable local disputes. To attempt too much may lead to doing too little, given the risk of exhaustion and disillusionment from too many humanitarian ventures. Moreover, in garnering public support for the use of such force, it is necessary for decision makers to show that they took such a step only after they had exhausted all reasonable alternative courses of action: simple persuasion, diplomatic or economic pressure, resort to regional organizations, appeals to international legal bodies, and so forth. Even in the anarchic world of international relations, guns must always be regarded as the last step rather than the first, as an option only when all others have proved unavailing.

From a purely moral point of view, it is not a small thing for leaders to ask their citizens to put their lives at risk or even to expend some of the national treasure on actions abroad. Before sending their troops into harm's way, leaders have an obligation to attempt every possible peaceful alternative. At the very least, attempting such last-ditch efforts helps to deal with what Senator John Glenn (D-Ohio) has called the "Dover test."[28] Dover, Delaware, is where the bodies of U.S. servicemen and women killed overseas are first taken. The "test" referred to is offering a reasonable explanation to their parents about why their sons or daughters had to die in the nation's service and in some perhaps obscure place. President Bush, in a speech to the cadets at West Point in January 1993, effectively addressed this matter. It was important to keep in mind, he said, that in humanitarian actions, "the potential sacrifice be one that can be explained and justified. We must never forget that using force is not some political abstraction, but a real commitment of our fathers and mothers and sons and daughters, brothers and sisters, friends and neighbors. You've got to look at it in human terms."[29]

The principle of last resort also applies, however, to those laying *claims* on the international community for rescue. There is a standard provision in international law that is usually invoked when cases are brought before arbitration panels or other international judicial bodies involving the putative mistreatment of foreigners by a host country. Called the "rule of local remedies," it asserts that before an international legal forum can become involved in such a dispute, the appellate party must demonstrate that it has exhausted all the available opportunities for redress of its grievances provided by the municipal legal system. The commonsense rationale for the rule of local remedies is that a dispute ought to be settled at the lowest possible level of authority and be taken to a higher body only if doing so is the one remaining option for achieving justice. Not incidentally, as a legal principle, the rule of local remedies is also designed to prevent citizens from powerful countries from using their privileged position, in consort with their governments, to press doubtful claims of special rights within a weaker host country.[30]

The rule of local remedies equates in many ways with what we have called the principle of last resort, particularly as it applies to those under travail. Even where obvious abuses have taken place in a country, and even when these can be traced to official policies of that country's government, all reasonable measures must be taken by the affected parties to ameliorate their plight, using the resources available to them, before they call on the international community for assistance. There are certain, almost self-evident rationales behind this stipulation. Almost every country in the world has at least some dissatisfied local groups that may be tempted to avoid a time-consuming and difficult effort to achieve their demands by working within their own country's institutions. Instead, they call on the international community to intervene to secure their "rightful" goals. This has been a pattern followed at times, for example, by spokespersons for the Irish Republican Army during the long period of the "troubles" in Northern Ireland.

The situation of the Kurds in Iraq provides an appropriate reference point to discuss the principle of last resort. Some within the Kurdish population had always dreamed of outright independence and a separate Kurdish state, but the bulk of the Kurds' political efforts have apparently been devoted to achieving a reasonable measure of autonomy for the Kurdish population within Iraq. Indeed, the Baghdad regime has, at various times over the years, seemed prepared to accept such an outcome. In the early 1970s the regime announced a tentative agreement with the Kurdish leadership governing language rights, guaranteed Kurdish political participation in the national government and a wide range of economic benefits. An Autonomy Law for the Region of Kurdistan was officially announced and put into effect on March 11, 1974. This agreement was effectively suspended the following year. After Saddam Hussein consolidated his power in Iraq after 1979, the position of the Kurds became increasingly desperate, even though Hussein occasionally made gestures to Kurdish demands, particularly during the Iran-Iraq war.[31]

Ever since the so-called "Anfal campaign" in 1988, however, in which Baghdad used poison gas against a number of Kurdish villages in order to quell all resistance, the policy of Saddam Hussein has been one of unrelieved brutality and even extermination of the Kurds. From a historical point of view, it can reasonably be argued that the Kurds in northern Iraq had gone a considerable distance in trying to reach an accommodation with Hussein. But his unyielding hostility to granting them any shred of autonomy or even decent treatment made an international effort to protect them not only right but indeed the only alternative available.

As far as the principle of last resort applying to intervenors as opposed to the victims, the events leading up to Operation Just Cause, the American intervention in Panama in December 1989, seemed to reflect an adherence to this principle by the Bush administration, and if so may account for the widespread public acceptance of that action. Over a period of time, the United States resorted to freezing Panamanian government assets in the United States, and it instituted other economic sanctions against the Noriega regime as well. Washington repeatedly offered Manuel Noriega a more or less graceful way out of the conundrum in which he increasingly found himself: safe passage out of Panama, taking with him most of his considerable financial assets, and a comfortable exile in Spain free from the perils of extradition to the United States for drug trafficking. Perhaps equally important, the United States attempted to engage the Organization of American States to put pressure on Noriega to step down, particularly after the fraudulent "elections" of May 1989, and thus avoid American military action of the type the OAS had always found so objectionable. As Secretary of State James Baker recalled, "I felt it was important to give the OAS a chance—if no other reason than to make it clear, should force be necessary, that the United States had exhausted every peaceful, diplomatic alternative."[32] The OAS condemned the electoral fraud and set up a mediating team that visited Panama three times over the next several months in a vain attempt to resolve the crisis. Eventually, however, as one OAS official said, they had to concede that "we have failed miserably."[33] Under the circumstances, the eventual launching of Operation Just Cause could reasonably be seen as a genuine "last resort" undertaken only when all other measures had proven fruitless.

A case in which a last-resort effort managed to avoid a forceful intervention is clearly that of Haiti in September 1994. Just prior to the planned dispatch of American forces to Haiti, President Clinton sent former President Jimmy Carter, Senator Sam Nunn, and former Joint Chiefs of Staff Chairman Colin Powell to negotiate with the Cedras regime on peaceful departure. As one analysis suggested, "If [the mission] failed, and the President had given the order to invade, he could at least contend he had really exhausted every possibility of reaching a peaceful settlement."[34] This is perhaps unduly cynical, but in any case, the last-minute peaceful resolution of the Haitian crisis meant that Senator Glenn's Dover test would never have to be faced.

The Tanzanian intervention in Uganda in 1979 is one final example of an intervenor apparently adhering to the principle of last resort. Despite Amin's appalling record of human-rights abuses, the international community basically stood by and allowed him to proceed, save for a few minor gestures such as an embargo on imports of Ugandan coffee by the United States. The one country that took an increasingly hard stand against Amin's depredations was neighboring Tanzania under the leadership of Julius Nyerere. Nyerere's motivations for doing so were, as we have already discussed, the usual mix of altruism and self-interest, since Uganda offered a series of quixotic security challenges to Tanzania throughout the 1970s. The point for our present purposes is that despite Amin's increasing record of moral degradation as well as obstreperous foreign policy, Nyerere held his hand for eight long years before finally moving against Kampala militarily. Even then it was Amin who finally forced the issue, with his invasion of the Kagera Salient. On November 15, a large Tanzanian force began the process of ousting Ugandan troops from the Salient and shortly after that, they entered Uganda itself. By January 1979, there were some 20,000 Tanzanian soldiers in the country, and in April, they occupied Kampala, whereupon Amin fled the country.

THE FACT OF IMPURE INTERVENORS

The previous three standards for assessing both the decision to intervene and the results of intervention are derived out of classical Just War theory. We turn now to two additional aspects that must be taken into consideration in arriving at a verdict on rightful humanitarian intervention. In the last chapter, we observed that states undertaking what can realistically be called some type of humanitarian intervention typically display mixed motives in doing so. Factors of self-interest and altruism typically combine to produce the decision to intervene. We also suggested that this need not be an occasion for condemnation, so long as substantive humanitarian good can be seen to have emerged from the action taken. There is a separate, though related, principle that needs to be considered in passing judgment on the bona fides behind a given intervention, however, and that has to do with what might be called the "dirty hands" of the intervenor. The issue is this: If the intervening state has had a past record of complicity in the crimes of a targeted leader or regime, does this nullify its claim now to be doing good? At the very least, should our verdict on the legitimacy of such an intervention be conditioned by past associations?

One of the most apt cases in which to address this issue concerns the French relationship with the late Jean Bedel Bokassa, self-styled "emperor" of the Central African Republic (CAR). As part of the general pattern of French policy toward Africa (discussed earlier), successive governments in Paris had maintained close relations with the leaders of the CAR following its independence from French rule in 1960—first, with David Dacko and, then, with Bokassa—after Bokassa ousted Dacko in a coup in January 1966. One factor in the French relationship with Bokassa was their appreciation of his valiant service with the French army in Indochina, as well as their concern with maintaining access to the considerable production of uranium in the CAR. The support for Bokassa took the form of general economic and political assistance (including French officials serving in important administrative posts) despite his increasing move toward autocracy. Eventually, relations with him took on a distinctly personal note when it was revealed that French President Giscard d'Estaing had received a gift of diamonds from Bokassa, as well as certain commercial opportunities for himself or his family, in return for his support of the African leader.[35]

As his rule unfolded, Jean Bedel Bokassa became an increasingly unwelcome embarrassment to the French government, particularly after he proclaimed himself emperor of the newly styled "Central African Empire" in December 1977. The ceremony was modeled on the coronation of Napoleon Bonaparte in 1804 and reportedly cost over a quarter of the total foreign exchange earnings of the CAR at the time.[36]

Rumors began to circulate that he engaged in cannibalism, even claiming that he served human flesh to visiting dignitaries under the guise of "beef." The final straw came when more than one hundred schoolchildren were killed in April 1979 for protesting against having to buy school uniforms made by one of Bokassa's own factories. In September 1979, some 1,800 French commands were flown to the capital of Bangui while Bokassa was away on a visit to Libya, and they restored David Dacko as president. Initially, Paris maintained the fiction that Dacko had himself taken the initiative in ousting Bokassa, with French troops being dispatched at his request. But the French government quickly dropped this subterfuge and admitted that it had been the mover of events and had acted on entirely "humanitarian" grounds (no claim of "self-defense" was seen as necessary or credible). An important aspect of the situation was that an earlier Commission of Inquiry composed of representatives of five African states had indicted Bokassa as having personally participated in the massacre of the schoolchildren. Undoubtedly as a result, subsequent international criticism of the French intervention was virtually absent (only Benin, Chad, and—predictably—Libya lodging protests).[37]

In gauging this whole episode, particularly the French record of complicity in supporting a man whom they eventually felt compelled to depose because of his appalling human rights record (which tarred the French reputation as well), several observations seem appropriate. It is only fair to recognize that the David Dacko whom Bokassa overthrew was hardly a paragon of virtue himself, and many besides the French felt that Dacko's ouster was a welcome event at the time because of the increasingly authoritarian and economically disastrous aspects of his regime. Bokassa at first committed himself to a series of wide-ranging reforms in order to improve the lot of the people of the CAR. Here, too, one can accept that Paris saw the new CAR leader as a person worth supporting. Moreover, the Organization of African Unity was, until very late in the day, firmly in Bokassa's corner, and its opinion had to count for something (or perhaps a lot).[38] From this perspective, an argument can be made that French support for Bokassa—even in view of his increasingly "disagreeable" behavior—was hardly surprising.

At the same time, it may fairly be said that Paris waited a long time, probably too long, before taking action against an individual with a particularly loathsome record and for whom they had a record of support. Even so, the French *did* eventually act, and in the process, they contributed to a potentially happier future for the citizens of the Central African Republic. It is of some note in this regard that Dacko lasted only a short time as the successor to Bokassa, and a more progressive regime began to govern the affairs of the republic, with at least some initially positive effects on the life of the people there. A more general conclusion is that if we wait for saints to undertake humanitarian action, we may wait for quite a long time. French hands were hardly clean in the *l'affaire* Bokassa, but the good that they finally did should receive at least modest applause. It is, after all, better to do good late in the day than to do no good at all.

This observation can be equally applied to the Kurds in the Middle East and, more specifically, with the efforts of other states to help them following the Gulf War in the spring of 1991. In the face of a brutal military assault by Baghdad against a Kurdish rebellion in northern Iraq, hundreds of thousands of Kurds fled toward the Turkish border and toward Iran as well. Conditions in the former area were particularly harsh, with as many as a thousand people dying daily in the mountains from the extreme cold and lack of food and medicine. In response, the UN Security Council adopted Resolution 688 on April 5, which condemned the Iraqi repression of the Kurds as a "threat" to international peace and security and demanded that it cease forthwith. To help the besieged Kurds, a widespread international relief effort ("Operation Provide Comfort") was undertaken along the Turkish-Iraqi border to provide basic foodstuffs, tents, medicines and so forth, to the refugees. Shortly after that, the United Kingdom, the United States and various other countries intervened with air and ground forces (which at their peak numbered over 21,000 from thirteen nations) to establish so-called safe havens in northern Iraq to which the Kurds could return. Iraqi forces were compelled to withdraw from the area where these havens were located, and a "no-fly" zone was also established in which no Iraqi aircraft were allowed to fly north of the 36th Parallel. Eventually, the allied military units in northern Iraq were replaced by a UN force of lightly armed peacekeepers, but a rapid deployment force of some 2,500 troops from eight nations continued to be based in southeastern Turkey to deter future Iraqi moves against the Kurds.[39]

Aside from the somewhat ambiguous legal authority granted by Resolution 688—which was not grounded in any specific provision of the UN Charter—the international community's efforts to help the Kurds is generally cited as one of the most prominent recent examples of humanitarian intervention. There is no doubt that these efforts did pay substantial dividends in reducing the suffering of the Kurdish people. Some 25 million pounds of food, water, medical supplies, clothing and shelter were provided. A major effort at restoring the infrastructure in Kurdistan, particularly sanitary conditions and electrical facilities as well as roads and communications, was undertaken by a team of international civil engineers.[40] At present, the Kurds enjoy a type of de facto autonomy in much of Iraqi Kurdistan and, at least for now, are relatively free from the threat of direct oppression by the forces of Saddam Hussein. At the same time, it is only fair to recognize that the past (and in some cases even current) behavior of the intervening powers was hardly a model of altruistic consistency in reacting to the travails of the Kurds.

The Kurds, of course, had long been engaged in a struggle for their rights against the brutal Baghdad dictatorship, but this campaign had received only sporadic support from other countries and at times was openly betrayed. The United States, for example, had mounted a CIA operation in the early 1970s to support the Kurdish cause, but in the so-called Algiers settlement of 1975, she abruptly abandoned her Kurdish "allies" to the tender mercies of the Iraqis as part of a deal that involved a normalization of relations between Iraq and still another American ally, Iran. In response to criticism of this about-face, Secretary of State Henry Kissinger observed that "covert action should not be confused with missionary work."[41] It seems clear that the United States, along with a number of other states, have often regarded the Kurds as a convenient "bargaining chip" in dealing with the Iraqi government. This pattern was seen once again on February 15, 1991, when President Bush issued a veiled declaration that seemed—once again—to be an encouragement for the Kurds to assert their independence: "There's another way for the bloodshed to stop, and that is for the Iraqi military and *the Iraqi people* to take matters into their own hands to force Saddam Hussein the dictator to step aside and to comply with the United Nations resolutions and then rejoin the family of peace-loving nations."[42] Although the administration later denied it, this statement seemed a not-so-subtle invitation to the Kurds to take up arms against their oppressors in Baghdad in service to the general American interest in removing Saddam Hussein as a threat to Middle Eastern stability.

It need hardly be said that Turkey herself, on whose territory allied military units were based in support of the Kurdish safe havens, has had a distinct ambivalence as well in her attitude toward the Kurdish cause. Ankara's main interest has been to minimize a possible "spill-over" effect from the Iraqi Kurds' independence struggle on the demand of

Turkey's own Kurds (20 percent of the country's population) for a greater degree of self-determination. As part of this strategy, the Turks have not been loath to undertake major cross-border raids into Iraq to deal with Kurdish separatist forces. Iran, too, which deserves credit for harboring a very large number of Kurdish refugees (on the order of one million), expressed a strong desire for a "resolution" of the Iraqi-Kurd conflict that would lessen the burden of having so many unwanted guests. At the most general level, all the states of the region—and others outside the region as well—are basically committed to the retention of a unified Iraqi state, even if this may confound Kurdish demands for self-determination. American spokespersons even suggested that Western-style democracy in Iraq "might be more destabilizing than stabilizing" and that efforts toward broader political participation in Iraqi political life should be allowed to proceed at their "own pace."[43]

Given that the Kurds, on many occasions, have been regarded more as the objects than the subjects of policy, the problem of "dirty hands" here is not easily resolved. Particularly because there was media coverage of the suffering of Kurdish refugees along the Turkish-Iraqi border in the spring of 1991, there seems little question that leaders in various countries—and the populations that they represented—felt something had to be done. The French Foreign Minister, Roland Dumas, for example, drew a parallel between the Holocaust and "crimes against humanity" and Saddam Hussein's mistreatment of the Kurds, which, in his view, suggested a "right to intervene" in response to gross violations of human rights.[44] Moreover, there is some evidence that a "guilty conscience" at past manipulations of the Kurdish cause may have played a role in the international community's coming to the rescue of the Kurds in 1991.[45] For proponents of humanitarian intervention, it would have been far cleaner if this action had represented only a logical continuation of past, genuine support for Kurdish rights. As noted in the discussion of the French relationship with Jean Bedel Bokassa, things are rarely so simple in the real world of affairs, and it could be argued that the mixed record of outside support for the Kurds in the past did not in itself invalidate the bona fides of this particular rescue mission at this particular time.

THE FACT OF IMPURE VICTIMS

A final issue that bears on judgments about the legitimacy of a given humanitarian intervention must be frankly faced. Oftentimes, the victims who need to be helped are themselves not entirely guiltless or pure in their actions and motives. The controversy that surrounds the whole notion of humanitarian intervention might be lessened if it was invariably just a matter of succoring those who are innocent and above reproach. In a few instances this may indeed be the case, but it is generally rare to find so neat a constellation of good and bad. This is not an argument for doing nothing, however. Even in relative terms, there may be a very large difference between the actions and motivations of one party compared to the other, and rightful humanitarian intervention must be based—or can be based—on a calculation of the *degree* of difference between the parties.

Take the situation of Rwanda. The basic fact is that the Hutu majority in that country embarked in the spring of 1994 on a systematic program of killing as many Tutsis as they could. The scope of the massacre that ensued—at least 500,000 slaughtered—overshadowed by a wide margin the Tutsis' own failings. During the colonial era first under the Germans and later the Belgians, the Tutsis, although only about 14 percent of the population, acquired a dominant position in Rwandan society and attempted to maintain this favored status at the expense of Hutu rights even when independence came. Once a Hutu government came into power, there were a series of attempts by Tutsi guerrilla forces to restore their tribe to authority. In 1990 the Rwandan Patriotic Front (RPF) launched a series of cross-border incursions from Uganda that were defeated (ironically) only with foreign assistance from France, Belgium, and Zaire.[46]

With the onset of the massacres of spring 1994, the RPF launched yet another major invasion of Rwanda from its bases outside the country, and because of its strong discipline and fighting ability, gradually acquired control over all of the country except for an area in the southwestern part of Rwanda. Now, it can hardly be claimed that the intervention of the RPF was simply for purposes of protecting its own people. Clearly, one of its goals was to reassert Tutsi influence in Rwandan politics and economics more generally. Moreover, there have been some cases of brutal RPF killings of their Hutu rivals both at the time and in the period since, notably in cooperation with the forces of Laurent Kabila in the eastern Congo (directed at Hutu refugees there).[47] Still, as argued, the point here is to compare the *relative* character of Hutu and RPF behavior. The main goal of the Hutu militants was systematically to eliminate the Tutsis from Rwandan life. The government established by the RPF in Kigali after their military success, by contrast, was a broad-based coalition with a majority of the cabinet posts being held by moderate Hutus. Moreover, the RPF's invasion had the unmistakable effect of bringing to a halt an enormous slaughter. The occasional depredations of RPF troops pale by comparison, and the leader of those forces, Paul Kagame, had issued specific instructions to his troops to avoid abusing civilians and violating the rules of war. That there were occasional departures from these strictures cannot be defended, but the overall record of the RPF emerges, nevertheless, as comparatively benign.[48]

A second prominent example of what we have called here the "impure victims" factor has to do once again with the Kurds of Iraq. One can hardly deny that the Kurds have been the victims of an unusually brutal campaign of oppression by Saddam Hussein, and that the international community's effort in Operation Provide Comfort to help the Kurds was both necessary and legitimate. At the same time, the history of the Kurds presents a depressing record of factional infighting, cynical reliance on other parties (even Saddam Hussein himself) to further selfish interests, and human rights abuses committed by the Kurds themselves against their own compatriots.

The Kurds have long been divided into two main political groups: the Kurdistan Democratic Party (KDP), currently led by Massoud Barzani, and the Patriotic Union of Kurdistan (PUK), headed by Jalal Talabani. In part, the KDP and PUK have differed on genuine grounds of ideology, social bases of support (rural versus urban), and contrasting views about how to deal with the regime in Baghdad. A good deal of the infighting among the Kurds, however, has involved less-elevated matters of economic self-interest (including control of customs revenues and lucrative smuggling operations) and political power plays having to do with the relative status of Massoud Barzani and Jalal Talabani within Kurdistan and in the international community more generally. As one close observer of the Kurdish situation has observed, Barzani, for one, has proved "unable to see the larger interest of Iraqi Kurds outside the parochial concerns of his tribal and family alliances."[49]

Perhaps the epitome of this politics of cynicism took place in the fall of 1996 when the KDP actually entered into a deal with Saddam's forces to cooperate in crushing the PUK. Helped by an initial deployment of some 40,000 Iraqi troops, together with large quantities of tanks and artillery, the KDP and its partner in Baghdad succeeded for a time in capturing the important cities of Erbil and Sulaimaniya and even Talabani's hometown of Koi Sanjak. An estimated 200,000 new refugees began to flee toward the Iranian border. As part of its arrangement with Baghdad, the KDP allowed Iraqi intelligence units to penetrate much of Kurdistan in the search for dissenters and defectors.[50] Moreover, Iraqi security forces were now able to target local Iraqis who had worked for international humanitarian aid organizations on the grounds that they were guilty of "treason."[51] Although the PUK later recaptured much of the territory it had lost (aided by equipment and supplies provided by its traditional Iranian ally), the whole KDP-Saddam arrangement was almost a textbook example of an "oppressed" people providing every opportunity to those doubtful about humanitarian intervention to feel that they were right all along.

Particularly discouraging to those who favored Operation Provide Comfort was evidence that human-rights abuses in Iraqi Kurdistan were attributable not just to Saddam Hussein, but could sometimes be laid at the door of the Kurdish factions themselves. Amnesty International, for example, after a three-year study, issued a report in 1995 that detailed various human rights abuses committed by Kurdish leaders against their own people, including torture, political assassination, and even killing peaceful demonstrators.[52] These particular actions took place in the so-called autonomous zone of Iraq, the relative independence of which was guaranteed by outside military forces, especially those of the United States. There is ample evidence as well that the Kurdistan Worker's Party (PKK), operating both in Turkey and northern Iraq, does not shy away from taking extreme measures against Kurds it considers tacitly in collaboration with the Ankara government. It is unlikely that many who are familiar with Saddam Hussein's abuses of the Kurds—including the use of poison gas against Kurdish villagers—would want to equate the Kurds' own human-rights failings with those of the Baghdad regime. Nevertheless, the case for humanitarian support of the Kurds would undoubtedly be easier to make if their own actions hadn't been at times so morally ambiguous and self-defeating. As one Western diplomat said, "the biggest goal of [the no-fly zone] was to protect them from Saddam Hussein. What it hasn't done is protect them from themselves."[53]

Even in one of the best-known cases of contemporary humanitarian intervention, the move by Indian forces into East Pakistan in December 1971 in order to end the horrendous atrocities being perpetrated by the Pakistani army on the Bengali people, the problem of "impure victims" raises itself, at least in modified form. Some might question whether it is appropriate even to raise such a question in this context, given the scale of suffering that had been visited on the Bengalis in the previous nine months by the military regime of President Yahya Khan. Yet it is only fair to recognize that the Awami League and its Bengali supporters were also capable of doubtful actions. The twists and turns of Sheik Rahman's statements on what he really envisioned for the future of East Pakistan—whether full independence, partial autonomy, or simply better economic treatment—had the effect of contributing to the paranoia of the leadership in Islamabad and thus contributed to the escalation of the crisis. Far more serious were the actions of certain Bengali militants following the outbreak of hostilities on March 25, 1971. The following day, various Bengali elements of the East Pakistan rifles and police defected and began slaughtering thousands of Pakistani troops as well as some of the non-Bengali population. Thousands of bodies from the non-Bengali group were found in the main towns outside Dacca.[54] These actions, to be sure, paled before the far-larger crimes of the Pakistani military, but they were sobering reminders that in this type of ethnic struggle, virtue almost never totally lies on one side of the issue.

CONCLUSION

The last two chapters have focused on two essential questions: What are the factors that may persuade a state or states to commit (or not to commit) to some sort of humanitarian intervention? How may we gauge the legitimacy of such an intervention both in terms of the process of decision making and in terms of the evident results of the action? Since we have touched on a wide variety of cases, quite different in content and circumstance, it might be well to offer a few summary comments here that can perhaps help tie together the threads of the discussion.

The first point that needs mentioning is that, with the possible exception of Somalia, none of these cases was what might be called an "ideal type" of the action known as humanitarian intervention. In theory, a "pure" humanitarian intervention is an effort to relieve massive human suffering, particularly denial of basic human rights, and one in which the intervention adheres to the three basic tenets of Just War doctrine set out here: right intention, proportionality, and last resort. As to the first criteria ("massive suffering"), neither Panama nor Haiti would seem to have reached this level. With respect to the Just War criterion, it is evident that the requirement of "right intention" has been only partially met in most of our examples. It is virtually absent in the case of the Vietnamese invasion of Cambodia and only partially present in most of the others (e.g., Uganda, Bokassa).

That almost all of our cases have featured "mixed motives," on the other hand, should not be an occasion for surprise, as we have suggested earlier. Michael Walzer made the essential point some years ago: "Clear examples of what is called 'humanitarian intervention' are very rare. Indeed, I have not found any, but only mixed cases where the humanitarian motive is one among several. States don't send their soldiers into other states, it seems, only in order to save lives."[55] Thus, what we have been dealing with here are situations in which at least *some* humanitarian motive seems to have been generally present in the decision to intervene, where there were patent violations of "core" human rights, and, finally, where some demonstrable humanitarian good was achieved by the intervention. Using these more restrictive criteria of humanitarian intervention, the cases studied here do seem proper (if imperfect) candidates for examination, given the paucity of totally "pure" examples of such intervention.

Another way in which to approach the question is to suggest that in cases of genuine mass suffering, the obligations of the international community to offer rescue approaches the level of a *duty*. In other, less dramatic situations, that community may have a *right*, if not strictly a duty, to intervene if "demonstrable humanitarian good" can be achieved. Naturally, there are likely to be far more examples of the right than of the duty, and this raises the problem of "selectivity," that is, why go in here and not there? By the very nature of the problem, there will never be an entirely satisfactory formula that provides definitive guidance on this matter, but it has been demonstrated in our case studies that interventions in "limited" humanitarian crises are far more likely to take place if aspects of the intervenor's own self-interest are involved as well. Thus, the United States moved against Haiti and Panama because non-humanitarian concerns fleshed out the genuine human rights issues present, whereas in Chile, there seemed little direct benefit to the material interests of the United States in deposing Pinochet.[56] Supporters of humanitarian intervention—in cases both major and "minor"—may bemoan the inconsistency here, and critics of such intervention may ironically seize on this phenomenon as well to attack the very idea of humanitarian action abroad. As has already been observed, however, if we wait for perfect consistency in the affairs of states, we are likely to be in for a long wait, and the best can wind up being the enemy of the good.

An emphasis on the humanitarian good that was achieved even by what might be called "approximations" of humanitarian intervention remains, in any case, the most crucial variable employed here, invoking, in particular, the principle of proportionality. That is, did the use of military force in violating another country's sovereignty—never a step to be taken lightly—produce such proportional humanitarian benefits that the normal proscription against such intervention could be said to have been rightly set aside? In some of our cases, these benefits were very large indeed (Cambodia, Uganda, East Pakistan), whereas other interventions produced tangible but more modest effects (Haiti, Panama, the Kurds). There is, of course, always the matter of the time frame in which we assess such benefits. British scholar Nicholas Wheeler agrees that "*humanitarian outcomes* are as significant as *humanitarian motives* in determining the humanitarian character of interventions."[57] At the same time, Wheeler makes a distinction between the short-term and long-term success of humanitarian intervention and suggests that unless the latter is achieved, the intervention may be called into question. He offers a query against both the interventions in Somalia and in support of the Kurds on these grounds. This is not, however, our position, which is that doing good in the short term is justification enough for a humanitarian intervention, even if a long-term solution to the conditions that gave rise to a human-rights crisis in the first place remains uncertain.

NOTES

1. Garrett Hardin is one of the best-known critics of the presumed morality of massive food aid programs. For a representative sample of his arguments in this regard, see *Promethean Ethics* (Seattle, WA: University of Washington Press, 1980) and *Living Within Limits* (New York: Oxford University Press, 1993).

2. A most impressive discussion of all the ramifications of Just War doctrine may be found in Robert Phillips, *War and Justice* (Norman, OK: University of Oklahoma Press, 1984).

3. One of the best-known analysts of humanitarian intervention, Tom Farer, stresses three key factors in passing judgment here: the identity of the intervenor, the intervenor's goals, and compliance with certain procedural safeguards. In identifying truly legitimate interventions, his basic principles are that there be no alternative means to a forceful intervention; that in the

absence of intervention, irreparable injury will be done to the target society; that minimum force be employed; and that the canons of proportionality be followed (meaning that less damage will be caused to the affected society by the intervention than by inaction). These are all essentially variations on Just War doctrine as well. Tom Farer, "A Paradigm of Legitimate Intervention," in *Enforcing Restraint*, ed. Lori Fisler Damrosch (New York: Council on Foreign Relations Press, 1993), 316–17, 327.

4. Phillips, *War and Justice*, 21.

5. Fernando R. Tesón, *Humanitarian Intervention* (Irvington-on-Hudson, NY: Transnational Publishers, 1985), 115.

6. Robert C. Johansen, "Limits and Opportunities in Humanitarian Intervention," in *The Ethics and Politics of Humanitarian Intervention*, Stanley Hoffmann, Robert C. Johansen, and James Sherba (Notre Dame, IN: University of Notre Dame Press, 1996), 77. Tesón himself seems to agree with this formulation, saying that the basic element in judging humanitarian interventions is whether human rights have been protected by the action.

7. For a good overall summary of the development of policy toward Somalia, see John Hirsch and Robert Oakley, *Somalia and Operation Restore Hope* (Washington, DC: United States Institute of Peace Press, 1995), 149–73.

8. William Shawcross, *The Quality of Mercy: Cambodia, Holocaust, and Modern Conscience* (New York: Simon and Schuster, 1984), 68.

9. Ibid., 71.

10. Gary Klintworth, *Vietnam's Intervention in Cambodia in International Law* (Canberra: Australian Government Publishing Service, 1989), 19–22.

11. Gareth Porter, "Vietnamese Policy and the Indochina Crisis," in *The Third Indochina Conflict*, ed. David Elliott (Boulder, CO: Westview Press, 1981), 109.

12. A good description of this period may be found in David P. Chandler, *A History of Cambodia*, 2nd ed. (Boulder, CO: Westview Press, 1992), 227–39.

13. Shawcross, *The Quality of Mercy*, 76.

14. Ibid., 108.

15. Amnesty International Report, *Human Rights in Uganda* (London: June, 1978), 2.

16. Caroline Thomas, *New States, Sovereignty and Intervention* (New York: St. Martin's Press, 1985), 101.

17. Ibid., 118. It must be acknowledged here that Obote shortly returned to his old authoritarian ways, and over the next five years, the human-rights situation in Uganda greatly deteriorated.

18. Thomas, *New States, Sovereignty and Intervention*, 92.

19. For a representative example of this criticism, see Natalino Ronzitti, *Rescuing Nationals Abroad Through Military Coercion and Intervention On Grounds of Humanity* (Dordrecht, Netherlands: M. Nijhoff Publishers, 1985), 102–6, as well as Farooq Hassan, "Realpolitik in International Law: After Tanzanian-Ugandan Conflict 'Humanitarian Intervention' Reexamined," *Willamette Law Review* 17 (Fall, 1981).

20. Adam Roberts, "Humanitarian War," *International Affairs* 69 (July, 1993). 442.

21. Michael Levitin, "The Law of Force and the Force of Law: Grenada, the Falklands, and Humanitarian Intervention," *Harvard International Law Journal* 27 (Spring, 1986), 654.

22. "After Noriega," *The Economist* (January 16, 1990), 17.

23. Cited in Fernando R. Tesón, *Humanitarian Intervention* (Irvington-on-Hudson, NY: Transnational Publishers, 1985), 181–82.

24. Marie Alexandrine Martin, *Cambodia,* trans. Mark W. McLeod (Berkeley: University of California Press, 1994), 175.

25. Chandler, *A History of Cambodia*, 229.

26. Martin, *Cambodia*, 217–18.

27. A further argument that might be advanced in favor of "proportionality" in this case would be that a tentative democratic regime was introduced to Cambodia following the Paris accords of 1991. The coup by Hun Sen's forces in the summer of 1997 did represent a setback to the stabilization of the country, but in late 1998, a new power-sharing arrangement was introduced (following fresh elections) between Hun Sen and his principal rival, Prince Norodom Ranariddh, that gives some promise of a better future for the Cambodian people.

28. George Church, "Destination Haiti," *Time* (September 26, 1994).

29. United States, Library of Congress, Congressional Research Service, *The Use of Force: Key Contemporary Documents* (Washington, DC: GPO, October 17, 1994), 33.

30. Ian Brownlie, *Principles of Public International Law*, 3rd ed. (Oxford: Clarendon Press, 1979), 495–505.

31. Arthur Campbell Turner, "Kurdish Nationalism," in *Ideology and Power in the Middle East*, eds. Peter J. Chelknowski and Robert J. Pranger (Durham, NC: Duke University Press, 1988), 406–10.

32. James Baker, *The Politics of Diplomacy* (New York: G. P. Putnam's Sons, 1995), 183.

33. Cited in Joshua Muravchik, *Exporting Democracy* (Washington, DC: The AEI Press, 1992), 172.

34. Church, "Destination Haiti."

35. Claude Wauthier, "France in Africa: President Giscard d'Estaing's Ambitious Diplomacy," *Africa Contemporary Record* 12 (1979–80),

A120–27. D'Estaing paid an official state visit to Bangui in March, 1975, on which occasion Bokassa referred to him as my "dear cousin."

36. Cristopher Clapham, *Africa and the International System* (Cambridge: Cambridge University Press, 1996), 188.

37. Sean D. Murphy, *Humanitarian Intervention* (Philadelphia: University of Pennsylvania Press, 1996), 108. Bokassa lived for a number of years in exile but later returned to the CAR. After serving a term in prison for his crimes, he died in Bangui in November, 1996.

38. After the French intervention, the new Central African ambassador to the United Nations referred to the "bitter disappointment of my country over the culpable silence of the United Nations and of the Organization of African Unity regarding the suffering of the people of the Central African Republic in face of massive and flagrant violations of human rights in the name of the sacred principle of nonintervention in the internal affairs of states." Cited in Fernando R. Tesón, *Humanitarian Intervention*, 2nd ed. (Irvington-on-Hudson, NY: Transnational Publishers, 1997), 197.

39. Christopher Greenwood, "Is There a Right of Humanitarian Intervention?" *The World Today* (February, 1993), 35–36.

40. Kurt Campbell and Thomas Weiss, "Military Humanitarianism," *Survival* (September/October, 1991), 456.

41. Daniel Schorr, "Telling It Like It Is: Kissinger and the Kurds," *Christian Science Monitor* (October 18, 1996), 19.

42. Lawrence Freedman and David Boren, "Safe Havens for Kurds in Post-war Iraq," in *To Loose the Bands of Wickedness,* ed. Nigel Rodley (London: Brassey's, 1992), 46. Emphasis supplied.

43. Ibid., 65.

44. Murphy, *Humanitarian Intervention*, 189. French President François Mitterrand echoed the same argument when he argued, "when we observe flagrant human rights violations on a massive scale, we cannot stand idly by. We have a duty to put a stop to these situations." Ibid., 190.

45. President Bush made much of the altruistic motives of the United States in helping the Kurds at this point. In a press conference, he emphasized that "all we are doing is motivated by humanitarian concerns. . . . Some might argue that this is an intervention into the internal affairs of Iraq, but I think the humanitarian concern, the refugee concern, is so overwhelming that there will be a lot of understanding about this." *New York Times* (April 17, 1991).

46. An excellent survey of the history of Rwanda as background to the events of 1994 is Gerald Prunier, *The Rwanda Crisis: History of a Genocide* (New York: Columbia University Press, 1995).

47. Donald G. McNeil, "Reports Point to Mass Killings of Refugees in Congo," *New York Times* (May 27, 1997).

48. Raymond Bonner, "How Minority Tutsi Won the War," *New York Times* (September 6, 1994), A6.

49. Kanan Makiya, "Betrayal in Iraq," *New York Review of Politics* (October 17, 1996), 10.

50. Henri J. Barkey, "Kurdish Geopolitics," *Current History* (January, 1997), 2–3.

51. Bill Frelick, "US Must Rescue Kurds Who Trusted US Employers," *Christian Science Monitor* (November 8, 1996), 19.

52. Amnesty International, Press release, February 27, 1995.

53. David Rohde, "The Kurds Get in Their Own Way Under the Wing of US Protection," *Christian Science Monitor* (April 7, 1995), 7.

54. *The Sunday Times (London)* (June 13, 1971).

55. Michael Walzer, *Just and Unjust Wars* (New York: Basic Books, 1977), 101.

56. Former Congressman Stephen Solarz and military analyst Michael O'Hanlon consider which situations may call for obligatory humanitarian intervention today, and they find very few in this category (Burundi being a possible exception). At the same time, they suggest that "humanitarian imperatives combined with other critical factors, such as a U.S. interest in promoting hemispheric democracy and stemming drug and refugee flows into this country, *can* justify intervention in which moral considerations alone might not. This was the case in both Haiti and Panama in recent years." "Humanitarian Intervention: When Is Force Justified?" *The Washington Quarterly* (Autumn, 1977), 3. Emphasis in original.

57. Nicholas J. Wheeler, "Humanitarian Intervention and World Politics," in *The Globalization of World Politics*, eds. John Baylis and Steve Smith (New York: Oxford University Press, 1997), 403. Emphasis in original.

CHAPTER 7

Going It Alone or Going It with Others

In considering the whole issue of humanitarian intervention, there is still another question that needs to be addressed, and it has such a wide array of both ethical and practical implications that it seems best to devote a separate chapter to its discussion. This has to do with the institutional framework within which potential humanitarian intervention can or should take place.

It is hard to dispute the conventional wisdom that a broadly collective framework is the ideal way in which to proceed, for reasons we will discuss. "Collective intervention . . . is by definition intervention that has been authorized by some international body having widespread legitimacy. . . . Intervention by such an organization, duly authorized, is widely seen as proper, even desirable."[1] At the same time, on both moral and utilitarian grounds, there is reason to question whether legitimate humanitarian intervention *always* has to proceed as a collective enterprise. Moreover, there are a series of variants for action that go beyond the simple unilateral-multilateral formulation, and these deserve careful attention as well.

The argument that a given humanitarian intervention normally is best undertaken by a multilateral force, and under the auspices of an international mandate—especially as provided by the United Nations—rests on certain fairly elementary and almost intuitively obvious premises. First, judgments on whether a situation warrants a potential outside intervention are, as a general matter, more likely to be well taken if there are a number of parties involved in the decision. Collective wisdom, in other words, is almost always superior to the possibly skewed judgment of a single state. Second, multilateral interventions are less likely to arouse violent reactions from local political forces, or even by the society at large, than a display of power by one intervenor alone. Sensitivities about violations of the national sovereignty, for example, may be rather more muted if it is the fabled "international community" that is displaying the mailed fist. From this perspective, collective intervention is almost always more efficient, or can be more efficient, than unilateral efforts.

A further claim of efficiency, as well as legitimacy, is that a multilateral effort is far more likely to gain the open, or at least tacit, consent of the majority of states, and such status is important for the intervenors to be able to achieve their objectives. As the case of the Vietnamese invasion of Cambodia in 1979 suggests, a unilateral intervenor may of course be prepared to ignore the protests of the world community at its actions in order to consolidate its goals. A steady drumbeat of criticism about its behavior from other states is, however, generally a deterrent to the state's even undertaking a defensible intervention in the first place. Clearly, this was one of the reasons that the Indian government tarried so long in 1971 before moving against Pakistan's repression of the Bengalis.

The argument for multilateralism in humanitarian intervention rests, above all, on the proposition that such a format is the best guarantee against potential abuses by states that use "humanitarianism" as a cover for pursuing their selfish national interests. Who can doubt, for example, that if the Soviet moves against Hungary and, later, Czechoslovakia had depended on an affirmative vote in the General Assembly or Security Council, these cynical exercises would hardly have gone forward? Similarly, there was almost no period in which the United States could have gotten genuine majority assent by the United Nations for its intervention in Vietnam, nor, for that matter, for its operations in the Dominican Republic in 1965. This assertion obviously relates to some of the other arguments for multilateralism cited earlier, but it remains as perhaps the most powerful single reason for collective action in humanitarian intervention. It does so additionally because unfettered unilateralism in decisions on intervention raises the prospect of an escalating instability in world affairs, given the suspicions, and possible inclinations to react forcefully, that may be felt by other states in the face of such behavior.[2]

All of this has its obvious logic, but even so, there are some cautionary notes that ought to be memtioned here. Michael Reisman is surely on the mark when he comments that "because rights without remedies are not rights at all, prohibiting the unilateral vindication of clear violations of rights when multilateral possibilities do not obtain is virtually to eliminate those rights."[3] To insist that no humanitarian intervention may go forward without the imprimatur of the international community may frequently lead to a type of paralysis and moral surrender. That community is, after all, riven by a variety of political, social, and economic disputation, and it may be the rare situation indeed when it can arrive at unanimity about the need and justification for interventionary action. One of the best-known students of the United Nations system, Inis Claude, puts the point rather effectively: "Collective irresponsibility in the use of force is not out of the question, nor is collective timidity and indecisiveness. . . . Collective gun-shyness is perhaps as likely to be encountered as unilateral trigger-happiness and is not necessarily more conducive to world order."[4]

The cases of East Pakistan and Idi Amin's Uganda are once again apt reference points here. A variety of states lamentated the atrocities taking place, but their offering of sympathy was hardly accompanied by concrete proposals or offers of action. It was left to India and Tanzania to undertake the actual measures to end the suffering, even though they clearly had not submitted their plans for approval to some international body. Julius Nyerere rather effectively defended his actions in ordering his troops into Uganda as follows: "What we did was exemplary at a time when the Organization of African Unity found itself unable to condemn Amin. I think we have set a good precedent inasmuch as when African nations find themselves collectively incapable of punishing a single country, then each country has to look after itself."[5] The bottom line, then, is that "a policy of consensualism is often a policy of the lowest common denominator."[6]

Even when the United Nations or another collective body moves itself to support a humanitarian intervention, there remains the possibility that the decision taken may not be appropriately arrived at or may contain internal flaws and contradictions. After all, as the old saying has it, a camel is a horse designed by a committee. One writer particularly sympathetic to the concerns of the developing world even suggests that actions taken by, say, the Security Council may have a built-in bias. "Intervention as mandated by Security Council decisions could be used [as] a tool by the five permanent member states, who represent the status quo. Because intervention has historically been seen as protecting the powerful against change by maintaining the status quo, developing countries are naturally suspicious of it."[7] Since the United Nations is widely seen by the developing world as a prime forum in which it can raise its concerns, this analysis is suggestive indeed.

It must also be recognized that in the current community of nations—and absent a genuine and permanent "international police force"—there are only a relative handful of states that have enough discretionary military power to take the lead in humanitarian intervention, especially when these involve relatively distant regions. It is certainly preferable to have an international consensus for forceful interventionary action, but there are surely situations in which one or more powerful states have to take the lead even in the absence of such consensus. One might even offer the proposition that these powers have a special *obligation* to do so, on the assumption that great power brings great responsibility. Admiral Alfred Thayer Mahan, the noted American sea-power theorist, put the matter rather grandiloquently some one hundred years ago. "The possession of power is a talent committed in trust, for which account will be exacted; and . . . under some circumstances, an obligation to repress evil external to its borders rests upon a nation, as surely as responsibility for the slums rests upon the rich quarters of a city."[8]

Mahan's thinking was actually quite common in discussions on humanitarian intervention in the earlier part of this century, and his assertion was taken as being almost self-evident, given the mores of the time. Consider the following comment from Ellery Stowell, author of the best-known treatise on humanitarian intervention to be found in the interwar period (and a fervent supporter of the legitimacy of such action). Decisions on intervention, according to him, "must be left to those powers who exercise a paramount direction over world affairs—that is, to the great world powers. Sometimes they act in concert. Each of the world powers also has a particular region outside of Europe where it often exercises this police power as if by a tacit mandate from the other powers."[9]

Such thinking is, to put it mildly, hardly fashionable today, and there is no question that it reflects a highly hierarchical and Western-centric view of international relations. The reference to great powers' obligation but also *right* to intervene is hardly an accepted norm of the contemporary system. The concept of spheres of interest in which these powers should have a more or less free hand to operate is also not high on the list of desired phenomena today. There is in fact much to object to in the analyses offered above. Mahan, after all, was a famous (or notorious) imperialist and supporter of American expansion. His sentimental reference to the "duty" of the United States to banish evil and suffering—just as the rich should help the poor—hardly concealed his identity as a strong American nationalist. The basic point, however, is that a full acceptance of the Mahanian credo, particularly given its source, contains many obvious dangers and invitations to excess. Even Stowell recognized this fact at times. He allowed as how "it is evident that power so vast is in danger of being abused. If it is unwisely used to interfere unnecessarily with the independence of the less powerful sovereign states, it will constitute a menace to society no less serious than that which it is intended to ward off."[10] A comment to which many today, particularly in the developing world, could only murmur "amen."

Even so, it seems unavailing, perhaps even counterproductive, not to recognize that certain major states, as a practical matter and in some cases even as a moral matter, will necessarily have to play the prominent role in using the international community's "police powers" to deal with quite unacceptable abuses of basic human rights. If they are unwilling to accept such a challenge, it is unlikely, indeed, that there will be a long list of candidates to take their place. Having said this, there are ways in which the practical demands of power can be accommodated to contemporary norms of collective decision making and the legitimization of forceful action.

Aside from genuinely collective measures taken under the auspices of the United Nations, two in particular suggest themselves. The first involves situations in which a single state is willing to or is convinced that it should intervene in a humanitarian emergency, but before doing so, it receives at least pro forma sanction from the international community (typically the United Nations) before acting. To be sure, such approval often may be no more than a reluctant acceptance of the inevitable, but it offers at least some protection against unrestrained abuse of the interventionary power. Given contemporary international mores, it seems in fact that countries are reluctant to undertake major interventions without at least some cover in the form of legitimization by outside authority.

Two relatively recent examples that might be cited in this regard involve, respectively, the French intervention in Uganda in June 1994 ("Operation Turquoise") and the dispatch of American troops to Haiti later in that same year. Before acting, the French lobbied at the United Nations for approval of Operation Turquoise, and Resolution 929 in fact provided such sanction, along with fairly restrictive stipulations about the length of the French operation. Also, when the Clinton administration decided on a forceful solution (if necessary) to the crisis in Haiti, it received, in the form of Resolution 940, authorization for military action against the Cedras regime. To be sure, Resolution 940 spoke of a "multinational force," and in obeisance to this wording, the United States secured commitments from seventeen other Caribbean and Latin American nations to provide a patina of some 1,500 troops to the main American force of about 20,000. As it was, last-minute negotiations persuaded the Haitian junta not to resist the invasion force, and advance units began to arrive in Haiti without opposition on September 19. It might be noted that in the case of Rwanda, Resolution 940 did not specifically require a "multinational" force; even so, the French government, in seeking still more protection against criticism of its actions, arranged for at least a token number of troops from other countries to be involved as well. Thus, she was able to get commitments from Senegal, Guinea-Bissau, Chad, Mauritania, Egypt, Niger, and Congo to offer a small contingent of forces to supplement her own and to provide Operation Turquoise with at least a fig leaf of cover that it was a truly international operation.[11]

The basic argument behind accepting—or even applauding—the idea of great power interventions but under some type of international mandate, has been developed, among others, by Stevenson McIlvaine, who formerly served as Deputy Chief of Mission at the United States Liaison Office in Mogadishu, Somalia, from 1992 to 1994. He speaks of the need for an "assertive multilateralism" in which "one country is the dominant player, [taking] the lead under a vague U.N. imprimatur. . . . When one Western power takes the lead and is willing to run the thing, it can be done effectively. But when it is just the U.N., the U.N. can monitor the situation, they can be a presence, but they can't make things happen. They can't make peace."[12] The cynics might question whether the Somalia version of "assertive multilateralism," particularly its success in "making peace," was the best example that McIlvaine could have used to advance his case, but the force of his argument remains nonetheless.[13]

A second variant to a truly international intervention is for the locus of decision making to be concentrated within regional organizations with a special geographical and political interest in a local crisis. This concept, in fact, has a long purchase within the context of the United Nations Charter, which set out essentially three variants for the legitimate use of force: as authorized and carried out by the Security Council, as undertaken by individual states under their right of self-defense (Article 51), and as directed by regional or subglobal organizations. Chapter VIII of the charter states clearly that "nothing in the present Charter precludes the existence of regional arrangements or agencies for dealing with such matters relating to the maintenance of international peace and security as are appropriate for regional action." Moreover, it refers to the possibility of the Security Council actually taking the initiative in activating such regional organizations for military purposes. One of the ambiguities here has always been the relationship between the United Nations and the regional groups. Did the latter actually have to get the *approval* of the former before they could take forceful action? In any event, in the period since 1945, there have been a series of interventions by regional bodies that establish an interesting precedent for such action, including the Arab League's actions in Lebanon, the OAU's efforts in Chad, and perhaps especially, the case of Liberia.

In the summer of 1990, the long-simmering resentments of most Liberians against the authoritarian rule of Samuel Doe resulted in the outbreak of a civil war in which various anti–Doe factions competed for support. Liberia gradually began to sink into anarchy, with mass starvation and disease rampant an increasing reality: Over the next several years, the estimate is that around 150,000 people, mostly civilians rather than combatants, lost their lives, with another 700,000 becoming refugees in neighboring countries. In response to this unfolding tragedy, the Economic Community of West African States (ECOWAS) deployed a large force to the country in August 1990. The motivations for this action were several, including the destabilizing effect of the large movement of refugees as well as the presence in Monrovia of a number of non-Liberian nationals at risk. There was clearly a core humanitarian purpose involved as well, however, involving the plight of the Liberian people themselves. In a statement justifying the intervention, ECOWAS spokesmen emphasized that the move was designed "first and foremost to stop the senseless killing of innocent civilian nationals and foreigners, and to help the Liberian people to restore their democratic institutions. ECOWAS intervention is in no way designed to save one part or punish another."[14]

The reaction of the United Nations, and of the international community more generally, to the ECOWAS intervention was consistently favorable. The Bush administration, in explaining why it would not become involved itself, insisted that this was "an African problem" requiring "an African solution" and praised the willingness of a regional organization such as ECOWAS to take the lead in dealing with the Liberian crisis.[15] Virtually all the other African states outside ECOWAS also lent their support. It is important to recognize, however, that this was not a case of ECOWAS acting in response to a prior United Nations mandate. Indeed, it was not until November 1992, that the Security Council passed Resolution 788 giving ex post facto approval to the ECOWAS intervention and establishing an arms embargo against the Liberian factions in the bargain. Secretary-General Boutros Boutros-Ghali some months later reaffirmed the official UN blessing for an action that had been taken without its initial approval: "Liberia continues to represent an example of systematic and effective cooperation between the United Nations and regional organizations, as envisaged in Chapter VIII of the Charter. The role of the United Nations has been a supportive one. Closest contact and consultation have been maintained with ECOWAS, which will continue to play the central role [in Liberia]."[16]

The belated passage of Resolution 788 might seem to be a case of making a virtue out of necessity, but it remains that the ECOWAS intervention in Liberia still stands as a particularly important example of a regional organization dealing with a regional humanitarian crisis. The fact that the intervention was by neighboring states, of course, did not mean that it would necessarily follow a smooth path. Indeed, in the years since 1990, the Liberian crisis continued to simmer. Despite the presence of some 12,000 troops from ECOWAS (constituted as ECOMOG, or the "ECOWAS Ceasefire Monitoring Group"), various attempts at a political solution proved ephemeral, and the number of civilian casualties and refugees continued to mount. ECOMOG itself was not immune from the fighting, and in December 1995, 64 of them were killed by the militia of one Roosevelt Johnson. The following April a tenuous coalition regime virtually collapsed, and Monrovia once again descended into anarchy. Finally, under ECOMOG's close supervision, open elections were held in August 1997, and one of the most brutal militia leaders, Charles Taylor, won an overwhelming victory.

Evidence suggested that large numbers voted for him not in spite of his brutality but because of it: he was seen as one person willing to use all "necessary" measures to ensure stability at long last for the beleagured country. Whether Taylor will, in fact, prove able to govern effectively—with at least minimum regard for basic human rights—remains an open question at the moment.[17]

The Liberian model of intervention, it might be observed, actually seemed to represent something of a compromise itself between overtly unilateral and comfortably collective action. It was ECOWAS that was the formal institutional structure behind the dispatch of troops to Liberia, but all informed assessments of this action suggest that it was certainly Nigeria that was the decisive influence behind the decision for intervention. Nigerian units comprised the largest percentage by far of the intervening force. A resolution of the Liberian crisis was seen by Lagos as critical to its broader foreign policy concerns and, not incidentally, acceptance by other regional states of Nigeria's decisive role in the region. The general direction of Nigerian policy in West Africa could be seen as well in her later intervention in Sierre Leone to restore democratically elected President Ahmed Kabbah to power following a military coup against his regime. In that instance, Nigeria proceeded in the absence of an ECOWAS (or United Nations) mandate, even though Nigerian Foreign Minister Tom Ikimi stressed that the goal of the operation was simply to restore "legitimate government, peace, and security." He also said that the action in Sierre Leone was necessary to prevent further instability in Liberia itself.[18]

There is a considerable body of opinion that suggests that in the continuing tension between the necessity to act in the face of humanitarian crises, and the often cumbersome decision-making procedures of general international organizations, reliance on regional groupings is an attractive compromise for several reasons. Such an approach presumably deals with some of the fears about openly unilateral interventions for selfish purposes, since it does, after all, support the notion of collective action. Moreover, regional organizations may well have a more acute understanding of the complexities and modalities of a local emergency than do more distant actors; their subsequent intervention may be more acceptable as well precisely because the intervenors are from the region. This discussion of the Liberian case, of course, suggests that such outcomes are not always easily achieved, even when the intervention is both collective and regionally-based.

In the ongoing debate between unilateralism and collectivism—in reacting to humanitarian crises—the case of Liberia leads logically to the proposition that in dealing specifically with the problem of "failed states," some form of multilateral action is generally the best way to proceed. The complexity and likely duration of an effort essentially to rebuild a whole society and political system are apt to tax the patience of a single intervening power beyond its endurance and its capabilities. Given the prospect—not to mention the reality—of a growing number of failed states, the international community needs to contemplate a variety of modalities by which it can react to these crises.

One notable recent study suggests that there is, in fact, a need for a new variant on the old trusteeship system prevalent in an earlier period that would constitute a type of "conservatorship." The domestic analogy in this regard is that of "guardianship," in which the affairs of an incompetent individual are taken over by public authority in order to protect his interests. The most modest type of conservatorship would be one in which various forms of assistance in governance would be offered to whatever relics of central authority remain in the targeted country. More ambitious would be a scheme in which crucial governmental functions would be, at least temporarily, handed over to outside authority. Finally, there could be a reprise, in essence, of a direct trusteeship, whereby the entire society and political system would be under the direction of such authority until local institutions could be reconstituted. Whichever of these three models might be pursued, their guiding spirit would be not to destroy the sovereignty of the failed state but, in fact, to restore it.[19]

An early example of "conservatorship" might be said to be the United Nations operation in the Congo in the early 1960s. UN troops were originally sent to supervise the withdrawal of Belgian forces from their former colony, but these troops stayed on for four years "because it was generally believed that without [their] presence the country would have fallen into total disorder." Over time, the United Nations virtually dominated the central administration of the country.[20] A more recent—and perhaps more relevant—case of conservatorship in operation was the United Nations Transitional Authority in Cambodia (UNTAC). This was essentially a combination of models two and three, as outlined above. United Nations authorities took over responsibility for certain key governmental functions in Cambodia, but their writ ran larger than this to include virtual temporary veto power over all aspects of Cambodian political life. The central purpose of UNTAC was to rebuild central institutions in the country and allow Cambodia to arrive at a point in which it could govern itself once UNTAC left.[21] The jury is still out on the ultimate results of these efforts. A coup by Hun Sen in the summer of 1997 effectively shattered the uneasy functioning of the coalition regime that was a key effort of the UNTAC operation. But a new political arrangement, perhaps promising greater stability, came in late November 1998, following new Cambodian elections. Hun Sen was now the unquestioned leader of the country, but his principal political rival, Prince Norodom Ranariddh, was accepted as speaker of the National Assembly, and, not incidentally, the Khmer Rouge forces were in a virtual stage of collapse.[22] The whole Cambodian affair, in any case, stands as an unusually prominent example of the international community's attempt to come to grips with the problem of the failed state.

FORCES AT THE READY

A key issue in the argument over unilateralism versus multilateralism in humanitarian intervention—and the different variants of each—has so far not been directly broached. This deals with both the availability and the effectiveness of armed forces in carrying out such interventions. Whatever position one adopts in terms of the unilateral-multilateral spectrum, there are important problems that present themselves in this regard.

For those who assert the necessity of a unilateral capacity by some states to intervene in the face of humanitarian emergencies, one of the critical difficulties that has always confronted such a stance has been essentially both moral and political. That is to say, how do democratic leaders deal with the so-called Dover principle, which we have already discussed and that (rightly) confronts all leaders of military forces in explaining to the mothers and fathers of those who die or are injured in foreign assignments why such a sacrifice was legitimate? How do they do so particularly when that assignment was to carry out humanitarian tasks with perhaps only a loose connection to the traditional national interest? A common solution that has been offered is the establishment of volunteer and elite units within the country's armed forces specifically earmarked for (potentially coercive) humanitarian missions abroad. Such "national units," as they are sometimes called, would attract recruits as a consequence of special pay and benefits, as well as the prestige that would presumably accrue to their being identified as responsible for unusually challenging humanitarian tasks. The impact and utility of these special forces would be magnified if their establishment was coordinated with similar units in various other countries prepared to contribute to international humanitarian action, especially in terms of agreed-on tactics and equipment.

It is sometimes argued that the military in countries such as the United States would, in the post-Cold War era, be relatively quick to adopt the above proposal, since their mission (or missions) in the new international system are somewhat hazy, and humanitarian work would be a new reason for being—and for continued budgetary support. In an address by former President George Bush to the UN General Assembly in September 1992, he, in fact, made much of the fact that under his administration, the U.S. military would be increasingly configured for various types of humanitarian missions, involving increased assets, formal training at the military academies, and even revised doctrine.[23] The existence of permanent national units assigned to humanitarian operations would also help in some way to legitimize whatever personal sacrifice was required. If those so affected had, after all, volunteered for these missions, accepting the risks involved but doing so because of the good to be done (and the special benefits accruing to them), their families could take some comfort from this fact. The sorrow at personal loss in these circumstances would hardly be washed away. Yet some real meaning could be given to this loss, which might well be absent if the average soldier was simply assigned to some obscure mission, the justification for which appeared to be murky.[24]

There is certainly an appealing case to be made for a series of states establishing and maintaining national units for humanitarian missions. Even so, there still remain a good many problems in adapting this idea to a country such as the United States. In an era in which much "political hay" is made about the "overextension" of American interests in the world—and the unfair burdens of this situation—establishing units within the American armed forces committed to international good work would be in some sense swimming upstream against an important segment of public opinion. Some responses testified to this state of mind during a series of Pentagon focus groups convened in several cities, which revealed considerable skepticism "by parents and their sons over the military's new humanitarian and peacekeeping missions."[25] Some military recruiters and Pentagon officials have also expressed concerns about the possible effect in attracting new recruits to the armed forces, if such missions should receive special emphasis. Perhaps just as important is the professional resistance within American military circles to developing units for humanitarian work. Of course, generals are always accused of preparing to fight the last war, but the prevailing ethos within the military seems to be that their primary—perhaps even sole—mission is to prepare for regular combat operations. One of these generals recently argued that every minute troops spent training for and conducting peace operations detracted from their preparedness for war.[26]

This discussion has focused on the issue of individual states having at least a theoretical capacity for unilateral humanitarian intervention. If we focus more on multilateral actions, particularly under the aegis of the United Nations, different, but no less pressing, problems present themselves. It is commonplace that every UN mission involving the use of military force is a vexing ad hoc enterprise in which the Secretary-General has to lobby member states to contribute troops. Moreover, there are invariable logistical and even tactical difficulties that confront the operation of such a force. Shashi Tharoor, a UN official working on peacekeeping operations, vividly summarizes the current situation:

> It is clear that if the world wants the United Nations to serve, even occasionally, as a fire brigade, it will have to do better than the present system, under which fire breaks out, the aldermen on the Security Council agree it needs to be put out, and the fire chief is then sent out to hire firemen, rent fire engines, find hoses of the right length and look for sources of water to put into them—while hoping that, when he has what he needs, the house has not already burned down and there will still be enough survivors to rescue.[27]

How to deal with this situation? Two possible solutions are often cited.

The first is to develop a scheme by which the so-called national units within member countries would be permanently earmarked for United Nations duty only, as called for in Articles 43 and 45 of the Charter. Under this system, such units would remain outside the normal national command structure and would not be assigned to any other duties not specifically authorized by the United Nations. Former Secretary-General Boutros Boutros-Ghali was active in suggesting the creation of a UN rapid deployment force consisting of such units. Under his formulation, they would be of battalion-size, trained to similar standards and operating procedures, share common communications equipment, and train together in regular joint exercises.[28] Sweden has long maintained such a force, and as a consequence, Swedish soldiers have been unusually active in a broad range of humanitarian and peacekeeping missions.[29]

The attractiveness of such a proposal is that it would create a body of trained and experienced troops readily available for multilateral humanitarian missions. A typical provision of this concept is that the member country agrees not only to absorb all expenses for the maintenance of such units, but also to cover their costs when sent on foreign operations as well, which would go some way toward solving the UN's perennial budgetary crisis for humanitarian work. While this is technically an appealing notion, the idea of a permanent force-in-being composed of separate national units depends, of course, on the political will of the governments involved and on their constituents' commitment to and confidence in United Nations decision making. This may obtain in some states, such as the Nordic countries, Ireland, and Canada, but it seems to be absent in a number of other potential participants, particularly among the major powers.

The second solution to the problem of having forces conveniently available for United Nations humanitarian operations is rather more radical than simply having a set of separate national units on call. This would involve the creation of a genuine, permanent international interventionary force, that is, an actual "United Nations army." In 1993, for example, Brian Urquhart, a UN official of long standing, floated a suggestion for a light-infantry force of about 5,000 volunteers who would be under direct UN command and who would be available for duties beyond traditional peacekeeping.[30] Both the Dutch and Canadian governments have also offered suggestions for a "United Nations Legion" that would be at the permanent disposal of the organization. A tentative basis for such a development might be found in Article 47 of the Charter, which established a Military Staff Committee (MSC) "to advise and assist the Security Council" on all questions relating to measures taken under Chapter VII on international peace and security. The MSC is composed of the chiefs of staff of the permanent members of the Security Council and, in theory, could provide a command framework for a standing United Nations force. In fact, in the years immediately after World War II, the MSC, working on the basis of Chapter VII, devoted a good deal of attention to the creation of a multilateral force from the three principal services of the armed forces and involving all the five permanent members of the Security Council. The force contemplated was impressive, with between 1,200 and 1,300 aircraft, from eight to twenty army divisions, and various naval units as well.[31] To be sure, this was not really a scheme for a permanent United Nations army as such, since the forces involved would have remained under national command authority until needed in a crisis. In any event, it proved impossible, with the worsening of the Cold War, for the MSC to achieve agreement on the establishment of such a force, and the later activities of the MSC were relatively nominal.

Depending on one's political viewpoint, the creation of an actual United Nations army of some sort would be either the best or the worst of all worlds. Certainly, it is the most logical direct answer to the challenge of having multilateral forces ready for use in humanitarian emergencies, especially since in terms of training and doctrine, it would be a more coherent body than a cobbled-together force of national units.[32] Support for the idea of a permanent international standing army has sometimes come from surprising sources. Former President Ronald Reagan, in a speech at Oxford University in December 1992, offered at least a veiled endorsement of the concept. "The world's democracies must enforce stricter standards of international conduct. Is this not a moral cause and a great undertaking as profound as the struggle against totalitarianism? What I propose, then, is nothing less than a humanitarian velvet glove backed by a steel fist of military force."[33]

The political objections to such a development are so obvious as to hardly need mentioning: Given the radical fringe's current alarm about UN "black helicopters" operating over the United States, it is not hard to imagine their emotions when confronted with the *reality* of a permanent UN standing army, emotions likely to be shared in some degree by those generally less extreme in their political orientation. It is important in this regard that the Clinton administration has come out directly against the idea and has dismissed the idea of American units earmarked for United Nations duty as well. In a major policy statement in May 1994, it was stated flatly that "the U.S. does not support a standing UN army, nor will we earmark specific U.S. military units for participation in UN operations."[34] There are other, more professional objections to the idea of a standing UN army. Ambassador Charles Lichenstein, former Deputy U.S. Representative to the United Nations, was typically direct in this respect. "Let me say it bluntly. My fundamental problem with a standing U.N. military is that I don't think there is anything more difficult in the world than building a successful, professional, battle ready military force. The U.N. first has to perfect the technique of organizing a two-car funeral, then we might want to consider giving it serious additional duties to undertake."[35] One needn't be quite as cynical as Lichenstein in assessing the possibilities of a United Nations standing force, but there is no historical record for such a truly international army being created and operating effectively.

One interim step that might meet the above objections would be to concentrate, at least for the time being, on the creation of a permanent humanitarian military force within the context of regional organizations, such as the West European Union, the Organization of African Unity, and so forth. The practical and political difficulties of working at this level might well be less than when the focus is on a genuine world army; in fact, there is already some precedent for such entities. The United Kingdom, for example, has proposed the creation of a European Reaction Force (ERF) under the auspices of the West European Union, autonomous from NATO, to deal with situations outside the geographical domain of NATO where military force was considered appropriate and European interests were involved.[36] Its establishment would represent a logical extension of the basic idea of national units, except that in this instance, they would operate entirely within a multilateral framework and under a common command structure.

Whatever final position one takes on the issue of forces-in-being for undertaking humanitarian action, a solution (or solutions) to the problem of capabilities must be high on the agenda of those who support the whole notion of humanitarian intervention. In some cases, the easiest job is simply to identify those likely cases in which such intervention would be justified. It is generally more difficult to establish concrete ways in which humanitarian intervention can go forward. This is true no matter what position one takes toward the perennial issue of unilateral versus multilateral action in dealing with humanitarian crises.

NOTES

1. Evan Luard, "Collective Intervention," in *Intervention in World Politics*, ed. Hedley Bull (Oxford: Clarendon Press, 1984), 157.

2. Stanley Hoffmann offers the novel suggestion of a treaty whereby a "qualified majority of signatories" could determine when circumstances warranted a collective humanitarian intervention. This group would report on their findings to the UN Secretariat and to the Security Council, which would have the subsequent power to order an end to the intervention once it had achieved its purposes. Stanley Hoffmann, "Sovereignty and the Ethics of Intervention," in *The Ethics and Politics of Humanitarian Intervention* (Notre Dame, IN: University of Notre Dame Press, 1996), 24.

3. Michael Reisman, "Sovereignty and Human Rights in Contemporary International Law," *American Journal of International Law*, 84 (October, 1990), 875.

4. Inis Claude, *States and the Global System* (New York: St. Martin's Press, 1988), 142.

5. Fernando R. Tesón, *Humanitarian Intervention* (Irvington-on-Hudson, NY: Transnational Publishers, 1985), 166.

6. Marc Trachtenberg, "Intervention in Historical Perspective," in *Emerging Norms of Justified Intervention*, eds. Laura Reed and Carl Kaysen (Cambridge, MA: American Academy of Arts and Sciences, 1993), 31.

7. Virginia Gamba, "Justified Intervention? A View from the South," in ibid., 119.

8. Alfred Thayer Mahan, *Some Neglected Aspects of War* (Boston: Little, Brown and Company, 1907), 107.

9. Ellery Stowell, *Intervention in International Law* (Washington, DC: John Byrne and Company, 1921), 279.

10. Ibid., 285.

11. I have drawn on Sean Murphy's discussion of the Rwandan and Haitian cases for most of the information presented here. See his *Humanitarian Intervention* (Philadelphia: University of Pennsylvania Press, 1996), 243–56, 260–75.

12. Miller Center of Public Affairs, University of Virginia, *Miller Center Report* (Summer, 1995), 11.

13. The model of a major power intervening but under the cover of multilateral authority doesn't always pan out, as demonstrated by the case of Grenada. The United States claimed that it sent its forces to that island under the auspices of the Organization of Eastern Caribbean states, but this hardly kept the Security Council from condemning the invasion by a vote of eleven to one (the United States exercised its veto). David Wippman, "Enforcing the Peace: ECOWAS and the Liberian Civil War," in *Enforcing Restraint*, ed. Lori Fisler Damrosch (New York: Council on Foreign Relations Press, 1993), 184.

14. Christopher Greenwood, "Is There a Right of Humanitarian Intervention?" *The World Today* (February, 1993), 37.

15. Wippman, "Enforcing the Peace: ECOWAS and the Liberian Civil War," 159.

16. Murphy, *Humanitarian Intervention*, 164.

17. Mary Fitzpatrick, "Liberia's Tenuous Election," *Christian Science Monitor* (August 1, 1997), 20; Jennifer Ludden, "Unsteady Liberia Takes Another Fall," *Christian Science Monitor* (April 9, 1996). For a relatively upbeat assessment of Taylor's first year in power, including his establishment of a Human Rights Commission, see Abiodum Onadipe, "Liberia: Taylor's First Year Report Card," *Contemporary Review* (November, 1998), 236–40.

18. Antony Goldman, "Is Nigeria a Coup Cop or Bully in Sierre Leone?" *Christian Science Monitor* (June 5, 1997), 6. As it happened, it took a full ten months for the rebel regime in Sierre Leone to be ousted, and Kabbah re-

sumed office only in March, 1998, with widespread fighting still going on in various parts of the country. "Grisly Message," *The Economist* (August 8, 1998), 40.

19. Gerald B. Helman and Steven R. Ratner, "Saving Failed States," *Foreign Policy* (Winter, 1992–93).

20. Luard, "Collective Intervention," 167–68.

21. For a good discussion of UNTAC's activities in Cambodia, see Michael Doyle, *UN Peacekeeping in Cambodia: UNTAC's Civil Mandate* (Boulder, CO: Lynne Rienner Publishers, 1995).

22. Seth Mydans, "Familiar Rite, Familiar Politics in Cambodian Assembly," *New York Times* (November 26, 1998), 3.

23. Frederick C. Cuny, "Humanitarian Assistance in the Post-Cold War Era," in *Humanitarianism Across Borders*, eds. Larry Minear and Thomas Weiss (Boulder, CO: Lynne Reiner Publishers, 1993), 161.

24. For a discussion of the idea of special national military units for humanitarian actions, see Tom Farer, "Intervention in Unnatural Humanitarian Emergencies: Lessons of the First Phase," *Human Rights Quarterly* 18 (February, 1996), 20–21.

25. Business Executives for National Security (BENS), "Peacekeeping: Perils and Prospects," (New York: September 29 and October 16, 1995), 14.

26. Ibid., 11. It is interesting that shortly before President Bush's speech on humanitarian operations to the General Assembly in 1992, General Colin Powell, Chairman of the Joint Chiefs, had questioned the whole idea of the American army being converted, at least in part, to humaniarian work.

27. Shashi Tharoor, "Should UN Peacekeeping Go 'Back to Basics'?" *Survival* 37 (Winter, 1995–96), 63.

28. Ibid., 62.

29. The early Swedish experience with such units is addressed in *Swedish Stand-By Forces in the Service of the United Nations* (Stockholm: Ministry of Foreign Affairs, 1982).

30. Adam Roberts, "From San Francisco to Sarajevo: The UN and the Use of Force," *Survival* 37 (Winter, 1995–96), 25.

31. Richard Connaughton, "Military Intervention and UN Peacekeeping," in *To Loose the Bands of Wickedness*, ed. Nigel S. Rodley (London: Brassey's, 1992), 170.

32. For a detailed proposal along these lines, see Carl Kaysen and George Rathjens, *Peace Operations by the United Nations: The Case for a Volunteer UN Military Force* (Cambridge, MA: American Academy of Arts and Sciences, 1996).

33. Cited in Adam Roberts, "From San Francisco to Sarajevo: The UN and the Use of Force," *Survival* 37 (Winter, 1995–96), 448.

34. United States, Library of Congress, Congressional Research Service, *The Use of Force: Key Contemporary Documents*, "The Clinton Administra-

tion's Policy on Reforming Multilateral Peace Operations," (Washington, DC: GPO, October 17, 1994), 45.

35. Business Executives for National Security (BENS), "Peacekeeping: Perils and Prospects," 8.

36. Connaughton, "Military Intervention and UN Peacekeeping," 179–80.

CHAPTER 8

Humanitarian Intervention Reconsidered

This book has dealt with the issue of humanitarian interventions for the most part as a matter that affects the community of nations generally, and certainly the fundamental moral significance of this issue bears on many, if not all, of the states in that community. At the same time, some special attention has been given to the role of the United States in such interventions, given this country's current position of unusual power and prominence. In this concluding chapter, therefore, I want to revisit not only the issue of humanitarian intervention generally, but also the potential—and perhaps the duty—for the United States to contribute to an ever-expanding regime of rightful attention to ending, or at least ameliorating, grave human-rights crises.

American involvement in and commitment to humanitarian intervention may well be at risk given the temper of our times, which seems to suggest that ethical political action is a virtual contradiction in terms. The sterility of much of the recent dialogue on this country's political life was perhaps best caught in an extraordinary diatribe offered by a well-known columnist for a major national newsmagazine shortly after American military pressure led to the removal of the Cedras regime in Haiti in September 1994. The fact that President Clinton had long hesitated before he decided on a policy of force (if necessary) had, according to this analysis, "done massive, perhaps irreparable damage to his presidency, to his party—and, worse, to America's status in the world." Former President Jimmy Carter, who played a major role in the peaceful resolution of the Haitian crisis, was contemptuously dismissed as the "Prince of Peace." There was a grudging acceptance that the Haitian intervention might have some beneficial results, but we were told not to "bet the farm" on it. The time-worn argument was repeated: in running a foreign policy, "the protection of national *interests* seems a lot more solid than the promulgation of national *principles*, however worthy."[1]

From where does such venom arise? The fact is that the American intervention in Haiti succeeded in removing a repugnant military dictatorship and offered the Haitian people some relief from the barbarisms of the Cedras regime. In a best case analysis, it may have even sowed the seeds of some minimal democratic governance to that unhappy land. Moreover, that there should have been some appropriate uncertainty over how to deal with a human-rights crisis, and that a peaceful effort to resolve it was better than using bullets, seems hardly surprising or objectionable. I would suggest that the real source of the above angst over the Haitian intervention lies in a common phenomenon today, which is an impossibly elevated set of standards by which we can—or ought to—judge humanitarian intervention. This is a point that has been discussed earlier, but it bears repetition. In effect, the suggestion is that unless such intervention is free of ambiguity and produces a balanced and uniformly attractive set of results, it has been a "failure," a "debacle," a "waste" of American resources and energy.

Consider, for example, the range of comment on another example of American participation in humanitarian intervention: Operation Restore Hope, the effort to deal with the Somali crisis. The conventional wisdom about this operation has evolved in such a way that Operation Restore Hope is now regarded by many, if not most, as a cautionary tale against any further exercises of the same sort. Somalia is widely described as a classic example of "mission creep" in which the earlier purposes of the intervention became lost in a fruitless attempt to remake the Somalia political structure, one result of which was the loss of a number of lives, including more than thirty Americans.

Such commentary cannot be dismissed totally out of hand. Certainly, every fatality is a human tragedy, and there seems little doubt that UNOSOM's understanding of the complex Somalia clan structure left a lot to be desired. But buried beneath all the rhetoric about the "failure" of Operation Restore Hope is the elementary fact that a great many Somalis were saved from an early death by the efforts of the international community. A former Assistant Secretary of State for Africa estimates the number as, at a minimum, around 250,000. He also suggests that Operation Restore Hope made at least some progress in knocking the Somali political impasse off dead center and thus creating the conditions for an eventual political settlement of some sort.[2] These successes, most especially the first one, place the issue of American casualties in Somalia in a rather different light. Some 58,000 Americans died in Vietnam in a supposed effort to help the Vietnamese people. Thirty-six American soldiers made the supreme sacrifice in Somalia, and as a result, several hundred thousand Somalis were indeed helped: they were given a chance at life.

There is yet another factor in the cynicism often expressed in this country about humanitarian interventions, and it deals with the notion that the United States is supposedly committing a very disproportionate and unfair share of its resources to these illusory adventures. Such thinking is only part and parcel of a more general impression about the overall level of foreign aid the United States government dispenses overseas. One poll revealed that most Americans thought foreign aid consumed about 15 percent of the Federal budget and that most favored cutting that to about 5 percent. Respondents also guessed that expenses for UN peacekeeping consumed about 22 percent of the American defense budget and supported reducing this to about 15 percent. Actually, both foreign aid expenditures, and peacekeeping expenses as part of the Defense Department's budget, are well under 1 percent. The United States actually ranks behind virtually every other industrial democracy in the amount of support it allocates for overseas assistance (twenty-two other nations devote larger percentages of GNP to foreign aid than the United States does).[3]

The "unfair burden" argument takes on a special asperity when the matter of the American contribution to UN-sponsored operations is addressed. Again, the common complaint is that this contribution has been and continues to be excessive. Of course, the idea of "excessive" is subjective, but it is instructive to consider that when UN peacekeeping activity was at its height (in the middle 1990s), there were some 67,000 United Nations personnel stationed around the world in peacekeeping operations. Of this number, exactly 963 were from the United States, based mostly in Macedonia and at a hospital in Croatia. As for its cost, Washington's share of the UN peacekeeping budget for all of 1994 amounted to approximately $1 billion (which was less than one-half the cost of a new attack submarine being built for the American navy). Three years later, this had fallen to around $350 million, and American personnel involved in UN peacekeeping had remained at around nine hundred.[4]

The Clinton administration seemed to feel that it had to respond to the perceptions about the overly-generous commitment of American resources to UN operations when it issued Presidential Decision Directive 25 in May 1994. That document suggested that in the future, the United States would commit to ventures such as Somalia only if a daunting range of prerequisites was first met: such action had to be in the self-interest of the United States, American participation had to be essential to its success, adequate resources had to be at hand for the undertaking, the objectives of the mission had to be clear and have an identifiable point at which the United States could withdraw from participation, and finally, Congress had to give its support to the undertaking.[5] Even though PDD 25 was primarily designed to quiet the fears of the most vocal media and Congressional critics concerning American "over-commitment" to humanitarian action, it may have had an internal bureaucratic rationale as well. As Andrew Natsios, himself a former American official concerned with humanitarian relief, said, "humanitarian interventionism does not have a large career constituency in State or DOD [Department of Defense]."[6]

The cribbed language of PDD 25 was, as it happened, a good deal removed from the rhetoric that candidate Clinton employed in his presidential campaign. In a speech in April 1992, for example, he called for the creation of an international army, presumably under United Nations auspices, that would stand "at the borders of countries threatened by aggression, preventing mass violence against civilian populations, providing humanitarian relief and combating terrorism."[7] Perhaps we shouldn't make too much of the difference between candidate Clinton and President Clinton. The responsibilities of power inevitably alter the way in which decision makers deal with the real problems they now face. Moreover, the May 1994 statement of principles seems at odds with Washington's subsequent intervention in Haiti. The real issue here, however, is whether in the earlier declaration, Clinton and his advisers went too far in limiting the possibility of, and perhaps even more important, the duty of the United States to undertake humanitarian action in world affairs.[8]

One further theme in the current denunciation of humanitarian intervention deserves attention, especially because it displays a particularly twisted logic. In this instance, an essentially Darwinian stance is taken concerning the world's troubles. The notion is advanced that this is indeed a vale of tears, and that the capacity for human brutality and cruelty is such that it is well nigh hopeless to assume that we can make measurable progress in dealing with such a panoply of suffering. We are told to tend to our own knitting, to concentrate on the development and welfare of our own fortunately situated society, and to eschew the temptation to fritter away our resources on a vain attempt to cure the world's ills. For those within this school of a more intellectual or at least historical bent, reference is sometimes made to Secretary of State John Quincy Adams's response to the pressures on the American administration in 1821 to assist the Greeks in their war of independence against the Turks. Adams admitted that America's "heart, benedictions and prayer" would go out to any area where "the standard of freedom and independence has been or shall be unfurled." Nevertheless, he said, the United States "goes not abroad in search of monsters to destroy. She is the well-wisher to the freedom and independence of all. She is the champion and vindicator only of her own."[9]

In one sense, such an argument is almost self-evident. The international community is indeed replete with examples of human suffering, and to attempt to remedy all of these equally and at the same time is to copy Don Quixote's vain exercise in tilting at windmills. In the classic formulation, by attempting to do too much, we may wind up doing too little—the best can become the enemy of the good. Even so, the above thinking is on balance a virtual contradiction in terms. It suggests that if we can't solve everything, then we shouldn't even attempt to solve something. The currently fashionable idea that there must be an "exit strategy" before we attempt any form of humanitarian intervention in order to prevent "over-reach" and "mission creep" is particularly bizarre. Reduced to its essentials, this is really an argument against intervening at all, since human-rights crises are inherently unpredictable. To establish a date for departure prior to involement allows the villains of the piece to lie low for a time, anticipating their chance to resume power, confident that the intervening forces will shortly be disappearing over the horizon.

The attitude of all or nothing would have some interesting consequences if adopted in, say, American domestic life. For example, it is commonplace that a large percentage of the homicides committed in the United States are never solved and their perpetrators go unpunished. Does this mean that we should remove murder as a felony offense within the legal system? The point is obvious: until the arrival of the Millennium, there will always be human tragedies around the world that are ignored and whose creators will never face judgment, at least in this life. This hardly removes our duty, however, to deal with at least *some* of these tragedies and *some* of these perpetrators, within the limits of our resources and the possibility of effective action. There can hardly be a more pathetic philosophy than one that proclaims that since we can't do everything, we will therefore do nothing.

THE CHIMERA OF REALIST THEORY

A crucial element in the current captious debate about humanitarian intervention, and the American role in such operations, clearly concerns varying concepts of the "national interest." Most "realist" writers assert that the national interest is almost self-evidently a matter of the narrow economic and security concerns of the state. Whatever increases the physical safety of the nation, therefore, or sustains or expands the economic prosperity of that nation, is *a fortiori* in the national interest. Other goals represent at best a diversion from that central consideration. A representative reflection of that position could be seen in testimony that Henry Kissinger offered before the Senate Foreign Relations Committee during the debate in the mid-1970s over the plight of Soviet Jews. The secretary of state had gone through an uncomfortable session of being browbeaten by Senators for his supposed indifference to human rights abuses in the Soviet Union, especially the Soviet regime's attitude toward Jewish emigration. Finally, in exasperation, the former professor tutored the committee on some basic realities in international relations. He spoke of the nation's very survival as the ultimate purpose of American foreign policy. He insisted that in his dealings with the Soviet leaders, he always had given and would continue to give his primary attention to reducing the threat of a nuclear war between the superpowers. If in doing so he had to downplay or mute American objections to some features of Soviet internal life, he made clear that this was a tradeoff of which he was unashamed.[10]

There was a certain force to Kissinger's depiction of his responsibilities, but at the same time, we must recognize that a realist definition of the national interest is no more than an abstract formulation, and it need have no particular claim on our sensibilities in either tradition or logic. The national interest is what we say it is, particularly in a pluralistic democratic society, and if that society determines that the relief and succor of oppressed peoples has to be counted as an important national objective, who can say that such a position is inherently "wrong" or misplaced?

In the most extreme case, societies have the inherent right to imperil their very existence if in so doing, they feel they are serving a cause that is integral to their sense of self-worth and reason for being. A good example of such a situation came with the Danish people's decision in 1943 to forestall German plans to deport all Danish Jews to concentration camps. There were only about 8,000 Jews living in Denmark (about 0.2 percent of the population). Under the semi-autonomous Danish government that was allowed to function by the dispensation of Berlin—a uniquely favorable arrangement for a country under German occupation—no Jewish property was expropriated nor were Jews removed from Danish governmental posts. The SS commander in Denmark, Karl Best, on instructions from Hitler, finally decided, however, to "settle" the Jewish question in Denmark in late September 1943 by rounding up the entire Jewish population and shipping them east. Word of this decision was leaked to Danish Social Democratic leaders, and in an extraordinary action, virtually the entire Danish population cooperated first in hiding and then ferrying the threatened Jews across the water to Sweden.[11] Given the Nazi temperament when faced with opposition, the Danes were putting the very fate of their country and society at risk in helping their Jewish compatriots. Numerous arrests and executions took place after the rescue, but the collective decision was to first answer the call of conscience and only then worry about the consequences.

There is a good deal of evidence that the American people themselves generally have not lost a proclivity for worrying about the conditions of others, in particular those who are less favored in other countries. Many Americans may be under the impression that the United States is doing more than its share in dealing with foreign crises, but this hasn't necessarily translated into an indifference to the welfare of others. One study showed that an "overwhelming majority" supporting UN peacekeeping in principle, and two-thirds of those questioned agreed that "when innocent civilians are suffering or are being killed, and a UN peace operation is being organized to try to address the problem, in most cases the US should be willing to contribute some troops, whether or not it serves the national interest."[12] Another survey revealed general public support for humanitarian assistance as well as involvment of American troops as long as the American commitment was not long term one. The number who adamantly opposed any type of quasi-humanitarian intervention by the United States was less than one-third of those polled. Despite the opposition among many in Congress to United Nations activities generally, the Chicago Council on Foreign Relations also found that a majority of Americans viewed "strengthening the United Nations" as a very important foreign policy goal of the United States.[13]

What these findings suggest is that given a high standard of moral leadership by American officials, and in particular a strong and unashamed appeal not to the worst but to the best instincts of the American people, there may be more popular support for at least some types of humanitarian intervention than is widely supposed. Ironically, the cynicism that may have to be overcome here is not so much that of the people as a whole but that of their leaders, who often seem prepared to adopt the lowest-common-denominator in setting out the foreign-policy goals of the United States. One striking fact about the United States's initial reluctance to become involved in the Bosnian crisis is that both the Washington foreign-policy establishment and the elite press argued that there was almost no public support for doing so. In fact, polls consistently suggested that a majority of Americans *did* support an active United States role in Bosnia. In short, "support for U.S. intervention went largely unreported, while the gap between the evidence in the polls and the discussions in the press and political discourse remained wide."[14]

This gap between the leaders and the led seems to have been a regular feature of the foreign-policy debate in recent years. The survey by the Chicago Council on Foreign Relations in fact concluded that "there are more traces of altruism among the public than among leaders." As recently as 1990, 58 percent of the general public felt that "promoting and defending human rights in other countries" should be a "very important" goal of the United States (compared to 42 percent for those styled as opinion leaders).[15] A study by the Program on International Policy Attitudes at the University of Maryland offered even more dramatic evidence on this point. Fully 84 percent of those questioned agreed with the statement that "sometimes the US should be willing to make some sacrifices if this will help the world as a whole."[16] The potential willingness of many Americans to offer continued assistance in humanitarian crises may, in fact, be cited as one of the most attractive aspects of the American character. The efforts of some "expert" commentators to cast scorn on its applicability (and, by implication, its naiveté) seem particularly unattractive.

It may be argued, in sum, that the traditional American commitment to helping the less fortunate, and even to the spreading of the benefits of democracy, still holds a powerful appeal despite the rhetoric of withdrawal being offered currently by certain powerful voices in Washington and elsewhere. Such a stance is based on at least a tacit recognition that the country can achieve its full moral identity only if it gives some reasonable attention to the fate and welfare of others. Perhaps this impulse comes from the fact that this is basically a country of immigrants, and that if the United States retreated from its obligations to the progress of mankind, it would in effect represent a repudiation of one of the basic themes in the country's history.

Even Henry Kissinger now seems to offer some grudging recognition of this proposition, at least in accepting that the American people *want* to feel that they have a moral relevance to the rest of the world. In his discussion of the evolution of diplomatic practice, Kissinger analyzes the American experience in the early years of this century by saying that Teddy Roosevelt's pure *realpolitik* did not lead the United States to a truly fruitful international involvement because its unvarnished appeal to self-interest did not engage the American idea of "exceptionalism": the idea that this country somehow had a special moral identity and thus was uniquely capable of moral leadership. In a tribute to President Woodrow Wilson's rather different philosophy, Kissinger argues that "Americans could be moved to great deeds only through a vision that coincided with their perception of their country as exceptional. . . . [Wilson] grasped that America's instinctive isolationism could be overcome only by an appeal to its belief in the exceptional nature of its ideals."[17]

The flaws in realist theory are limited not just to its rather cramped definition of the national interest, but they extend to its whole conception of international relations as well. There is ample evidence, for example, that states often undertake actions that have little evident connection with their narrow self-interest. The very extensive provision of emergency food aid to afflicted countries around the world is only one example, even though in certain instances, by a generous stretch of logic, such policies might be seen as contributing to selfish national concerns, such as providing a market for our farmers' agricultural surplus. In many instances, however, it is virtually impossible to demonstrate how such food aid provides any tangible material benefit to the donor country other than a sense of doing good in a calamitous situation.[18] More generally, the realist arguments contain a central logical contradiction. On the one hand, they offer an assertion about how states *do* behave; on the other hand, they provide advice about how states *should* behave. The latter is evidently inconsistent with the former: if all states do follow the realist paradigm, there should be no need for such guidance. The obvious point, then, is that many states do not follow (or at least not all the time) the narrow dictates of self-interest. Instead, they are sometimes open to the appeals of humanitarianism, such as providing famine relief described above.

THE CHANGING CHARACTER OF INTERNATIONAL RELATIONS

One may go further than this, however, and suggest that such feelings of duty may be significantly on the rise. The admitted travails of our age have actually disguised a most significant development in the character of international relations, the existence of which should be the occasion for at least modest celebration. The degree of attention to, and even the heated debate about, humanitarian interventions in recent years may be a sign of some real progress in the standards of the international system and in the practice of international politics generally. Particularly given the brutalities of the twentieth century, it might seem quixotic, even bizarre, to speak of "higher standards" in the conduct of world affairs. Despite the lamentable record of our time, however, it is not totally fatuous to suggest that there are at least some reasons for hope in humanity's progress.

Perhaps chief among these is an increasing acceptance of *responsibility* in the trials and tribulations of others. Clearly, revelations about the Holocaust played an important role in contributing to this trend, particularly given the guilt so many parties felt about not having done more to prevent it. Sir Hartley Shawcross, the British prosecutor at the Nuremberg trials, indirectly admitted that more could and should have been done to help the Jews of Europe; saying so, he implied that the lessons of the Holocaust must be given great weight in shaping responses to future atrocities. "The rights of humanitarian intervention on behalf of the rights of men trampled upon by a state in a manner shocking the sense of mankind has long been considered to form part of the recognized law of nations."[19]

We have already discussed how this sense of rightful involvement has been increasingly reflected in formal documents, such as the various United Nations human-rights treaties, the Helsinki Accords, the Geneva agreements on humanitarian law, and others. A smaller but no less significant piece of evidence attesting to it has been the establishment of organizations such as the International Crisis Group (ICG) in London in 1995 under the leadership of fabled relief worker Fred Cuny. The ICG's focus is on the development of a strategy and then a detailed set of recommendations for averting or at least limiting major human rights crises. Its goal is to persuade governments to carry out these recommendations—if necessary by military force.[20] It is worthwhile to reflect a bit more on the basic change in *sensibilities* that underlies all these developments. Not so long ago, after all, various types of human disasters were accepted as almost being the natural order of things. They were certainly not regarded as requiring action to redress by one's own state.

Consider, for example, the terrible Irish famine of the 1840s. It is estimated that almost a million people starved to death in Ireland as a consequence of the potato crop failure. This calamity took place not in some obscure corner of the non-European world, but in Europe itself. Despite this fact, there was little in the way of organized international relief efforts to deal with its effects, although some private groups in the United States and other countries did offer some help. The British government, which then controlled Ireland, attempted to provide basic food relief to the most afflicted, but at the same time, it allowed the continued *export* of large quantities of cereals from the island because of London's reluctance to interfere with the free operation of laissez faire economics.[21] It is impossible to imagine today that such a relatively insouciant approach—either by the British government or the international community—would be tolerated. It is instructive to compare international relief efforts to allay famine in Ethiopia in the 1980s with the lack of action on the Irish famine more than a century earlier. Ethiopia was certainly a far more obscure place than Ireland (at least to those in the West), and yet a major operation was undertaken to help those in need. Moreover, such assistance was offered despite the fact that the Ethiopian regime of the day was hard-line Marxist-Leninist and made a habit of describing the political iniquities of the Western food donors in the most strident fashion.

There are other examples that could be cited of the change of attitudes from an earlier era to the present. In 1989, the Chinese government decided to crush the student protest movement in that country, and in the process of clearing Tiananmen Square in Beijing, Chinese troops killed or wounded several thousand people. There was a good deal of military violence, accompanied by large numbers of arrests, in other areas of China as well. The international community reacted with outrage at these events. Economic sanctions, and cutting off normal diplomatic exchanges with the PRC by a number of countries, including the United States (at least for a time), were a testament to the intense feeling the Chinese government's actions had aroused. The shadow of Tiananmen still hangs over Beijing's relations with many regimes around the world.

Every human death is certainly a tragedy, but compare the suffering of the Chinese dissidents in 1989 with that experienced by an earlier generation of Chinese protesters. In response to the corruption and ineptitude of the Manchu dynasty, the so-called Taiping rebellion broke out in 1851. Until it was suppressed almost a generation later, the standard estimate is that almost twenty million people died in the fighting between the Manchu regime and the rebels. To the extent that the international community took note of this catastrophe, it was to give political and military support to the Manchus, since the great powers preferred an enfeebled and vulnerable Chinese regime to one organized along much tougher lines by the forces for change. The Manchus would undoubtedly have collapsed without this support, and the net result of foreign involvement was to prolong a terrible period of instability and warfare for the Chinese people.[22] That indifference to the effect of their actions on Chinese society could hardly stand in greater contrast to the concerns about the rights of the individual in China expressed by a number of states in 1989, some 140 years later.

If changing values within the international system make a growing regime of humanitarian interventions more conceivable, at least in moral terms, it may rightly be argued that with the passing of the Cold War, such interventions have become increasingly feasible as well. During the lamentable era of East-West confrontation, even genuinely well-meant interventions to aid the population of a target state ran the risk of inadvertent escalation as one superpower or the other reacted with suspicion (the Congo in 1960 perhaps being a representative example). There are currently some 35,000 troops from various NATO countries in the former Yugoslavia. While the effect of their efforts at peacemaking may be debated, their very presence is of great historical significance. It is inconceivable to think of such a large force being accepted by, say, the Brezhnev leadership of the Soviet period or even during Gorbachev's tenure for that matter, given historic Russian ties to the Serbs. Indeed, their dispatch would likely have been the occasion for a major East-West confrontation. It is notable in this connection that a small contingent of Russian troops are actually participating in SFOR. More generally, the end of the Cold War has apparently led to less tolerance for "convenient dictators," who even while guilty of substantial abuses of their own citizens, were nevertheless welcomed as assets by the superpowers in their mutual competition (Marcos, Mobutu, and the Shah, as well as Castro and Saddam Hussein, being prime examples).[23]

A SYSTEM OF QUALIFIED SOVEREIGNTY

Many of these specific developments are only part of a more general underlying phenomenon that has been with us for some time. It is one to which we have given some attention in these pages, and it involves the increasing erosion of the traditional concept of state sovereignty. Former UN Secretary-General Perez de Cuellar, in a speech given shortly after international intervention to help the Kurds, put the basic proposition well: "We are clearly witnessing what is probably an irresistible shift in public attitudes toward the belief that the defense of the oppressed in the name of morality should prevail over frontiers and legal documents."[24]

It must be recognized that the very concept of "sovereignty" has actually been rather limited in time and place. Even within the Western tradition of political thought, it only came into full play with the peace of Westphalia in 1648. From the fall of Rome in the fifth century and extending for more than a thousand years, the primary emphasis was on the idea of a united Christendom rather than the special rights of the various segments of this community. It was Westphalia that enshrined the doctrine of sovereignty and, with it, the accompanying rule of non-intervention as the prevailing norm among states. One important factor here was that the use of force was now linked to the pursuit of narrowly defined state interests rather than grander religious or ideological purposes.[25]

That the diminution of this classical version of sovereignty is an empirical fact today hardly seems in dispute. From a *normative* perspective, this can only be considered a welcome development. But it is necessary to proceed carefully here. Michael Walzer and others are surely right in maintaining that nation-states still have a role to play in securing the liberty of their citizenry, in sustaining the national cultural heritage, and, perhaps above all, in giving a sense of identity and purpose to a group of individuals with felt common bonds. None of this should or need go away. But there is a need for a formal acceptance of a new concept of sovereignty. The new concept would represent a middle way between abandoning the undoubted value of diversity and accepting continued abuses by regimes that operate under a cloak of their right to total freedom of action. This new paradigm might be styled "qualified sovereignty," and it is our contention here that it is the norm toward which the community of nations should increasingly strive.

The concept of qualified sovereignty represents an attempt to marry the two traditions referred to—the idea of an essentially unified human community, on the one hand, and a system of essentially independent actors, on the other. Under such a regime, the principle of non-intervention would still be given serious weight, and for a variety of reasons already referred to, including the threat of widespread instability in world affairs as well as the inherent normative claims of sovereign self-governance. States would still have considerable leave to pursue their own particular goals and interests, and to sustain their particular sense of community. Indeed the noted Article 51 of the United Nations Charter needs to be seen in this light. In giving states a legitimate right of self-defense, Article 51 was really reaffirming the notion that states could defend the values of their citizenry against foreign aggression. In some ways, Charles de Gaulle's vision of a "Europe of nations" catches the essential idea of qualified sovereignty here. De Gaulle was obsessed with maintaining what he considered the special character of the French nation, "l'idée Français." At the same time, he was far from rejecting various forms of closer cooperation with the other European states. His call for a Europe "from the Atlantic to the Urals" was an open commitment to a broader European framework of activity. To be sure, de Gaulle's foreign policy is often remembered more as an exercise in obstructionism than in vision, and there is no doubt that he often left it unclear how and when French interests could legitimately be subordinated for the good of the whole. Nevertheless, the basic idea behind de Gaulle's thinking deserves some respectful attention as we attempt to define what a regime of qualified sovereignty would really involve.[26]

What it would entail, primarily, is that states would no longer have full authority over their own citizens where issues of basic human rights are concerned. If these rights be substantially limited, then claims of sovereign power could no longer be sustained, and the state would open itself to rightful action from the international community. The term "qualified" sovereignty also has another, related aspect. In order to "qualify" for the full rights and privileges of sovereignty, states would need to accept certain basic norms of democratic governance and humanitarian treatment of individuals. Unlike traditional international law, therefore, sovereignty would not automatically be granted simply on the basis of certain "objective" criteria, such as exclusive jurisdiction over a fixed and populated territory, a stability of organization and administration, and so forth. These would be the *necessary* ingredients in receiving recognition of sovereignty but they would not be *sufficient*. At this stage in the evolution of international relations, it is high time that a government's systematic abuses of various categories of individuals no longer be accepted in terms of the classical rights of both sovereignty and non-intervention.

As described here, the doctrine of qualified sovereignty actually derives out of a fairly pronounced tradition in Western political thought. Even John Stuart Mill, who was generally opposed to the notion of humanitarian intervention, may be counted in this tradition. He made an exception to his general rule, however, in the case of relations between so-called Christian states and barbarous ones, the latter beyond the pale of civilized nations. In this instance, as, for example, in interventions by European regimes to remedy abuses attributable to the Ottomans, Mill accepted the idea of the legitimacy of such action. Even in relations among Christian states, Mill accepted that intervention might sometimes be defended on the basis that a people was struggling to attain its liberty against an oppressive regime, although in this instance, he could support intervention only if another outside power had first intervened on behalf of the regime in question.[27] In essence, of course, the idea of qualified sovereignty equates with the cosmopolitan theory of state legitimacy that we discussed in an earlier chapter. It is a theory whose time has come, to which there can be or should be little demur today.[28]

AN INTERNATIONAL POLICING AUTHORITY

In making a case for a regime of qualified sovereignty—and for an accompanying commitment to humanitarian intervention when necessary—we are really suggesting that the traditional concept of "police powers," a fundamental feature of domestic societies everywhere, be applied (at least partially) to the international system. The police in municipal polities are charged with seeing that societal norms are enforced and that the innocent are protected from the depredations of the wicked. Above all, functioning police systems are designed to ensure that there is a degree of regularity and order in everyday life, within which individuals may pursue their interests to the best of their ability. Naturally, there is a price to be paid for such systems: individuals agree to surrender total sovereignty over their affairs in the interests of sustaining a civil society in which all may flourish. This surrender of total liberty to do as one wants (or might want) has long been seen as essential to any notion of an ordered and productive society. Both Hobbes and Locke, although in very different ways, made this essential point long ago.

The notion of police powers actually has some provenance within international law, and not surprisingly, it has often been referred to by supporters of the right of humanitarian intervention. Thus, in the early 1920s, Ellery Stowell argued that the international community had such powers, which "justifies any curtailment of the rights which are ordinarily enjoyed by the separate states, provided the action to be taken seems reasonably necessary for the protection of the common safety."[29] The most obvious and least controversial example of police powers in international relations is obviously collective efforts to thwart aggression, such as the Allied effort against the Nazis and Japanese in World War II and the more recent international coalition formed to reverse the Iraqi move into Kuwait. In this instance, the "common safety" referred to by Stowell basically connotes the safety of states—that is, the protection of their sovereignty against external threats. Any logical expansion of international police powers as part of a regime of humanitarian intervention would, however, go beyond the issue of state sovereignty and would include the welfare of the individual citizenry in various principalities. Such a norm may be connected to, but is also quite discrete from, the legal protection of regime independence. Thus, there may be massive suffering by individuals within a given society even in the absence of any external aggression.

The theory behind the use of international police powers in such situations is analogous to that used to defend domestic police activity: By helping one (or many), one is in effect helping all by sustaining a civil society. We have discussed earlier, for example, the existence of massive international refugee flight as one potential trigger for humanitarian intervention, particularly when such events are the result of conscious repressive policies by a government. It is widely accepted that refugee crises have multiplier effects that have an impact on the welfare of a number of state or societal actors. Forceful action to prevent or stop such crises are a legitimate contribution to the maintenance of international civil society.

One very important premise behind the operation of domestic police powers has an equal application to the use of such powers within the international system; in fact, it goes some way toward answering some of the principal objections to the concept of humanitarian intervention that we have already addressed. When crime takes place within a municipal system, the police do not stand by idly simply because the crime in question may be a reflection of deep societal problems that can only be ameliorated over a long period of time. The assumption is that crime has to be dealt with in and of itself if social conditions are not to deteriorate further. Similarly, in international relations, a number of human-rights crises can easily be seen as reflecting profound societal factors that will not easily be dealt with, certainly not in the short run. As discussed earlier, critics of humanitarian intervention often hold this view to argue that nothing at all should then be done, since the problem cannot be immediately "solved." Aside from being an invitation to moral paralysis, such a stance virtually equates with a willingness to tolerate a permanent status quo of injustice and suffering around the world. This is not a prospect that is likely to prove comfortable even to the most hardened observers as a logical extension of their position.

There are obviously some problematical aspects to our calling for an international "police authority" similar to that found in domestic society, even if the argument here accepts that such an authority would be more modest in its extent and operation than the municipal variant. Domestic police operate (at least in theory) within an established judicial system that provides guidelines for their activity and, perhaps more important, provides protection against police abuse. In democratic polities, the basic norms to be enforced are the result of legislative action, which—again, in theory—reflect a consensus within society. The police also typically have "the bigger battalions," that is, sufficient force to enable them to deal with even the most powerful domestic lawbreakers such as organized gangs. Perhaps above all, the police have a *legitimacy* that generally goes unquestioned, even if there may be complaints about certain of their individual actions.

As noted, this is a somewhat idealized portrait of police powers in domestic society, and there are many countries around the world where one or more of these elements is distinguished mostly by its absence.

Nevertheless, taken as a general description of municipal police systems, it is evident that substantial differences exist between these regimes and an incipient international police authority. There is no international "legislature" to pass "laws" accepted as binding and legitimate by everyone. There is a structure of international law, but on many of the most important questions involving humanitarian intervention, there continues to be widespread disagreement about what that law allows or even dictates. Moreover, the International Court of Justice and its regional variants are only a pale echo of a fully developed municipal legal system. For the most part, the ICJ can only hear cases in which the parties agree to its jurisdiction, not a very promising system for punishing wrong-doers.[30] In a world of often powerful sovereign states, it is not easy to establish a preponderance of force that can compel such states to alter their behavior. In practice, it has been the relatively weak and undeveloped principalities that have been the targets of humanitarian intervention rather than the great powers. Finally, the widespread acceptance of the *legitimacy* of domestic police powers hardly finds its reflection in international relations, or to the same extent. This is undeniably related to the fact that police typically operate within some sort of felt sense of community and a social compact. There may be an emerging notion of a distinct international community, but it is still only in a nascent stage.

All these represent formidable difficulties in developing any international police authority that would be a reflection, at least in part, of the police powers that exist within domestic society. At the same time, we should remember that even within Western countries, the notion of a permanent, professional police establishment is relatively recent. In Great Britain, for example, it wasn't until the passage of the Metropolitan Police Act in 1829, at the urging of Home Secretary Robert Peel, that such an establishment came into being (soon to be referred to simply as Scotland Yard). Moreover, it might be argued that the various schemes discussed earlier for creating an actual standing UN military capability under Chapter VII of the Charter, or at least for developing forces specifically assigned to United Nations actions ("national units"), provide at least the beginning of a potential policing authority. It doesn't seem fatuous to suggest, in any case, that as the idea of a true "international community" gradually becomes a reality rather than just a concept, the acceptance of some type of such authority may not be far behind.

A SUMMING UP

The central assertion of this book has been that a sense of responsibility for the welfare of others is a distinguishing feature of the human personality, and that this characteristic has increasingly been reflected in the operations of the international political system. To be sure, there is no call to be Pollyanish about the degree to which we are now consistently acting as if we were our brother's keeper. Clearly, there continues to be a series of outrages in the world today that go relatively unnoticed, especially if they receive little or no attention from the media, and for which there is little pressure to offer remedy.

We must also accept that the transformation of the international system, from one in which states have virtually unalloyed control over their own affairs to a regime of what we have called qualified sovereignty, will hardly proceed in a straight line and will present many difficulties and ambiguities. Secretary-General Perez de Cuellar, in the speech quoted earlier, touched on the central challenge. He suggested that this was an issue that had to be considered both prudently and boldly.

> In a prudent manner, because the principles of sovereignty cannot be radically challenged without international chaos quickly ensuing. In a bold manner, because we have probably reached a stage in the ethical and psychological evolution of Western civilization in which the massive and deliberate violation of human rights will no longer be tolerated. It falls to us, therefore, to forge a new concept, one which marries law and morality.[31]

In arriving at such a "marriage," it is important to accept that humanitarian intervention, especially if we define it as the application or threat of force, will properly be used only as a last resort in response to truly intolerable situations that seem to admit of no other solution. Stanley Hoffmann is surely right when he comments that "many people, even when they are dissatisfied with and engaged in a struggle against their government, are deeply suspicious of outside interference, unwilling to substitute one form of intrusion into their lives for another, or at least hostile to foreigners who claim a right to intrude in order to protect what may well be unpopular minorities against oppressive majorities."[32] There is, in fact, no suggestion here that humanitarian intervention should ever become a step casually to be taken. Indeed, as international standards for the protection of human rights become—we hope—more widely accepted, true humanitarian interventions might become relatively rare phenomena. In a number of other cases that present more ambiguous moral circumstances, or especially when prudential considerations militate against the use of military force, there are a variety of less-drastic options available that recognize the force of human-rights considerations, but at the same time, avoid the inevitable complications of outright intervention.

Under the rubric of "compellance," the international community has at its disposal an impressive range of measures that it can take to persuade the target state to engage in a cost-benefit analysis that results in more enlightened conduct. Among the most promising types of compellance is what might be called a general policy of "isolation," particularly through diplomatic ostracism or economic boycott. The first of these addresses the desire of even the most dubious regimes to have some degree of "respect" and legitimate recognition from the family of nations. Marc Trachtenberg summarizes the point quite effectively:

> Much of the political meaning of [humanitarian] intervention derives from the fact it stigmatizes its target as less than civilized and thus as not worthy of the respect that civilized states have for each other. Indeed, it is because it carries this connotation even today that the threat of intervention—that is, the threat of stigmatization, of being placed outside the circle of the civilized nations—can carry real weight as a means of enforcing international norms.[33]

The second form of isolation touches on the practical consequences of a state being cut off from an increasingly interrelated international economic system, with all that implies in terms of foreign investment, standard trade relations, and so forth. To be sure, there are some moral difficulties in applying economic isolation to an offending regime, particularly since the effect of this particular step may fall far more heavily on the heads of the oppressed than on the oppressors. As one perceptive analysis has it, "economic sanctions [may] have been imposed by the international community too readily because they are perceived as an easy, low-cost option." Yet they inevitably involve "the threat or use of physical harm against civilians and hence [are] an activity that requires careful ethical appraisal."[34] The issue here, as in all cases of applied morality in international affairs, requires a careful balancing of the long-term good to be achieved versus the short-term pain inflicted even on the innocent.

Even so, policies of isolation remain as a potentially compelling alternative to a too-ambitious regime of humanitarian intervention. Their appeal, as Robert Jackson says, is that they are "a way of avoiding the use of military force, respecting the traditional doctrine of nonintervention, and upholding the value of self-determination while still sanctioning human rights and other emergent international standards of conduct."[35] Their effectiveness, of course, depends on the relative economic vulnerability of the targeted country, on the particulars of the decision-making process in that country, and on the willingness of states to maintain a united front in imposing a regime of isolation. As Jackson's comment suggests, however, they present an especially attractive alternative to those who as a general matter are quite skeptical about forcible humanitarian intervention.

From their perspective, a strategy of isolation properly involves the international community in pressuring a regime to reform itself, but ultimately, it is the responsibility—and the right—of the indigenous society itself to fight for, or to insist that, such reforms take place. In this sense, what has been called "positive non-intervention" may be the functional equivalent of humanitarian intervention but without use of military force from a particular intervenor or intervenors. At its most successful, it can express a powerful sense of the priority of human-rights concerns on the international agenda.[36] Perhaps the best recent example of using isolation against a government obviously guilty of fundamental human rights violations is that of South Africa. Over a period of years, the increasing economic costs of maintaining apartheid, as well as the embarrassment at being excluded from routine activities such as international sporting events, evidently pushed the Pretoria regime toward a fundamental reexamination of its basic ideology.

In all of this, to repeat a point made at various stages in our analysis, it is incumbent on those states with the greatest *capacity* for humanitarian action on the world stage (of whatever variety) to accept the *responsibility* to act that such power conveys—and for no nation more than the United States. It is plain there are powerful forces in this country that argue against a wider humanitarian role for the United States. As Senator John Warner (R-Virginia) put it, "We simply cannot respond over and over again to these contingencies [that] lack a clear linkage to our national security."[37]

Quite an opposite stance toward American responsibilities in the world was offered by the American Catholic bishops at about the same time as Warner's comment. In the bishops' statement, they dismissed the notion that narrow interpretations of international law provided a cover under which the United States could stand aside in the face of great human-rights abuses: "The principles of sovereignty and nonintervention may be overridden by forceful means in exceptional circumstances, notably in the cases of genocide or when whole populations are threatened by aggression or anarchy."[38] As an expression of the essential rationale for and legitimacy of humanitarian intervention, that language can hardly be improved, and considering the audience toward which the bishops' words were directed, the strong implication was that the United States had to assume its proper role in reacting to "exceptional circumstances."

The world is a far from perfect place today, but there are reasons to hope that a more refined international consciousness may be developing and that the building blocks of at least a better world may be at hand. Philosopher Robert Phillips offers a moving summary of the basic impulse to accepting humanitarian obligations: "The virtue of charity is . . . central to the moral life because only through self-giving love (which entails a forgetfulness of self) is the self fulfilled. This uncalculated giving is obviously not confined *a priori* to any particular group or political configuration but is potentially directed to all."[39] Americans have an opportunity—and an obligation—to make a major contribution to this expanding sense of duty. The cynics question whether states can ever truly "do good" in international affairs, but not even to make an attempt at doing good is the ultimate expression of a self-defeating moral apathy. Robert Kennedy, in his 1968 campaign for the Democratic presidential nomination, liked to quote these famous lines from George Bernard Shaw, "Some men see things as they are and ask why? I see things that never were and ask why not?" The ultimate test of a nation's foreign policy lies in its ability to recognize what ought to be changed, what can be changed and what cannot, and to take action based on this distinction. We can expect no more than this, but certainly no less.

NOTES

1. Joe Klein, "Empathy for the Devil," *Newsweek* (October 3, 1994), 39. Emphasis in original.

2. Chester Crocker, "The Lessons of Somalia," *Foreign Affairs* (May/June, 1995), 2–8. Another study emphasizes how Somalian politics has now been substantially decentralized but is hardly anarchic. A variety of local organizations now perform the essential functions of governance. Ken Menkhaus, "Somalia: Political Order in a Stateless Society," *Current History* (May, 1998), 220–24.

3. "An Emerging Consensus" (Center for International and Security Studies, University of Maryland: July 10, 1996), 7.

4. "U.N. Stepping Back from Interventions in Hot Spots," *San Francisco Chronicle* (March 28, 1995), A7; United States, Department of State, Background Notes, "United Nations" (Washington, DC: GPO, September, 1997). Overall UN peacekeeping operations had fallen considerably by the fall of 1997, with a total of about 20,000 personnel from various countries now involved.

5. "New U.S. Peacekeeping Policy De-emphasizes Role of the U.N.," *New York Times* (May 6, 1994), A1. In a macabre circumstance of timing, President Clinton signed PPD 25 at the very moment that the massacre of the Tutsis was taking place in Rwanda.

6. Andrew Natsios, "Illusions of Influence," in *From Massacres to Genocide,* eds. Robert I. Rotberg and Thomas Weiss, (Washington, DC: The Brookings Institution, 1996), 160.

7. "New U.S. Peacekeeping Policy De-emphasizes Role of the U.N.," A4.

8. It is only fair to recognize that Clinton has hardly been the only president to demonstrate considerable ambivalence in his attitude toward humanitarian action. An earlier example of Presidental schizophrenia on this matter could be seen in President Bush's speech to the cadets at West Point on January 5, 1993. He observed that "the United States should not stand by with so many lives at stake [with reference to Somalia] when a limited deployment of US forces . . . could make an immediate and dramatic difference." But he added some pretty important qualifiers. American actions, he said, had to be "buttressed by the forces of other countries and acting under the full authority of the United Nations" and "without excessive levels of risk and cost." United States, Library of Congress, Congressional Research Service. *The Use of Force: Key Contemporary Documents.* Washington, DC: GPO, October 17, 1994, 32.

9. Cited in Norman Graebner, ed., *Ideas and Diplomacy* (New York: Oxford University Press, 1964), 88.

10. On this issue, see Cathal Nolan, *Principled Diplomacy: Security and Rights in U.S. Foreign Policy* (Westport, CT: Greenwood Press, 1993).

11. Lucy S. Dawidowicz, *The War Against the Jews 1933–1945* (New York: Holt, Rinehart and Winston, 1975), 372–74. The Germans managed to lay their hands on four hundred of the Danish Jews and sent them to the concentration camp at Theresienstadt. The Danish government demanded to inspect the conditions under which they were living at the camp, and a Danish Red Cross team paid a visit in June, 1944. As a consequence of the Danish interest in their fate, none of these Jews was sent on to Auschwitz, and the vast majority survived the war.

12. "United Nations Peacekeeping Survey" (Program on International Policy Attitudes, University of Maryland: April 19–23, 1995). Another survey by the Project on Foreign Policy and the Public at the University of Maryland found that 66 percent of those questioned would support sending U.S. troops to Burundi as part of a UN effort to prevent genocide there. "Poll on America's Role in the World," 5.

13. Andrew Kohut and Robert C. Toth, "Arms and the People," *Foreign Affairs* (November/December, 1994), 47, 57.

14. Richard Sobel, "Portraying American Public Opinion Toward the Bosnia Crisis," *Harvard International Journal of the Press and Politics* (Spring, 1998), 16–34. Sobel offers some interesting analysis about the reasons for this disconnect, but he does conclude that "a key factor in sustaining public support [for intervention] is the leadership role the president and Congress play. If the administration puts forward a consistent, convincing rationale for why the United States should send troops, the American people generally agree."

15. John E. Rielly, ed., *American Public Opinion and U.S. Foreign Policy 1995* (Chicago: Chicago Council on Foreign Relations, 1995), 18, 40. One former official once again stresses that presidential leadership is in fact decisive in gaining public support for humanitarian missions, and that this can be achieved given a clear and forceful statement of the human rights issues at stake. John Shattuck, "Human Rights and Humanitarian Crises," in *From Massacres to Genocide*, 173–74.

16. Steven Kull and Clay Ramsay, "U.S. Public Attitudes on U.S. Involvement in Haiti" (Program on International Policy Attitudes, University of Maryland: August 22, 1994), 10.

17. Henry Kissinger, *Diplomacy* (New York: Simon and Schuster, 1994), 44. This comment was offered with particular regard to American entry into World War I, and Kissinger's position is that Teddy Roosevelt's "realism" could not compete with the "idealism" of Wilson in gaining support for an action that was, from a strictly realist perspective as well, important to American interests.

18. See, for example, Robert McElroy's extremely interesting discussion of American food aid to Russia in the early 1920s in *Morality and American Foreign Policy* (Princeton, NJ: Princeton University Press, 1992).

19. Cited in Ann Thomas and A. J. Thomas, Jr., *Non-Intervention* (Dallas, TX: Southern Methodist University Press, 1956), 374. Shawcross's assertion about the "recognized law of nations" may be seen today in the international tribunals organized to deal with the atrocities committed in Rwanda and the former Yugoslavia.

20. William Shawcross, "A Hero of Our Time," *New York Review of Books* (November 30, 1995), 38.

21. Edward Norman, *A History of Modern Ireland* (London: Allan Lane, 1971), 114–15.

22. A standard history of these events is Michael Franz, *The Taiping Rebellion* (Seattle: University of Washington Press, 1972).

23. A proposal that has been floated at various times in recent years is the establishment of a sort of "Club Fled," a permanent Elbe, to assist in the removal of dictators such as Noriega, Duvalier, and others. While it is seemingly a somewhat whimsical idea, it has a certain logic, given the frequent difficulties of finding a country willing to accept a deposed tyrant. The Club Fled notion is mentioned in Thomas Gillespie, "Unwanted Responsibility," *Peace and Change* 18 (July, 1993), 238.

24. Cited in Guenter Lewy, "The Case for Humanitarian Intervention," *Orbis* (Fall, 1993), 627–28.

25. For an interesting discussion of this evolution in thinking, see Bryan Hehir, "The Ethics of Intervention," *Ethics and International Affairs* (1995).

26. For an excellent survey of the premises and unfolding of de Gaulle's foreign policy, see Edward Kolodziej, *French International Policy Under De Gaulle and Pompidou* (Ithaca, NY: Cornell University Press, 1974).

27. Pierre Laberge, "Humanitarian Intervention: Three Ethical Positions," *Ethics and International Affairs* (1995), 22–23.

28. The move toward a regime of qualified sovereignty is not just limited to the Western world. As David Wippman points out, the almost univeral African support for ECOWAS's activity in Liberia "suggests an increased willingness on the part of many African states to recognize that a blanket prohibition on outside intervention in a state's domestic affairs is no longer feasible or necessarily in the interest of most African states." David Wippman, "Enforcing the Peace: ECOWAS and the Liberian Civil War," in *Enforcing Restraint*, ed. Lori Fisler Damrosch (New York: Council on Foreign Relations Press, 1993), 192.

29. Ellery Stowell, *Intervention in International Law* (Washington, DC: John Byrne and Company, 1921), 279.

30. It is of interest that just before leaving office, UN Secretary-General Perez de Cuellar called for a "kind of court" comprised of unbiased persons free from governmental control to decide on circumstances in which the right of the international community to intervene in the domestic affairs of a state was justified. Anthony Parsons, "Conclusions and Recommendations," in *To Loose the Bands of Wickedness*, ed. Nigel S. Rodley (London: Brassey's, 1992), 225.

31. Guenter Lewy, "The Case for Humanitarian Intervention," *Orbis* (Fall, 1993), 627–28.

32. Stanley Hoffmann, "Sovereignty and the Ethics of Intervention," in *The Ethics and Politics of Humanitarian Intervention*, Stanley Hoffmann,

Robert C. Johansen, and James Sherba (Notre Dame, IN: University of Notre Dame Press, 1996), 19.

33. Marc Trachtenberg, "Intervention in Historical Perspective," in *Emerging Norms of Justified Intervention*, eds. Carl Kaysen and Laura W. Reed (Cambridge, MA: American Academy of Arts and Sciences, 1993), 24.

34. David Fisher, "The Ethics of Intervention," *Survival* 36 (Spring, 1994), 53. For an analysis of the morally problematical aspects of sanctions in the specific case of Haiti, see Albert C. Pierce, "Just War Principles and Economic Sanctions," *Ethics and International Affairs* 10 (1996).

35. Robert H. Jackson, "International Community Beyond the Cold War," in *Beyond Westphalia?* eds. Gene Lyons and Michael Mastanduno (Baltimore, MD: Johns Hopkins University Press, 1995), 82.

36. For an interesting discussion of these points, see Jack Donnelly, "Human Rights, Humanitarian Intervention and American Foreign Policy," *Journal of International Affairs* (1983), 324–28.

37. Jonathan S. Landay, "GOP Seeks Limits to Peacekeeping," *Christian Science Monitor* (February 13, 1995), 4.

38. *The Harvest of Justice Is Shown in Peace* (Washington: U.S. Catholic Conference, 1994), 16.

39. Robert L. Phillips, "The Ethics of Humanitarian Intervention," in *Humanitarian Intervention*, eds. Duane L. Cady and Robert L. Phillips (Lanham, MD: Rowman and Littlefield, 1996), 8.

Bibliography

Adelman, Howard. "The Ethics of Humanitarian Intervention." *Public Affairs Quarterly* (January, 1992).

Aldrich, Robert, and Connell, John, eds. *France in World Politics.* London and New York: Routledge, 1989.

American Jewish Committee. *American Jewish Yearbook 1934–35.* Philadelphia: American Jewish Committee, 1936.

Amnesty International Report. *Human Rights in Uganda.* London: June, 1978.

Bailey, Sydney D. *War and Conscience in the Nuclear Age.* New York: St. Martin's Press, 1987.

Baker, James. *The Politics of Diplomacy.* New York: G. P. Putnam's Sons, 1995.

Barkey, Henri J. "Kurdish Geopolitics." *Current History* (January, 1997).

Battiata, Mary. "War of the Worlds." *Washington Post* (June 30, 1996).

Baylis, John, and Smith, Steve, eds. *The Globalization of World Politics.* New York: Oxford University Press, 1997.

Bazyler, Michael J. "Reexamining the Doctrine of Humanitarian Intervention in Light of the Atrocities in Kampuchea and Ethiopia." *Stanford Journal of International Law* 23 (1987).

Beitz, Charles. *Political Theory and International Relations.* Princeton: Princeton University Press, 1979.

Beitz, Charles, et al., eds. *International Ethics.* Princeton: Princeton University Press, 1985.

Bell, Daniel A. "The East Asian Challenge to Human Rights: Reflections on an East West Dialogue." *Human Rights Quarterly* 18 (1996).

Bethell, Leslie. *The Abolition of the Brazilian Slave Trade.* Cambridge: Cambridge University Press, 1970.

Betts, Richard K. "The Delusion of Impartial Intervention." *Foreign Affairs* 73 (November/December, 1994).

Bills, David. "International Human Rights and Humanitarian Intervention: The Ramifications of Reform on the United Nations' Security Council." *Texas International Law Journal* 31 (Winter, 1996).

Bonner, Raymond. "How Minority Tutsi Won the War." *New York Times* (September 6, 1994).

Boutros-Ghali, Boutros. "Empowering the United Nations." *Foreign Affairs* (Winter, 1992/93).

Bowett, D. W. "Reprisals Involving Recourse to Armed Force." *American Journal of International Law* 66 (1972).

Boyd, Charles G. "Making Peace with the Guilty." *Foreign Affairs* (September/October, 1995).

Boyer, Peter. "Famine in Ethiopia, the TV Accident That Exploded." *Washington Journalism Review* (January, 1985).

Brigg, Herbert W. *The Law of Nations.* 2nd edition. New York: Appleton-Century-Crofts, 1952.

Brown, Chris. *International Relations Theory.* New York: Columbia University Press, 1992.

Brown, Peter G., and MacLean, Douglas, eds. *Human Rights and U.S. Foreign Policy.* Lexington, MA: Lexington Books, 1979.

Brownlie, Ian. *Principles of Public International Law*, 3rd ed. Oxford: Clarendon Press, 1979.

Buckley, Kevin. *Panama: The Whole Story.* New York: Simon and Schuster, 1991.

Bull, Hedley, ed. *Intervention in World Politics.* Oxford: Clarendon Press, 1984.

Burgenthal, Thomas, and Sohn, Louis. *International Protection of Human Rights, Cases and Materials: Basic Documents.* Indianapolis: Bobbs-Merrill, 1973.

Burns, Edward McNall, and Ralph, Philip Lee. *World Civilizations.* Volume II, 5th ed. New York: W. W. Norton and Company, 1974.

Burton, Michael L. "Legalizing the Sublegal: A Proposal for Codifying A Doctrine of Unilateral Humanitarian Intervention." *The Georgetown Law Journal* 85 (December, 1996).

Business Executives for National Security (BENS). "Peacekeeping: Perils and Prospects." New York: September 29 and October 16, 1995.

Cady, Duane L., and Phillips, Robert L. *Humanitarian Intervention*. Lanham, MD: Rowman and Littlefield, 1996.

Campbell, Kurt M., and Weiss, Thomas. "Military Humanitarianism." *Survival* (September/October, 1991).

Carnegie Commission on Preventing Deadly Conflict, *Preventing Deadly Conflict: Final Report*. Washington, DC: Carnegie Commission on Preventing Deadly Conflict, 1997.

Center for International and Security Studies. "An Emerging Consensus." College Park, MD: University of Maryland, July 10, 1996.

Cerna, Christina. "Universality of Human Rights and Cultural Diversity: Implementation of Human Rights in Different Sociocultural Contexts." *Human Rights Quarterly* 16 (1994).

Chandler, David P. *A History of Cambodia*. 2nd ed. Boulder, CO: Westview Press, 1992.

Chelknowski, Peter J., and Pranger, Robert J., eds. *Ideology and Power in the Middle East*. Durham, NC: Duke University Press, 1988.

Chopra, Jarat, and Weiss, Thomas. "Sovereignty Is No Longer Sancrosanct." *Ethics and International Affairs* (1992).

Choudhury, Golan. *The Last Days of United Pakistan*. Bloomington, IN: Indiana University Press, 1974.

Christiansen, Drew, and Lopez, George. *Morals and Might*. Boulder, CO: Westview, 1993.

Church, George. "Destination Haiti." *Time* (September 26, 1994).

Clapham, Cristopher. *Africa and the International System*. Cambridge: Cambridge University Press, 1996.

Claude, Inis. *States and the Global System*. New York: St. Martin's Press, 1988.

Conference on Security and Cooperation in Europe. *Report of the CSCE Meeting of the Experts on National Minorities*. Geneva, 1991.

Craig, Gordon. "No More Parades." *New York Review of Books* (April 20, 1995).

Crocker, Chester. "The Lessons of Somalia." *Foreign Affairs* (May/June, 1995).

Damrosch, Lori Fisler, ed. *Enforcing Restraint*. New York: Council on Foreign Relations Press, 1993.

Damrosch, Lori Fisler, and Scheffer, David, eds. *Law and Force in the New International Order*. Boulder, CO: Westview Press, 1991.

Dawidowicz, Lucy S. *The War Against the Jews 1933–1945*. New York: Holt, Rinehart and Winston, 1975.

Dodd, William E. *Ambassador Dodd's Diary 1933–38*. New York: Harcourt, Brace and Company, 1941.

Donnelly, Jack. "Human Rights, Humanitarian Intervention and American Foreign Policy." *Journal of International Affairs* 36 (1983).

_____. "Humanitarian Intervention: Law, Morality and Politics." *Journal of International Affairs* 37 (Winter, 1984).

_____. "International Human Rights: A Regime Analysis." *International Organization* 3 (Summer, 1986).

_____. *Universal Human Rights in Theory and Practice.* Ithaca, NY: Cornell University Press, 1989.

Dopppelt, Gerald. "Statism Without Foundations." *Philosophy and Public Affairs* 9 (Summer, 1980).

Doyle, Michael. *UN Peacekeeping in Cambodia: UNTAC's Civil Mandate.* Boulder, CO: Lynne Rienner Publishers, 1995.

_____. *Ways of War and Peace.* New York: W. W. Norton, 1997.

Duffy, Michael, and Goodgame, Dan. *Marching in Place.* New York: Simon and Schuster, 1992.

Dunn, John. "The Dilemma of Humanitarian Intervention." *Government and Opposition* 29 (Spring, 1994).

Eachus, Todd, and Livingston, Steven. "Famine, Floodlights and U.S. Foreign Policy: Reconsidering the CNN Effect in the Case of Somalia." Paper presented at the annual meeting of the International Studies Association (February, 1995).

Eisner, Douglas. "Humanitarian Intervention in the Post-Cold War Era." *Boston University International Law Journal* 11 (Spring, 1993).

Elfstrom, G. F. "On Dilemmas of Intervention." *Ethics* 93 (1982–83).

Elliott, David, ed. *The Third Indochina Conflict.* Boulder, CO: Westview Press, 1981.

Falk, Richard. "The Complexities of Humanitarian Intervention: A New World Order Challenge." *Michigan Journal of International Law* 17 (Winter, 1996).

Farer, Tom. "Intervention in Unnatural Humanitarian Emergencies: Lessons of the First Phase." *Human Rights Quarterly* 18 (February, 1996).

Feingold, Henry. *The Politics of Rescue: The Roosevelt Administration and the Holocaust 1938–1945.* New Brunswick, NJ: Rutgers University Press, 1970.

Felice, William. *Taking Suffering Seriously: The Importance of Collective Human Rights.* Albany: State University of New York Press, 1996.

Fisher, David. "The Ethics of Intervention." *Survival* 36 (Spring, 1994).

Fitzpatrick, Mary. "Liberia's Tenuous Election." *Christian Science Monitor* (August 1, 1997).

Forsythe, David. *The Internationalization of Human Rights.* Lexington, MA: Lexington Books, 1991.

_____. "The UN and Human Rights at Fifty: An Incremental but Incomplete Revolution." *Global Governance* 1 (1995).

Forsythe, David, and Pease, Kelly. "Human Rights, Humanitarian Intervention, and World Politics." *Human Rights Quarterly* (May, 1993).

Franck, Thomas, and Rodley, Nigel. "After Bangladesh: The Law of Humanitarian Intervention by Force." *American Journal of International Law* 67 (1973).

Franz, Michael. *The Taiping Rebellion.* Seattle: University of Washington Press, 1972.

Frelick, Bill. "US Must Rescue Kurds Who Trusted US Employers." *Christian Science Monitor* (November 8, 1996).

Fukuyama, Francis. *The End of History and the Last Man.* New York: Free Press, 1992.

The Gallup Organization. "Americans Upbeat, But Not Extraordinarily So." Princeton, NJ: May, 1997.

_____. "Small Business and Military Generate Most Confidence in Americans." Princeton, NJ: July, 1997.

Ganji, Manouchehr. *International Protection of Human Rights.* Geneva: Librairie E. Droz, 1962.

Gardner, Richard, Helman, Gerald, and Scheffer, David J. *Post-Gulf War Challenges to the U.N. Collective Security System: Three Views on the Issue of Humanitarian Intervention.* Washington, DC: United States Institute of Peace, 1992.

Garrett, Stephen A. *From Potsdam to Poland.* New York: Praeger, 1986.

Gentile, Giovanni. *Genesis and the Structure of Society.* Trans. H. S. Harris. Urbana: University of Illinois Press, 1966.

Gillespie, Thomas. "Unwanted Responsibility: Humanitarian Military Intervention to Advance Human Rights." *Peace and Change* (July, 1993).

Goldhagen, Daniel. *Hitler's Willing Executioners.* New York: Knopf, 1996.

Goldman, Antony. "Is Nigeria a Coup Cop or Bully in Sierre Leone?" *Christian Science Monitor* (June 5, 1997).

Gordenker, Leon, and Weiss, Thomas, eds. *Soldiers, Peacekeepers, and Disasters.* London: Macmillan, 1990.

Graebner, Norman, ed. *Ideas and Diplomacy.* New York: Oxford University Press, 1964.

Gray, Christopher M. "Humanitarian Intervention." *Current* (February, 1998).

Greenwood, Christopher. "Is There a Right of Humanitarian Intervention?" *The World Today* (February, 1993).

Haas, Richard. *Intervention.* Washington: Carnegie Endowment for International Peace, 1994.

Hall, William Edward. *A Treatise on International Law.* 4th ed. Oxford: Clarendon Press, 1895.

Hardin, Garrett. *Living Within Limits.* New York: Oxford University Press, 1993.

_____. *Promethean Ethics.* Seattle: University of Washington Press, 1980.

Harriss, John, ed. *The Politics of Humaniarian Intervention*. London: Pinter, 1995.

The Harvest of Justice Is Shown in Peace. Washington: U.S. Catholic Conference, 1994.

Hashmi, Sohail. "Is There an Islamic Ethic of Humanitarian Intervention?" *Ethics and International Affairs* 7 (1993).

Hassan, Farooq. "Realpolitik in International Law: After Tanzanian-Ugandan Conflict 'Humanitarian Intervention' Reexamined." *Willamette Law Review* 17 (Fall, 1981).

Hehir, Bryan. "The Ethics of Intervention." *Ethics and International Affairs* 9 (1995).

Helman, Gerald B., and Ratner, Steven R. "Saving Failed States." *Foreign Policy* (Winter 1992–93).

Henkin, Louis, et al., *Right v. Might*. New York: Council on Foreign Relations Press, 1989.

Herz, John. *International Politics in the Atomic Age*. New York: Columbia University Press, 1962.

Himes, Kenneth. "Just War, Pacifism and Humanitarian Intervention." *America* (August 14, 1993).

_____. "The Morality of Humanitarian Intervention." *Theological Studies* (March, 1994).

Hinsley, F. H. *Power and the Pursuit of the Peace*. London: Cambridge University Press, 1967.

Hirsch, John, and Oakley, Robert. *Somalia and Operation Restore Hope*. Washington, DC: United States Institute of Peace Press, 1995.

Hoffmann, Stanley. "Out of the Cold: Humanitarian Intervention in the 1990's." *Harvard International Review* (Fall, 1993).

Hoffmann, Stanley, Johansen, Robert C., and Sherba, James. *The Ethics and Politics of Humanitarian Intervention*. Notre Dame, IN: University of Notre Dame Press, 1996.

Howard, Rhoda. *Human Rights and the Search for Community*. Boulder, CO: Westview Press, 1995.

Huntington, Samuel. "The Clash of Civilizations." *Foreign Affairs* (Summer, 1993).

Immerman, Richard. *The CIA in Guatemala*. Austin: University of Texas Press, 1982.

Independent Commission on International Humanitarian Issues. *Winning the Human Race*. London: Zed Books, 1988.

Jackson, Robert. "Armed Humanitarianism." *International Journal* 48 (1993).

Jakobsen, Peter Viggo. "National Interest, Humanitarianism or CNN: What Triggers UN Peace Enforcement After the Cold War?" *Journal of Peace Research* 33 (May, 1996).

Jones, Dorothy. *Code of Peace*. Chicago: University of Chicago Press, 1991.

Kaysen, Carl, and Rathjens, George. *Peace Operations by the United Nations: The Case for a Volunteer UN Military Force*. Cambridge, MA: American Academy of Arts and Sciences, 1996.

Kaysen, Carl, and Reed, Laura W., eds. *Emerging Norms of Justified Intervention*. Cambridge, MA: American Academy of Arts and Sciences, 1993.

Kenney, George. "The Bosnian Calculation." *New York Times Magazine* (April 23, 1995).

Keynes, John Maynard. *The General Theory of Employment, Interest and Money*. New York: Harcourt, Brace and World, 1965.

Kishner, Tony. *The Holocaust and the Liberal Imagination*. Oxford: Blackwell, 1994.

Kissinger, Henry. *Diplomacy*. New York: Simon and Schuster, 1994.

_____. *The White House Years*. Boston: Little, Brown, 1979.

Klein, Joe. "Empathy for the Devil." *Newsweek* (October 3, 1994).

Klintworth, Gary. *Vietnam's Intervention in Cambodia in International Law*. Canberra: Australian Government Publishing Service, 1989.

Kohut, Andrew, and Toth, Robert C. "Arms and the People." *Foreign Affairs* (November/December, 1994).

Kolodziej, Edward. *French International Policy Under de Gaulle and Pompidou*. Ithaca: Cornell University Press, 1974.

Kovach, Bill. "Do the News Media Make Foreign Policy?" *Foreign Policy* (Spring, 1996).

Krauthammer, Charles. "Intervention Lite: Foreign Policy by CNN." *Washington Post* (February 18, 1994).

Kull, Steven, and Ramsay, Clay. "U.S. Public Attitudes on U.S. Involvement in Haiti." Program on International Policy Attitudes, University of Maryland: August 22, 1994.

Künnemann, Rolf. "A Coherent Approach to Human Rights." *Human Rights Quarterly* 17 (1995).

Laberge, Pierre. "Humanitarian Intervention: Three Ethical Positions." *Ethics and International Affairs* (1996).

Landay, Jonathan S. "GOP Seeks Limits to Peacekeeping." *Christian Science Monitor* (February 13, 1995).

Lapid, Ilana. "From the Hobbesian Floor to the Kantian Ceiling: UN Intervention as a Practical-Idealist Challenge." *Social Studies* (May, 1995).

Leurdijk, J. *Intervention in International Politics*. Leeuwarden, Netherlands: Eismas BV, 1986.

Levitin, Michael. "The Law of Force and the Force of Law: Grenada, the Falklands, and Humanitarian Intervention." *Harvard International Law Journal* 27 (Spring, 1986).

Lewy, Guenter. "The Case for Humanitarian Intervention." *Orbis* (Fall, 1993).
Lillich, Richard. "Forcible Self-Help by States to Protect Human Rights." *Iowa Law Review* 53 (1967).
_____, ed. *Humanitarian Intervention and the United Nations.* Charlottesville: University of Virginia Press, 1973.
Lippmann, Walter. *The Public Philosophy.* New York: Mentor Books, 1955.
Luban, David. "Just War and Human Rights." *Philosophy and Public Affairs* 9 (Winter, 1980).
Ludden, Jennifer. "Unsteady Liberia Takes Another Fall." *Christian Science Monitor* (April 9, 1996).
Lyons, Gene, and Mastanduno, Michael, eds. *Beyond Westphalia?* Baltimore: Johns Hopkins University Press, 1995.
Mahan, Alfred Thayer. *Some Neglected Aspects of War.* Boston: Little, Brown and Company, 1907.
Makiya, Kanan. "Betrayal in Iraq." *New York Review of Politics* (October 17, 1996).
Martin, Marie Alexandrine. *Cambodia.* Trans. Mark W. McLeod. Berkeley: University of California Press, 1994.
Matthews, Jessica. "Policy Vs. TV." *Washington Post* (March 8, 1994).
Maynes, Charles. "Containing Ethnic Conflict." *Foreign Policy* (Spring, 1993).
McDougal, Myres Smith. *Law and Minimum World Public Order.* New Haven: Yale University Press, 1961.
McElroy, Robert. *Morality and American Foreign Policy.* Princeton: Princeton University Press, 1992.
McNeil, Donald G. "Reports Point to Mass Killings of Refugees in Congo." *New York Times* (May 27, 1997).
Menkhaus, Ken. "Somalia: Political Order in a Stateless Society." *Current History* (May, 1998).
Mill, J. S. *Essays on Politics and Culture.* New York: Doubleday, 1962.
Miller Center Report. Miller Center of Public Affairs, University of Virginia, Charlottesville, VA: Summer, 1995.
Minear, Larry, and Weiss, Thomas G. *Humanitarianism and War.* Boulder, CO: Lynne Rienner, 1994.
Minear, Larry. "Humanitarian Intervention in a New World Order." *Overseas Development Council Policy Focus* 1 (February, 1992)
_____. *Humanitarianism and War.* Boulder: Lynne Rienner, 1994.
Minear, Larry, and Weiss, Thomas G., eds. *Humanitarianism Across Borders.* Boulder, CO: Lynne Rienner Publishers, 1993.
Moore, John Norton. "The Control of Foreign Intervention in Internal Conflict." *Virginia Journal of International Law* 9 (1969).
_____, ed. *Law and Civil War in the Modern World.* Baltimore: Johns Hopkins University Press, 1974.

Muldoon, James P. "What Happened to Humanitarian Intervention?" *Bulletin of the Atomic Scientists* (March, 1995).

Muravchik, Joshua. *Exporting Democracy.* Washington, DC: The AEI Press, 1992.

Murphy, Sean D. *Humanitarian Intervention.* Philadelphia: University of Pennsylvania Press, 1996.

Mydans, Seth. "Familiar Rite, Familiar Politics in Cambodian Assembly. *New York Times* (November 26, 1998).

Nafzinger, James A. R. "Humanitarian Intervention in a Community of Power Part II." *Denver Journal of International Law and Policy* 22 (Spring, 1994).

Nardin, Terry, and Mapel, David, eds. *Traditions of International Ethics.* Cambridge: Cambridge University Press, 1992.

Nardin, Terry, and Slater, Jerome. "Nonintervention and Human Rights." *Journal of Politics* 48 (February, 1986).

Natsios, Andrew. *U.S. Foreign Policy and the Four Horsemen of the Apocalypse.* Westport, CT: Praeger, 1997.

Neack, Laura. "UN Peace-keeping: In the Interest of Community or Self?" *Journal of Peace Research* 32 (May, 1995).

Neuman, Johanna. *Lights, Camera, War: Is Media Technology Driving International Politics?* New York: St. Martin's Press, 1996.

Nolan, Cathal. *Principled Diplomacy: Security and Rights in U.S. Foreign Policy.* Westport, CT: Greenwood Press, 1993.

_____. "The United States and Tsarist Anti-Semitism, 1865–1914." *Diplomacy and Statecraft* 3 (November, 1992).

Norman, Edward. *A History of Modern Ireland.* London: Allan Lane, 1971.

Oberdorfer, Don. "The Path to Intervention." *Washington Post* (December 6, 1992).

O'Hanlon, Michael, and Solarz, Stephen. "Humanitarian Intervention: When Is Force Justified?" *The Washington Quarterly* (Autumn, 1997).

Onadipe, Abiodum. "Liberia: Taylor's First Year Report Card." *Contemporary Review* (November, 1998).

Oppenheim, L. *International Law.* 7th ed. Ed. H. Lauterpacht. London: Longmans, Green, 1948.

Oppenheim, Lassa. *International Law: A Treatise.* New York: Longmans, Green and Co., 1905.

Osgood, Robert, and Tucker, Robert. *Force, Order, and Justice.* Baltimore: Johns Hopkins University Press, 1967.

O'Toole, Thomas. *The Central African Republic: The Continent's Hidden Heart.* Boulder, CO: Westview Press, 1986.

Parekh, Bhikhu. "Rethinking Humanitarian Intervention." *International Political Science Review* 18 (1997).

Paterson, Thomas, Clifford, J. Garry, and Hagan, Kenneth J. *American Foreign Policy*. Lexington, MA: D. C. Heath and Company, 1991.

Perusse, Roland. *Haitian Democracy Restored, 1991–1995*. Lanham, MD: University Press of America, 1995.

Phillips, Robert L. *War and Justice*. Norman: University of Oklahoma Press, 1984.

Pierce, Albert C. "Just War Principles and Economic Sanctions." *Ethics and International Affairs* 10 (1996).

Pollis, Adamantia. "Cultural Relativism Revisited: Through a State Prism." *Human Rights Quarterly* 18 (1996).

Program on International Policy Attitudes. "United Nations Peacekeeping Survey." College Park: University of Maryland, April 19–23, 1995.

Prunier, Gerald. *The Rwanda Crisis: History of a Genocide*. New York: Columbia University Press, 1995.

Radu, Michael. "The Pinochet Case: Anti-Communism on Trial." Philadelphia: Foreign Policy Research Institute E-Note (October 30, 1998).

Reisman, Michael. "Sovereignty and Human Rights in Contemporary International Law." *American Journal of International Law* 84 (October, 1990).

Report of the Chilean National Commission on Truth and Reconciliation. Trans. Philip E. Berryman. Notre Dame, IN: University of Notre Dame Press, 1993.

Reppas, Michael J. "The Lawfulness of Humanitarian Intervention." *St. Thomas Law Review* 9 (Winter, 1997).

Rieff, David. "The Lessons of Bosnia." *World Policy Journal* 12 (Spring, 1995).

_____. *Slaughterhouse: Bosnia and the Failure of the West*. New York: Simon and Schuster, 1994.

Rielly, John E., ed. *American Public Opinion and U.S. Foreign Policy 1995*. Chicago: Chicago Council on Foreign Relations, 1995.

Roberts, Adam. "From San Francisco to Sarajevo: The UN and the Use of Force." *Survival* 37 (Winter, 1995–96).

_____. "Humanitarian War." *International Affairs* 69 (July, 1993).

_____. "The Road to Hell: Humanitarian Intervention." *Current* (June, 1994).

Rodley, Nigel S., ed. *To Loose the Bands of Wickedness*. London: Brassey's, 1992.

Rohde, David. "The Kurds Get in Their Own Way Under the Wing of US Protection." *Christian Science Monitor* (April 7, 1995).

Ronzitti, Natalino. *Rescuing Nationals Abroad Through Military Coercion and Intervention on Grounds of Humanity*. Dordrecht, Netherlands: M. Nijhoff Publishers, 1985.

Rotberg, Robert I. "Clinton Was Right." *Foreign Policy* (Spring, 1996).

Rotberg, Robert I., and Weiss, Thomas G. *From Massacres to Genocide.* Washington, DC: Brookings Institution, 1996.

Schorr, Daniel. "Telling It Like It Is: Kissinger and the Kurds." *Christian Science Monitor* (October 18, 1996).

Shawcross, William. "A Hero of Our Time." *New York Review of Books* (November 30, 1995).

_____. *The Quality of Mercy: Cambodia, Holocaust, and Modern Conscience.* New York: Simon and Schuster, 1984.

Shue, Henry. *Basic Rights: Subsistence, Affluence and U.S. Foreign Policy.* 2nd ed. Princeton: Princeton University Press, 1996.

Sigmund, Paul. *The United States and Democracy in Chile.* Baltimore: Johns Hopkins University Press, 1993.

Smith, Jeffrey. "U.S. Mission to Rwanda Criticized." *New York Times* (September 5, 1994).

Smith, Michael. "Ethics and Intervention." *Journal of Ethics and International Affairs* 3 (1989).

Smock, David R. *Making War and Waging Peace.* Washington, DC: United States Institute of Peace Press, 1993.

Sobel, Richard. "Portraying American Public Opinion Toward the Bosnia Crisis." *Harvard International Journal of the Press and Politics* (Spring, 1998).

Stedman, Stephen John. "The New Interventionists." *Foreign Affairs* (Winter, 1992/93).

Stone, Julius. *Aggression and World Order.* London: Stevens, 1958.

Stowell, Ellery. *Intervention in International Law.* Washington, DC: John Byrne and Company, 1921.

Swedish Stand-By Forces in the Service of the United Nations. Stockholm: Ministry of Foreign Affairs, 1982.

Sweeney, John. "Stuck in Haiti." *Foreign Policy* (Spring, 1996).

Tesón, Fernando R. *Humanitarian Intervention.* Irvington-on-Hudson, NY: Transnational Publishers, 1985, 1997.

Tharoor, Shashi. "Should UN Peacekeeping Go 'Back to Basics'?" *Survival* 37 (Winter, 1995–96).

Thomas, Ann, and Thomas, A. J. *Non-Intervention.* Dallas: Southern Methodist University Press, 1956.

Thomas, Caroline. *New States, Sovereignty and Intervention.* New York: St. Martin's Press, 1985.

Tyagi, Yogesh K. "The Concept of Humanitarian Intervention Revisited." *Michigan Journal of International Law* 16 (Spring, 1995).

United Nations High Commissioner for Refugees. *The State of the World's Refugees 1995: In Search of Solutions.* New York: Oxford University Press, 1995.

United States, Department of State, Background Notes, "United Nations." Washington, DC: GPO, September, 1997.

United States, Library of Congress, Congressional Research Service. *The Use of Force: Key Contemporary Documents.* Washington, DC: GPO, October 17, 1994.

United States Mission to the United Nations. *Global Humanitarian Emergencies, 1997.* Washington: GPO, April, 1997.

Vattel, Emmerich. *The Law of Nations or the Principles of Natural Law.* Edited and translated by Charles Fenwick. Washington, DC: Carnegie Institute, 1916.

Vincent, R. J. *Human Rights and International Relations.* Cambridge: Cambridge University Press, 1986.

_____. *Nonintervention and International Order.* Princeton: Princeton University Press, 1974.

Von Glahn, Gerhard. *Law Among Nations.* 3rd ed. New York: Macmillan Publishing, 1976.

Walzer, Michael. *Just and Unjust Wars.* New York: Basic Books, 1977.

_____. "The Moral Standing of States: A Response to Four Critics." *Philosophy and Public Affairs* 9 (Spring, 1980).

_____. "The Politics of Rescue." *Social Research* (Spring, 1995).

Wauthier, Claude. "France in Africa: President Giscard d'Estaing's Ambitious Diplomacy." *Africa Contemporary Record* 12 (1979–80).

Weisband, Edward, ed. *Poverty Amidst Plenty: World Political Economy and Distributive Justice.* Boulder, CO: Westview Press, 1989.

Wheaton, H. *Elements of International Law.* London: B. Fellowes, 1836.

Woodward, Bob. *The Commanders.* New York: Simon and Schuster, 1991.

Woolsey, Theodore S. *American Foreign Policy.* New York: The Century Co., 1898.

Index

About the Author

STEPHEN A. GARRETT is Professor of International Policy Studies at the Monterey Institute of International Studies. He has previously taught at the University of Virginia, the American University of Beirut, and the Naval Postgraduate School. He has published five books and over forty articles on topics in international affairs.

ISBN 0-275-96581-3
90000>
EAN
9 780275 965815
HARDCOVER BAR CODE